WHITE BY DEFINITION

WHITE BY DEFINITION

Social Classification
in Creole Louisiana

Virginia R. Domínguez

RUTGERS UNIVERSITY PRESS
New Brunswick, New Jersey, and London

Second paperback printing, 1997

Library of Congress Cataloging-in-Publication Data

Domínguez, Virginia R.
  White by definition.

  Bibliography: p.
  Includes index.
    1. Creoles—Louisiana—Ethnic identity.   2. Afro-
Americans—Louisiana—Ethnic identity.   3. Louisiana—
Population.   4. Race awareness—Louisiana.   5. Miscege-
nation—Louisiana   6. Ethnicity—Louisiana   I. Title.
F380.C87D65   1986   305.8'044'0763   85–14609
ISBN 0–8135–1109–7

"DOG TURNED INTO CAT":

Oxford, England
 The Dean of Worcester College has found an unusual way
of getting around ancient rules that bar dogs from his college.
 The governing body voted last week that his dog, Flint,
is a cat.

—*San Francisco Chronicle*, November 10, 1975

CONTENTS

FIGURES

TABLES

PREFACE

I write this preface sitting in Jerusalem, a non-Jew in a Jewish state. The country's fourth national census is nearing completion. Of the ten questions on the short form, one catches my eye. "Are you," it asks, "(1) Jewish, (2) Moslem, (3) Greek Orthodox, (4) Greek Catholic, (5) Latin (Catholic), (6) Christian— other (specify), (7) Druze, (8) other (specify)?" There is no parallel question: "Are you (1) Jewish, (2) Arab, (3) Semitic (other), (4) Indo-European, (5) Negroid, (6) Mongoloid, (7) Oceanic, (8) other (specify)?" Nor is there a question, "How many of your great-grandparents were born Jewish?"

I am intrigued by the alternatives it offers to Jewish identity. Four are Christian denominations. One is a general term for followers of Mohammed. A sixth identifies a sociopolitical enclave of followers of a medieval leader who broke off from mainstream Islam. An Israeli Arab friend says it is a bureaucratic ploy to undermine Arab nationalism. The vast majority of non-Jews in Israel, he is convinced, if given the choice, would identify themselves as Arabs and not as followers of one or another religious leader. An Israeli Jewish friend says it is a bureaucratic ploy to undermine Jewish secularism. The question, he is convinced, plays upon different interpretations of what it means to be Jewish. The question is simply put: Are you or are you not Jewish? The secular Jew, Jewish by ancestry, finds it difficult not to check off the box identifying him as Jewish. But in the formulation of the question, Jewish is juxtaposed to Greek Orthodox and Latin Catholic, making it therefore a religious identification, to be used as such by religious interest groups against the wishes of the secular.

Sitting in Jerusalem, my mind wanders off both to the Law of Return and to the perennially debated proposal to establish by law once and for all who is a Jew. Under the former, anyone born to a Jewish mother who has not taken formal steps to adopt a different religion has the right to become a citizen of Israel the moment he or she arrives in the country as an immigrant. Under the latter, only those who convert to Judaism according to Orthodox interpretation of Jewish law will be accepted in Israel legally as Jews.

This book is about the conscious manipulation of identity throughout the history of Louisiana. But the longer I sit in Jerusalem the less this study seems to be particularly about Louisiana or even about that region of the New World with a history of European settlement and African slavery. Race is the issue in Louisiana. Religion or citizenship may be the issue elsewhere. All amount to criteria of social classification by which rights are differentially distributed. It has been the fashion in the last ten years to soften the assumed rigidity of those criteria by pointing to the flow of individuals across the boundaries of social categories. There is, after all, "passing," conversion, and naturalization. But I wonder if in the enthusiasm of the discovery we have not lost sight of the greater picture. Individuals cross boundaries that they do not individually create. Individuals manipulate criteria of classification in order to change their individual identities according to those criteria.

We need not fall back on the "naturalness" of identities—an emphasis on primordial sentiments or the assertions of sociobiology—if we shift the spotlight away from boundary crossings. The struggle over Jewish identity in Israel is between individuals acting collectively to exert political pressure through the institutions by which the population at large is regulated. The context is legal and bureaucratic as well as individual. The struggle is also historically rooted in a public opinion continually adjusting interpretations of the past in light of the circumstances of the present, and the present within the limitations of a past history. Naturalness need not be invoked. In fact, to the extent that it is invoked when it is possible to show that identities have been consciously manipulated, it is the presumption of naturalness that warrants explanation.

The research on which this book is based began in 1975 as a study of the ethnic identity of Louisiana Creoles. The literature at the time stressed the purely local, and frequently the folkloristic. There were biographical sketches, family genealogies, and descriptions of customs or lifestyles. Above all, most dealt either with white Creoles *or* colored Creoles, not with the existence of both types, the historical processes that led to their differentiation, or the existence of multiple claims to Creole identity. I set out to do fifteen months of archival research and participant observation in the city of New Orleans.

But as I collected data and pursued the analysis, the project underwent a fateful metamorphosis. The problem of Creole identity, it became clear, was deeply enmeshed in a more general struggle over the definition of the socially relevant identities. There was, on one hand, an obvious historical struggle over the criteria of social classification and, on the other hand, a widespread reluctance to recognize social classification as a man-made construction. The intervention of legal institutions in the struggle over social classification made the struggle seem more obvious, and the reluctance more a case of downright mystification. How, I asked, could the fact of historical manipulation of social identities itself be so manipulated?

ACKNOWLEDGMENTS

I want to thank, above all, the hundreds of Creole informants who put up with me when I asked trying questions, who extended a helping hand when the chips were down, who allowed me to enter their most private worlds although I was an outsider, and who contributed not only most of the substance of this volume but also many of its insights into social classification. I regret that the need to protect the identity of my informants keeps me from thanking them individually in print. I have used here only the names of individuals and families that appear in records readily accessible to the public. I am relieved only by the thought that those informants who contributed so much to this study know just who they are and how much these words of acknowledgment apply to them individually.

In addition, I am deeply indebted to Annelies Sheehan, my research assistant for more than a year, for her diligence, imagination, and constant enthusiasm, and to Emily Poriss, Virginia Tyce, Evelyn Pugh, Nell Borah, and Brother Louis of the Josephite Order for participating so cheerfully and actively in several of my data-gathering projects.

To the archivists of the Special Collections Division of the Howard-Tilton Memorial Library at Tulane, the Historic New Orleans Collection, the archives of the University of New Orleans, the Amistad Research Center at Dillard, the library of Xavier University, the archives of the Louisiana State University at Baton Rouge, and the Special Collections Division of the Eugene P. Watson Memorial Library at the Northwestern State University of Louisiana go very special thanks. For two years they welcomed my assistants and me with open arms, complied with our requests for manuscripts and records, and even suggested sources of information of which we had not been aware.

To my colleagues Raymond Smith and Marshall Sahlins of the University of Chicago, Munro Edmonson of Tulane, Sidney Mintz of Johns Hopkins, Harold Scheffler and Ellen Messer of Yale, Niara Sudarkasa of the University of Michigan, and Eileen Basker of the Hebrew University of Jerusalem, and to Marlie Wasserman, editor-in-chief of Rutgers University Press, I extend heartfelt thanks for pushing and nudging, encouraging and critiquing, believing in me and keeping me honest. I also wish to thank Alexander Hull and Rahel Rosen, who kindly examined the Creole and French texts and corrected my translations of them where necessary. I remain, of course, ultimately responsible for any muddles and flaws that may still appear in this volume. For permission to reprint parts of my articles that appeared in *American Ethnologist* 4 (1977): 589–602, I wish to thank the American Anthropological Association.

For financial support, I am doubly indebted to the National Science Foundation. A National Science Foundation Graduate Fellowship supported many months of academic preparation as well as almost a year of research in Louisiana. A special National Science Foundation Research Grant #BNS76-02955 supplemented the fellowship with allowances for research assistants, transportation, photocopying, and gifts for informants.

The volume, however, could not have been completed without the generous financial and moral support of the Harvard University Society of Fellows from 1976 to 1979 and of the Duke University Department of Anthropology since 1979. Together they have induced humility where arrogance once reigned supreme; they have shown me the artificiality of disciplinary boundaries and the value of interdisciplinary research; and most of all, they have taught me to question my own theoretical assumptions, to question the questions as well as the answers.

Chapter 1

INTRODUCTION

The tension between individual choice and social norm emerges as something of a false dichotomy, and might better be represented as a continued negotiation by actors of how to interpret the norms. . . . It allows us to see rules not merely as a set of constraints upon people, but as something that people actively manipulate to express a sense of their own position in the social world. —Michael Herzfeld in *American Ethnologist*, 1982

A recent Louisiana case attracted widespread national attention. In the fall of 1982 Susie Phipps, age forty-eight, went to court to have herself declared white. The headline in the *International Herald Tribune* read: "Woman Challenges a Race Law: 'Look at Me, I'm White'; Despite Fair Skin, She is Labeled 'Colored' under Louisiana Statute Based on Genealogy" (October 5, 1982).[1] In the December 3 *People* magazine, the headline read: "Raised White, a Louisiana Belle Challenges Race Records That Call Her 'Colored.'" Even in a small North Carolina paper, the *Durham Morning Herald*, there was the story and the eye-catching headline: "Woman Files Suit, Says She Is White" (September 15, 1982).

The details of Susie Phipps's life are noteworthy, but so is the form in which the "facts" were presented to the public. In each of the headlines quoted above, the papers hinted that there may be more than one basis for racial identification. The *International Herald Tribune* juxtaposed physical appearance to genealogy. *People* magazine found a contradiction in being raised white and being called colored. The Durham paper suggested a lack of agreement between self-identification and identification by others.

Recognition of the inexactitude of race continued in the body of each article. All report the State Bureau of Vital Statistics' claim that she is legally colored because her great-great-great-great-grandmother was a Negress and a number of other ancestors mulattoes, quadroons, and octoroons. They note, in addition, that the bureau rested its case on a 1970 Louisiana statute that made 1/32 "Negro blood" the dividing line between white and black. To put it in perspective, they informed the public that Louisiana law traditionally held that any trace of Negro ancestry was the basis for legal blackness.

Both *People* and the *Tribune* cited in some detail the expert testimony that anthropologist Munro Edmonson presented in court on Mrs. Phipps's behalf. According to the *Tribune*, he testified that there is no such thing as a pure race, no way to determine what percentage of Negro blood Mrs. Phipps's slave ancestor had and, thus, no way to determine what percentage black Susie Phipps is. In addition, the paper claimed Edmonson called the present law "nonsense" in an interview he granted outside the courtroom. According to *People*, he testified that the genealogy the bureau prepared to support its case was "impressive, [but that] it says nothing at all about Mrs. Phipps' race." He is quoted as saying that genes are "shuffled" before birth, making it at least theoretically possible for a child to inherit all his genes from just two grandparents. Then, as if to appeal to the public at large, the magazine went on to summarize parts of Edmonson's testimony that, it said, might "elicit a barrage of vigorous objections": that modern genetic studies show that blacks in the United States average 25 percent white genes and that whites average 5 percent black genes, and that by these statistics, using the 1/32 law, the entire native-born population of Louisiana would be considered black!

In the wording of these stories, there was a shade of cynicism or disbelief—insinuations that the concept of race contained in the 1970 statute and employed by the Bureau of Vital Statistics was out of date, unscientific, and yet encoded in the law. There were insinuations that this was an issue resurrected from the past that made no sense in contemporary American society. The plaintiff's zeal, after all, was matched by the bureau's perseverance—and this in a country where for about a generation there had been official racial equality under the law. The *Tribune* reported that her story, "a story as old as the country, has elements of anthropology and sociology special to this region, and its message, here in 1982 America, is that it is still far better to be white than black." It went on to say that the 1970 Louisiana statute in question "is the only one in the country that gives any equation for determining a person's race." "Elsewhere," it continued, "race is simply a matter of what the parents tell the authorities to record on the birth certificate, with no questions asked." The thrust of the argument was the same in the piece in *People* magazine: "Birth certificates in most states record race for purposes of identification, census, and public health. Most states, and the U.S. States Census Bureau, now follow a self-identification policy in registering race at birth. In Louisiana, however, a 1970 statute still on the books has snared Susie and thousands of others into racial classifications determined by fractions. . . . In Susie's case, . . . the state contended that other ancestors were mulattoes, quadroons, and octoroons— *outmoded* expressions denoting mixed blood (December 3, 1982, pp. 155–156; emphasis added). Months later, the *New York Times* reiterated the theme when it announced the repeal of the 1970 statute late in June 1983. It quoted the New Orleans state representative who wrote the law that replaces the 1970 statute, saying that the state legislature was moved to act "to reflect *modern* thinking" (June 26, 1983, sect. E, p. 41; emphasis added).

It is clear throughout the media coverage that the case hinges on competing and coexisting perceptions of the nature of racial identity: the possibility of purity, the arbitrariness of calculations, the nature of reproduction, and the mutability of the criteria of identity. But in and of themselves, these disputed points are not novel. After three decades of active struggle for equal civil rights, continued advances in human genetics that make talk of "blood" seem primitive or folklorish, and the publication of both scholarly manuscripts and popular books proclaiming the sociocultural basis of our concepts of race, a localized argument about one woman's racial identity hardly seems newsworthy.

The twist, so to speak, in this case is not racial identity per se, but rather the role of law. Louisiana was singled out by the press because it had a statute with an "operative equation for the determination of race" (New York Times, June 26, 1983, sect. E, p. 41), not because it is the only state in which there are varied, often competing bases for racial identification. The issue became one of constitutionality. Did the 1970 statute infringe on the rights granted citizens by the United States Constitution? Is one of those rights the freedom to choose what one is?

The appealing question is also a nagging one. There is, to begin with, the semblance of a contradiction. To speak of "what one is" is to imply that some identities are fixed, given, unalterable. A change of phrasing makes this clearer. "Freedom to choose what one wants to be" would contain an implicit denial of the fixedness of identity in that it suggests that it might be possible to realize one's wishes. "Freedom to choose what one is becoming" would convey a similar message. In this case, will and desire seem irrelevant, and extra-individual forces are patently evident in the very phrase "is becoming"; but the words openly assert a process of becoming. The activity would be continuous rather than completed. In both of these alternative forms, there is room for individual choice and action and, thus, room for conceptualizing freedom to choose one's identity. But how, after all, can we possibly conceive of freedom of choice if we take identities as givens? And if there is really no choice, how are we to interpret the legal granting of "choice"?

The United States Supreme Court has taken a pragmatic approach to this question in recent years. In 1944 (Korematsu v. United States, 323 U.S. 214)[2] and again in 1954 (Bolling v. Sharpe, 347 U.S. 497), the Court argued that racial classifications must be subject to strict judicial scrutiny because they deny equal protection of the law under the Fourteenth Amendment. And in 1964 (*McLaughlin* v. *Florida,* 379 U.S. 184; *Anderson* v. *Martin,* 375 U.S. 399), it held that racial classification is "constitutionally suspect." But in several more recent cases (cf. *Shapiro* v. *Thompson,* 394 U.S. 618 [1969]; *Sherbert* v. *Verner,* 374 U.S. 398 [1963]; *Bates* v. *The City of Little Rock,* 361 U.S. 516 [1960]), the Court has sustained statutes that define racial categories when it has deemed such statutes necessary for the purpose of realizing compelling and constitutionally acceptable state interests (cf. Davis 1976: 199–200).

Clearly the civil rights movement of the 1960s increased sensitivity to the existence of prejudice and led to the identification of invidious discrimination. But the issue then was the granting of rights to blacks, not the granting of the right to be white or black. The former had compelling state interest but carried ironic implications. Protecting the rights of blacks required the maintenance of a system for distinguishing blacks from whites, even though the system had come into existence for the purpose of disenfranchising those identified as black.

To redress a legal injustice, then, the Court permits racial classification by institutions. The question is whether the Court's pragmatic concern of protecting the rights of a sector of the population that has historically been subjected to systematic discrimination infringes on the rights of individuals to opt not to be racially classified and to identify themselves racially according to their own criteria of classification.

THE LIMITS OF CHOICE

A legal scholar might interpret the problem as conflict of rights and a geneticist as a human fabrication bearing little relationship to the "facts" of nature. But the problem is also the conceptualization of choice. A kind of folk existentialism pervades public opinion and surfaces as a legal contradiction.

The United States is ideologically committed to the propositions "that all men are created equal," and that all have "certain unalienable Rights, [and] that among these are Life, Liberty, and the pursuit of Happiness. Equality is reckoned as equality between individuals; rights are accorded individuals; and liberty is assumed to be freedom of and for the individual. It thus follows that choice is conceived in terms of the individual. Herein echoes Kierkegaard's notion of the self: "man is a creature of open possibility who is obliged to struggle unremittingly in order to 'become what he is' and who does so with no presiding 'essence' or laws to support the autonomy of the task" (Gill and Sherman 1973: 10). That there is also a legal system that shapes and limits individual action, then, appears to be a dilemma.

The analytic problem is by no means a new one, but it remains a recurrent issue in the social sciences. Witness the internal debates within British social anthropology, which have spanned much of the twentieth century. The structural-functionalism of Radcliffe-Brown assumed normative consensus, regarded society as a system of morals, logically prior to behavior, and did not "depict any intervening social process between the moral injunction and the pattern" (Barth 1966: 2). The functionalism of Malinowski and Firth countered with an emphasis on processes of exchange between individuals, competition as process, and the principles governing choice and the allocation of resources. Then as Leach and Needham strove for a reinterpretation of the concept of structure in more semiotic terms (thereby, nonetheless, affirming its ontological primacy), Barth reaffirmed the individual exercise of choice as an explanation of how social patterns or regularities are generated. It would be easy to describe the recurrent debate in Hegelian terms of thesis and antithesis and pay little attention to the content of the debate, or to depict it as the current epistemological concern of the discourse of a specific institutionalized profession. Sahlins might even argue that it is but a manifestation of "the endemic Western antinomy of a worldless subject confronting a thoughtless object" (1976: x). But the question itself is a critical one if we are to conceptualize individual choice as an observable social act in an ideologically and institutionally constituted society.

The task is a difficult one. Barth argues that we can resolve the difficulties incurred by models of normative consensus in explaining social change by adopting "the most simple and general model available to us . . . one of an aggregate of people exercising choice while influenced by certain constraints and incentives" (1966: 1). The terms *aggregate* and *constraints* are interesting and pivotal. *Aggregate* suggests individuation rather than a structurally integrated whole. The individuals who make up the aggregate behave individually, according to Barth, in "sequences of interaction systematically governed by reciprocity." As such, individuals appear as actors pursuing "self-interest" and maximizing gain.

In the Barthian formulation, constraints are part and parcel of each transaction. They include the rights and obligations of the set of statuses relevant to each situation (ibid.: 3) and the set of values that lead individuals in real life to seek something and prefer it to something of less value (ibid.: 5). It would be tempting to interpret those passages as acknowledging the role of social institutions and cultural logics of significance both on individual actors and on the structure of interactions. But that translation defies the whole point of his argument against viewing individual actions as mere instantiations of culture and society. Rather than treating the integration of culture as axiomatic—an allegation he makes of much anthropological writing—Barth insists that consistency in values, where that is itself a goal of the participating actors, is in fact generated in and through social transactions. But the process also allows for inconsistency and momentum for social change.

As such, the individual emerges refurbished and activated to the point of nearly dissolving any sense of an ideologically and institutionally constituted society. But at what expense? Asad has already pointed out in his reanalysis of Barth's early work on the Swat Pathans that Barth's failure to take into account ideological differences between social classes and the broader historical processes of social and political domination led him to a kind of functionalism that he himself decries. Society emerges as a "logically closed system . . . located at a point in linear time" (Asad 1972: 90).

It may be, as Kapferer has recently argued, that a transactional orientation like Barth's is at once too broad and too restrictive (1976). The simplicity of its model and the narrowness of the set of guiding concepts and assumptions may severely reduce the insights we are apt to get from their application to specific settings. Kapferer himself suggests that "it might lead to a neglect of aspects of social behavior—for instance, behavior's symbolic mode—which might be critical to successful explanation" (1976: 7).

The problem is evident in Barth's conceptualization of ethnic groups and boundaries (1969). There is no doubt that his documentation of significant flow of personnel across the boundaries of ethnic groups, and his interpretation of it as pivotal, revolutionized a field where many still spoke of primordial sentiment, biological ancestry, and cultural unity as the distinguishing features of ethnic groups (e.g., Narroll 1964; Glazer and Moynihan 1963 and 1975; Wilkie 1977). But he did not, or could not, satisfactorily engage the question of how ethnic boundaries are created and maintained in a society. For him, ethnic groups and identities are artifacts of the many interpersonal encounters and transactions in which individuals actualize their ethnicity or fail to actualize it in accordance with the cognitive "model" of the ethnic boundary they hold. The existence and maintenance of ethnicity would thus depend on how well the individual's ethnic self-conception conforms to the social reality he or she faces. At base, then, individual self-interest and manipulation of cultural attributes for personal ends become the explanation for ethnic boundaries.

The image has been compelling enough to foster a growing

literature on ethnicity that focuses on the flow of personnel across boundaries. But in the enthusiasm for the model, certain fundamental questions have remained largely unexplored. There is, for example, the troublesome question of why, if indeed ethnic groups are not biologically and culturally self-perpetuating, we should not simply consider them economic interest groups, social classes, or political organizations; or why members of ethnic groups under those conditions should continue to claim that the groups are biologically and culturally self-perpetuating; or why so many societies have generic terms to refer to the types of social categories that structure their interactions—why *varnas* and *jatis* in South Asia, *races* in the English-speaking world of the nineteenth century, and *class* in much of Latin America? And how and why do these generic terms change over time in the context of a single society? The unanswered questions have a theme in common: the implication that the individual exercise of choice takes place within sociohistorical environments that deem only certain kinds of choices possible.

The problem I address in this book is how to interpret the struggle between individuals actively trying to exercise choice over who and what they are and epistemological and institutional systems that seem to stand in their way. How frequently do such struggles take place? Under what conditions are individuals ever successful? And what makes certain manipulations possible when others do not even stand a chance?

I take an approach that is at once synchronic and diachronic, epistemological and institutional. I do so not simply to present a more complete picture of the nature of social identities and the role of individual actors in generating or manipulating them, but rather to present an adequate picture. It is simply not true that history can be added on to an analysis that was not conceived diachronically from the start. Chapters entitled "the historical background" reveal authors' implicit beliefs about the limited relevance of long-term historical processes. The history is tacked on, like a stage prop—visually helpful but structurally unnecessary.

If history is a depiction of social, economic, and political processes initiated at some time in the past, then any account of processes set in "real" time is history. It becomes something else as well when the goal is the exploration of an issue thought to be of analytical relevance elsewhere. This study, then, *is* history at the same time that it *uses* history. The setting is Louisiana; the issues are the definitions of identity, the forms they take, the way they are perceived, and the circumstances under which they change.

What is an identity? I take the position that social identities do not exist without public affirmation. Social identities are simply not who we are genetically nor how we as individuals think about ourselves. They are, I contend, conceptions of the self, constructed in time and place both epistemologically and socially in opposition to other such selves. What would otherwise explain how an individual could one day be white and the next day black? Or how and why human institutions deliberate proposals to redefine an identity?

But how do we follow the struggles and manipulations of identities? Geertz (e.g., 1975) has always argued that we need to focus on public webs of significance, and I, for one, have always found the conception aesthetically appealing but analytically obscure. How in the world do we locate not what is just "in people's heads" nor what is simply observable even by a total stranger, but rather those "public webs of significance"?

William James wrote in 1907 that "the universe has always appeared to the natural mind as a kind of enigma, of which the key must always be sought in the shape of some illuminating word or name" (James 1949 [1907]: 52). It is not a unique idea, but it is a useful one. Labeling theory has concentrated on the behavioral consequences of applying labels to individuals.

And yet social labels are clearly much more than cues for individual behavior.

James wrote of the "practical cash values" of words and of how they are "an indication of the ways in which existing realities may be changed" (ibid.: 53). Similar claims have been made for the emergence and use of personal names in different contexts— that they epitomize personal or social "experiences, historical happenings, attitudes to life, and cultural ideas and values" (Fortes 1955: 349), that they serve in the narrowest sense as symbols of identity (Isaacs 1975: 46), and that they function in the broadest sense as condensed symbols of native experiences of all of social reality (Turner 1967).

Clearly, as lexemes, social labels are conventional signs used in thinking and communicating. People think with them, through them, and about them. People use them in light of how and what they think of them and of how they think others think of them. In other words, they convey messages referentially and indexically (cf. Silverstein 1976).

It is not that labels are empty baskets, but that their intrinsic tie to context of usage—both in the micro and macro sense— means that they always capture some aspect of the social context of the moment in which they are used and that, in doing so, the identities they name are both affirmed and contextualized in each instance of usage. The fact that part of the message conveyed each time a term is used comes from the context of usage also means that there is never a single isolable meaning of a label. Changes in context can, and do, reorder priorities that then trigger reordering of distinctive features.

The periodic issuing of definitions of particular identities supports, rather than challenges, this interpretation. It is like statutory law itself. Definitions testify to the prevalence of nonconforming uses much like laws attest to the prevalence of illegal practices. Those who formulate and advocate particular definitions of identity seek, often unconsciously, to collapse description with prescription in much the same way in which those who formulate and advocate statutory changes in the law invoke rationality and fairness in order to bring about change. The analogy to law is especially relevant here, since so much of the struggle over identities at least in Louisiana takes place within the parameters of the law and the arbitrariness of such laws smacks of conscious manipulation. For most people, manipulation carries negative connotations. Moore (1978: 2) implies that it is those negative connotations that keep Americans, including most lawyers, married to an idyllic view of law, even though "no week passes in America without extensive public claims being made by political figures for the beneficial effects to be expected from new legislation they sponsor, as if there were no possible uncertainties in the results."

But manipulation as management and negotiation is, I contend, not only intrinsic to the legal system but also intrinsic to the system of social classification more generally. Manipulation is evident in the interaction between individual attempts to exercise choice and the epistemological and institutional constraints on the conceivability and realizability of individual choice. Manipulation is both the strategy and the result. It is individuals acting in recognition of "the system" and changing, in the process, some of the very terms on which the system operates. But it exists at once in the intersection between public opinion and the exercise of power politics. Like law itself, it is limited by the thrust of public opinion, conducted "with reference to culturally inscribed categories" (Comaroff and Roberts 1981: 20), and triggered by "the force of politically organized society" (Radcliffe-Brown 1952: 212).

IDENTIFYING THE CREOLE

The Louisiana Creoles, on whose ethnography this book is based, are people long identified with Louisiana, frequently romanticized in the popular literature, and only sporadically inspected by social scientists.[3] Famous and yet hard to pinpoint, they get both credit and blame for the emergence of jazz, New Orleans' Mardi Gras, Creole cuisine, grilled-iron lacework, and infamous Bourbon Street. And yet what is most curious about them, I shall argue, is not what they do but rather who and what they are.

European colonial expansion in the sixteenth, seventeenth, and eighteenth centuries gave rise to a number of Creole societies and Creole languages. We find self-identified Creole populations in the Dutch East Indies as well as the English-speaking West Indies, in the French colonies of Martinique, and Senegal, in the Dutch settlements of Malabar, Surinam, and Curaçao, in most of Latin America, and in coastal West Africa. Sectors of colonial societies, sometimes entire colonial populations, became known as Creole. Evoking romantic images of these outposts, M. H. Herrin wrote in 1952: "Whether we hear of the English Creole of the West Indian, East Indian, or West African colonies, the French Creole of Algeria, Martinique, or Senegal, or the Dutch Creole of Malabar, the name invariably provokes fancies of burning sins, of monstrous vegetations, of nights lighted by the Southern Cross" (1952: 31–32).

Common to these societies were structured economic, and often political, contacts with Western Europe, a self-image as pioneering societies surviving or thriving in nearly unlivable surroundings, and a heterogeneity of physical appearance, language, and cultural heritage. A single definition of the term *Creole* may have been adequate for all of these societies during the early stages of European expansion. But as the Creole populations of these colonies (or former colonies) established diverse social, political, and economic positions for themselves over the years, *Creole* acquired diverse meanings.

The *Academia Real Española* (Royal Spanish Academy of Arts and Letters) claims that the origin of the word is the Spanish term *criollo,* and that it was invented by Spanish explorers and settlers during the initial stages of the conquest of the West Indies. Its early uses in Spanish, according to the academy, suggest that it signified all locally born persons of nonnative origin. This included persons born of European parents in the islands as well as locally born children of African slaves (cf. McCants 1973: xxii). In his study, *Development of Creole Society in Jamaica, 1770–1820,* Edward Braithwaite derived *criollo* from the verb *criar,* meaning "to raise or to breed." According to Braithwaite, in the West Indies *Creole* referred only to those "born in, native to, committed to the area of living," whether white or slave (1971: xv). The 1869 edition of the French *Larousse* (vol. 5: 490–491) offers a similar description of the sense of *Creole.* Then during the second half of the nineteenth century and the first half of the twentieth, intellectual, ideological, and social movements in Europe and its former colonies exerted pressure on the racially undifferentiated conception of Creole. The changes were both classificatory and political.

Contrary to the 1869 edition's stress on the nonracial connotations of the term, the 1929 edition of the *Larousse* unequivocally stated that *Creole* was correctly used only in reference to the presumably white population of these colonial or formerly colonial societies. Moreover, it argued that when the term was used to refer to the black populations of Haiti, Reunion, and Mauritius, *Negro* followed it as noun. Thus, Haitian Creoles, for example, were "really" Creole Negroes and not simply Creoles. They were Negroes who resembled the "true Creoles." They may have spoken the language of the whites known as Creole, boasted an ancestry threateningly similar to that of white Creoles and often deeply interwebbed with it, and thought of themselves as French, Spanish, English, Dutch, or Portuguese in culture and allegiance. Still, the *Larousse* affirmed that they were Negroes and not Creoles (cf. Coleman 1945: xi; Lanusse 1945). Between 1869 and 1929, contributors to the *Larousse* breathed a changing air. The 1929 edition picks up a discernible structural shift in definitions of social labels and in the hierarchical arrangement of social categories. Whereas the 1869 edition attributed to *Creole* essentially the same senses as noun and adjective, the 1929 edition argued that different syntactic function signified semantic difference. Used as noun, *Creole* correctly designated only a Caucasian population; as adjective, by way of analogy it could be used to refer to non-Caucasian peoples of current or former colonies. In the 1929 edition of *Larousse,* race was assigned primacy over local birth or cultural allegiance as criterion of classification.

The result today is that a reputable dictionary like Webster's *New Twentieth Century Dictionary of the English Language* (1976) offers eight definitions for the term *Creole:*

1. originally, a native, especially of the West Indies, Central America, tropical South America, the Gulf States, or Mauritius, of nonnative descent;

2. a person of French or Spanish descent born in the Americas;

3. a person of Negro descent born in the Americas; usually a creole Negro;

4. a person descended from or culturally related to the original French settlers of Louisiana and New Orleans; hence, French as spoken by such people;

5. loosely, anyone from Louisiana;

6. a person descended from or culturally related to original Spanish settlers in the Gulf States, especially Texas;

7. loosely, a person of mixed Creole and Negro stock; and

8. (from Sp. Criollo) in parts of tropical South America, the child of a white father and a mestiza mother.

Of those definitions that apply to people of Louisiana (numbers 1 through 7), several stress local birth, most specify ancestry as a distinctive feature, and two employ cultural distinctions. Each combination of distinctive features delimits the conceptual boundaries of a category of people known as Creole. For Louisiana alone, seven such categories can be identified. Some appear ethnic, some racial, and some neither. Several are mutually exclusive. The question is whether this is a simple and plausible description of confusion or the result of manipulation at three levels—conceptual, institutional, and individual.

Who does what and within what limits? And how does that constant acting in view of the system alter the system itself? The chapters of this book document the manipulation of identity, the rationalization of those manipulations, and the social, economic, and political consequences of those manipulations. The book is divided into three parts. In Part I, "The Legal Domain," I explore the structuring of the system of racial classification as racial identities were defined and redefined over the years. Chapter 2 discusses the role of law in defining those identities, and Chapter 3 the linking of those definitions to a sociopolitical logic of significance. Part II, "The Political Economy of Labeling," explains the transformations of the referential values of Creole and the timing of those changes. Chapter 4 documents the emergence of a Creole identity only decades after the founding of the colony of Louisiana and links it to changes in the political economy. Chapter 5 examines the way in which racial polarization in the 1860s and 1870s led to a fundamental transformation of Creole identity. Chapter 6 analyzes the coexistence of conflicting interpretations today of who and what a Creole is. Finally, in Part III, I explore how individuals themselves both consciously manipulate the system of classification and are, in turn, subject to its internal logic. Chapter 7 debunks the myth of identity by ancestry, while Chapter 8 explains the inferential process on which most cases of individual manipulation rest.

THE FIELDWORK

Exploration of the patterns and processes of social classification required, first, a separation and, then, an intertwining of methods and themes. I shall identify the major ones briefly here and discuss some of the adaptations I consider necessary for research on social classification.

For a diachronic perspective on patterns of labeling, archival research is pivotal. In this study, a major question concerned previous uses of *Creole*. Toward that end, I conducted a survey of all published material about Louisiana in which the term *Creole* appeared in the title. The coverage was probably not exhaustive, but it did cover all materials on deposit at the Newberry Library in Chicago, the Library of Congress, Sterling Memorial Library at Yale, Widener Library at Harvard, the Howard-Tilton Memorial Library at Tulane, and the central Louisiana State University Library at Baton Rouge—in sum, at the major research libraries in this country and the local repositories. The definitions and descriptions of the Creoles that appeared in each of these items were then compiled and compared, and a clear pattern of historical change emerged.

A second stage of the research involved the analysis of historical manuscripts in the Special Collections division of the Howard-Tilton Memorial library at Tulane, the Historic New Orleans Collection, the Amistad Research Center, the University of New Orleans, the Louisiana State Museum, and the archives of the Louisiana State University in Baton Rouge and Natchitoches. In them, I focused on large collections of family papers donated to these archives by families who today regard themselves either as Creole or as French. Of particular interest was information on kinship, marriage, interracial relations, inheritance patterns, and social networks, as well as periodic discourses on definitions of the term *Creole*. In addition, I searched deliberately for connotations or associations of the term *Creole* throughout the nearly three centuries of Louisiana history.

The legal research was equally comprehensive and archival. Research assistants were employed to do legal research on adoption, marriage, paternity, and inheritance from which detailed histories of statutory and case law could be written. In addition, the research team conducted title searches of properties, analyzed probate records of French Creole families, determined where the French Creoles lived, when they moved, and where they moved since the early part of the nineteenth century using old city directories. Finally, research assistants ascertained the authenticity of many genealogical claims, wherever possible, using church and civil records. This part of the research lasted from April 1975 through the summer of 1977.

Fifteen months of fieldwork in New Orleans complemented the historical research. Fieldwork included collecting extensive data on households, analyzing social networks, and generally doing participant observation. I concentrated throughout the period on expressions of self-identity and on ways in which self-identified Creoles referred to others. Interviews and questionnaires supplemented the analysis of social classification and hierarchy.

Two aspects of the research demanded methodological flexibility: concern with the use of social labels in previous generations, and the size and diversity of the population that identifies itself as Creole today. Obviously those long since dead could not serve as informants in any traditional sense; neither could they be interviewed or observed in everyday social interaction. Information on the use of social labels in earlier time periods had to come from careful examination of letters, documents, legal cases, newspapers, literary works, and genealogical records. Although this yielded a large volume of relevant data, its quality was uneven. It is difficult, at best, to discern authors' intentions and biases from finished texts of this sort. The material is usable then only in conjunction with other forms of data—information on the social and economic backgrounds of the authors of those texts, and opinions and biases less cautiously given in personal letters to friends and relatives. Where possible, I use such information to qualify data on social labels obtained from these sources. I should add as well that the French and Spanish in these texts often look awkward to the modern eye. Their orthography and spelling are frequently inconsistent—even wrong by today's standards. I have, of course, made no attempt to "correct" them when I quote from them in this book. I have tried to be as faithful as possible in reproducing the originals. There is no foolproof method, but there are checks and balances.

The second methodological problem I faced at the outset was

a familiar one to sociologists and anthropologists engaged in studies of complex societies, urban and regional analyses. Who would constitute my data base given the size of the population in question? There were, and are, many more individuals who identify themselves as Creole than I could possibly interview, meet, or even observe. Metropolitan New Orleans, where most of them live, constitutes a population of more than a million people. And although there are certain residential clusters of Creoles in the metropolitan area, Creoles are distributed quite broadly throughout much of the city and its suburbs.

The standard answer frequently is random sampling, and indeed two studies of Creoles of Color (Palazzolo 1955; Wingfield 1961) fall into this mold. I myself have used some of the information they generated on the behavior and socioeconomic characteristics of these Creoles to draw comparisons with the present. But the technique severely limited their analyses of the differentiation of social identities in the larger society from which differentiation of their own social identities in large part derives.

The technique of random sampling, I concluded, is plagued with a structural disadvantage. It presupposes the existence of a clearly identifiable group or groups from which the sample is drawn, in effect ignoring the very question that a study such as this seeks to answer. For the question is not only what those people who identify themselves as Creole think or do, but rather how and why they identify themselves in a particular way and how their choice of social identity is related to social, economic, political, and cultural patterns of the society at large. Moreover, if self-identification were used as a basis for random sampling, the sample chosen would at best only be partially random. It would only be a sample of a self-determined group, not a sample of all those persons whose families have at one time or another considered themselves Creoles, or who have at some point in their lives identified themselves as such. Using the technique of random sampling, it would be extremely difficult, if not impossible, to document changes in the processes of identification and variations in the interpretation of social labels.

This study relied instead on what I call multiple, nonrandom samples. Individuals who identified themselves as Creole introduced me to others who either also identified themselves as Creole or whom my informants considered to be Creole. I consciously then employed the genealogical method to locate those who through one criterion or another qualified as Creoles. In this manner, I was able to collect information on more than ten thousand people and to interview formally or informally approximately a thousand.

Interviews included group discussions in the homes of both white and colored Creoles, school questionnaires and class discussions, and open-ended conversations with individuals both in private and in public. By combining the genealogical method with the technique of individual referral, I located individuals with significantly different opinions on the meanings of Creole identity and with diverse patterns of self-identification. All identified themselves, or were identified by others, as Creole. The goal was to determine the different types of people informants explicitly described as Creole or implied to be Creole in casual conversation. The results were different modes of self-identification, varying degrees of self-awareness, ongoing processes of change in social identification, and conflicts, myths, and controversies surrounding the epistemological and social bases for identification.

Part I

THE LEGAL DOMAIN

Chapter 2

DEFINING THE RACIAL STRUCTURE

I begin with an analysis of what appears to be a contradiction in terms: the continuous historical pattern of determining race by man-made law rather than by processes of nature. How and why does this take place? What are the conditions under which categories of identity are restructured, and how arbitrary are the legal systems of racial classification that emerge over different historical periods?

From 1718 to 1768, Louisiana was in the hands of the French. Like its vastly more prosperous sister colony of St. Domingue (now Haiti), it attracted European settlers and recruited African slaves. A legal distinction between free persons and slaves coincided in the early years with a distinction between Europeans and Africans. But as Europeans and slaves began to engage in sexual relations with each other in the first few decades of the colony's history, as they had in the much longer history of St. Domingue, a tripartite legal distinction emerged. In the overwhelming majority of these unions, the man was European and the woman a slave, often the man's legal property. Children born to such unions were legally slaves, because they were the offspring of slave mothers. But in a significant number of cases, the white father freed his slave children—and often also his concubine—by granting them legal freedom when they were his own property or by buying them their freedom from others when they were not. Once manumitted, they were free and therefore legally different from African slaves. But in the French colonial context, they did not emerge legally or socially as white. They were *gens de couleur libre,* free people of color.

Legally the population was divided into whites, free people of color, and slaves. From a strictly legal standpoint, the tripartite classification rested on the application of two different criteria of differentiation: possession or lack of possession of legal freedom, and descent or lack of descent from Africans. But the social processes that led to the emergence of free people of color—sexual unions between European settlers and African slaves and the manumission of their offspring—made it de facto a classification by ancestry. *Gens de couleur libre* became a near-synonym for offspring of mixed European and African unions. In 1732, all 6 free persons of color in New Orleans were labeled *mulatre(sse)*, words signifying racial mixture. By 1769 this was true of 68 of the 99 (68.7 percent) free persons of color in the city (total population of 3,190), and by 1778, of 248 of 353 (70.2 percent).

When in 1768 Louisiana came under Spanish control, Spanish laws perpetuated the tripartite distinction. On one hand, Spanish administration meant the subjection of Louisiana to long-standing stipulations about purity of blood. A legacy of medieval concerns abolished only in 1865, the concept of purity entitled only those "not having neither mixture nor race of Moors, Jews, heretics or convicts of the Inquisition" (Martínez Alcubilla 1891(7): 890–891) to enter particular professions and accede to certain offices. Purity of blood signified "absence of infidel ancestry" (Domínguez Ortiz 1955: 233). In the overseas possessions, however, as Martínez-Alier has pointed out, "in the end it was only those of African origin who were regarded as contaminated and thus to be avoided by those of 'pure blood'" (1974: 15). In this sense, Louisiana's free people of color were, by law, clearly differentiated from the rest of the free population.

On the other hand, the Spanish administration did little to dichotomize the population. It continued to recognize manumission of slaves and the right of children of free people of color to free status. It prohibited marriage between whites and all people of color but gave the authorities the power to grant dispensations from this impediment to marriage. One of Antonio de Ulloa's acts in his first year in office as first Spanish governor of Louisiana was to grant permission to a Frenchman to marry a Negro woman (Haskins 1975: 19–20). In addition, for nearly twenty years it failed to issue official regulations against concubinage between whites and people of color. Even the 1786 "Bando de Buen Gobierno" left the government's intent unclear. It ordered free-colored women to wear *tignons* (kerchiefs) so they would not be mistaken for white—a reminder of the purity-of-blood criterion. It also specified that it would proceed with severity against persons living in concubinage—an officially color-blind statement of support for the position of the Catholic church. Finally, it declared that it would not tolerate free Negro, mulatto, or quadroon women earning a living on "incontinence" (Gayarré 1886; Fortier 1892; Baudier 1939: 203)— in its phrasing an attack on colored prostitution that contained within it recognition of the separation of free people of color from the slave population. By 1803, 23.8 percent (1,335 residents) of the population of New Orleans was free-colored (cf. Davis 1806: 136).

The 1808 project of the Louisiana Civil Code acknowledged the existence of the three sectors of society and sought to prevent marriage across either of the two boundaries.

Civil Code 1808, page 24, article 8 states: "Free persons and slaves are incapable of contracting marriage together; the celebration of such marriages is forbidden, and the marriage is void; it is the same with respect to the marriages contracted by free white persons with free people of color" (cf. also Acts 1807, chapter 17-13.)

So strong was the correspondence between free-colored status and mixed ancestry that it influenced legal decisions early in the nineteenth century. The *gens de couleur* were presumed to be free under Louisiana law; blacks were not. The Louisiana Supreme Court declared in 1810 that "persons of color may be descended from Indians on both sides, from a white parent, or mulatto parents in possession of their freedom." Hence, the court added, the probability that a colored person was free was so great that he ought not to be deprived of freedom upon mere presumption, "but that perhaps a Negro plaintiff would be required to establish his right by such evidence as would destroy the force of the presumption arising from colour" (*Adele* v. *Beauregard* in Martin 1811: 183).

The 1825 Civil Code continued the prohibition on marriage between slaves, free people of color, and whites in Louisiana. Even so, intermating continued, and with it the size of the racially mixed population grew. The phrase "free people of color," upon whose meaning the antimiscegenation statutes depended, became more and more equivocal. In February 1857, a bill was introduced in the Louisiana state legislature that defined "person of color" as anyone with a "taint of African blood." The bill's sponsor argued that although the Civil Code explicitly prohibited marriages between free-colored and white persons, a clearer statute was needed to prevent miscegenous marriages between whites and those who looked white but who could be shown to have "a touch of the tarbrush." He reported in his presentation that "such marriages were not infrequent" in New Orleans, that they were in fact on the rise (*New Orleans Daily Picayune*, February 20, 1857; Everett 1950: 117–118). Although the bill did not pass, it was evidence of increasing white concern with the growth of a sector of the population of color that was physically Caucasian enough to pass for white.

Reconstruction altered the picture temporarily. The state legislature, dominated by colored southerners and white northerners, allowed antimiscegenation provisions to disappear from the 1870 revision of the Civil Code. Yet it is evident from white judges' rulings in the cases of *Hart* v. *Hoss and Elder* (26 La. Ann. 90) in 1874 and the *Succession of T. W. Colwell* in 1882 (34 La. Ann. 265) that repeal of antimiscegenation statutes was thought, by whites at least, contrary to the basic principles of Louisiana social structure.

E. C. Hart had lived for a number of years in concubinage with the plaintiff Cornelia, a woman of color. They had several children. In November 1867, Hart married Cornelia in Shreveport. The marriage was legal according to the state constitution of 1864 and the civil rights bill proposed by the United States Congress on June 13, 1866, as the Fourteenth Amendment to the U.S. Constitution. It was solemnized by a Roman Catholic priest in accordance with the forms of the Roman Catholic church. The same priest subsequently baptized the children at their father's request and with his consent (although he could not be present himself). Hart died some eighteen months later.

In this case, his collateral heirs sued to prevent Cornelia and her children from inheriting his estate. They argued that the children were permanently ineligible to inherit from Hart, as they had been conceived at a time when he was legally incapable of marrying Cornelia. Although one of the judges agreed with the collateral heirs, the opinion of the majority was to rule in favor of Hart's colored family. "No impediment would be in the way of white children becoming legitimated, standing in every respect under the same circumstances" (26 La. Ann. 97). Article 199 states that "children legitimated by a subsequent marriage have the same rights as if they were born during marriage."

In its long written opinion, the court stressed time and again that its ruling was the direct effect of the civil rights bill, which conflicted with, and overrode, traditional Louisiana law; the court thus argued that the ruling in effect did not come from within Louisiana but was "imposed" upon the state. In J. Morgan's dissenting opinion, there is clear though covert criticism of the civil rights bill.

> It is held by the majority of the court that what is known as the Civil Rights bill obliterates all State laws creating distinctions between inhabitants of the State on account of race, color or previous condition, and therefore the marriage between Hart and the plaintiff was not prohibited by the State laws at the time

of their marriage, and the marriage legitimates the children under the acknowledgments to be found in the record. *I do not so read the law.* I understand it to give to all citizens of the United States of every race and color without regard to any previous condition of slavery the right to make and enforce contracts, to sue, be parties, and give evidence, to inherit, etc., and to full and equal benefit of all laws and proceedings for the security of persons and property as is enjoyed by white citizens. Marriage is, with us, a civil contract; inheritance is regulated by law. White persons and persons of color may by this act contract marriage; colored children may inherit. This proposition I do not dispute. But I deny that the act in question professes to regulate the legitimation of children, or that it provides how the fact of legitimation shall be established, or what acts constitute legitimation, or that it pretends to alter our laws upon the subject of inheritance. It simply does away with all distinctions on account of race, color or previous condition.

Eight years later in the *Succession of T. W. Colwell* the court affirmed its earlier opinion and its criticism of laws that made miscegenation legal. Here the two legitimate sisters of the deceased, T. W. Colwell, fought against his colored children for his succession, an estate worth more than $60,000. The children claimed to be his forced and only rightful heirs; the sisters claimed that his marriage to the children's mother, a colored woman by the name of Delia McCalop, was not valid because it crossed racial boundaries. The court ruled reluctantly in favor of Colwell's children. Although the children were conceived and born at a time when the parents could not legally have married each other, the marriage was valid at the time it was celebrated and it had the effect of legitimating Colwell's children.

By the end of the nineteenth century, the situation had changed drastically. Not only were whites again in political power, but they also sought more than ever to separate the white population of Louisiana from the state's large population of color. Interracial marriages were again made illegal in 1894. And it is clear from legislators' deliberations that they were concerned with marriages between whites and racially mixed persons as much as between whites and blacks. The state legislature was particularly concerned with the specific case of a white man married to a "mulatress" (Saunders 1925: 27). Overt legal concern began to extend openly beyond the question of interracial marriage. White legislators sought to prevent all forms of continued sexual contact between the "pure" and the "impure," and it was clear by the turn of the century, if not before, that prohibiting interracial marriage alone would not achieve this goal. Thus, in 1908, the legislature passed a bill (Act 87 of the regular session, p. 105) making concubinage "between a person of the Caucasian race and a person of the negro race a felony, fixing the punishment therefore and defining what shall constitute concubinage."

Act 87, 1908—

Section 1. Be it enacted by the General Assembly of the State of Louisiana that concubinage between a person of the Caucasian or white race and a person of the negro or black race is hereby made a felony, and whoever shall be convicted thereof in any course of competent jurisdiction, shall for each offense be sentenced to imprisonment at the discretion of the court for a term of not less than one month nor more than one year with or without hard labor.

Section 2. Be it further enacted, etc. that the living together or cohabitation of persons of the Caucasian and of the negro races shall be proof of the violation of the provision of section 1 of this act. For the purpose of this Act concubinage is hereby defined to be the unlawful cohabitation of persons of the Caucasian and of the negro race whether open or secret.

Section 3. Be it further enacted, etc. that it shall be the duty of the judges of the several district courts of this State to specifically charge the grand juries upon this Act.

Section 4. Be it further enacted, etc. that all laws and parts of laws in conflict with the provisions of this Act be and the same are hereby repealed.

(Bill introduced by Mr. Hunsicker, act signed by H. G.

Dupré, speaker of the House, P. M. Lambremont, lieutenant governor and president of the Senate; and J. Y. Sanders, governor of the state of Louisiana.)

But Act 87 of 1908 would not prove to be sufficient to prevent interracial sexual unions. The case of *State* v. *Treadaway* (126 La. 500) in 1910 revealed its major loophole. Octave Treadaway was indicted for miscegenation, in violation of Act 87 of 1908. Treadaway was white; his companion, an octoroon. In the words of the Supreme Court of Louisiana, which finally resolved the case, "the sole question is whether an octoroon is 'a person of the negro or black race' within the meaning of this statute" (ibid.: 501). After long deliberation and extensive legal discourse on the definitions of the words negro and colored, the Supreme Court of Louisiana (affirming the lower court's judgment) acquitted the defendants. An octoroon, it argued, was simply not a negro.

The Louisiana Supreme Court's case rested on the distinction between the terms *negro* and *person of color*. It argued that a negro is necessarily a person of color, but a person of color is not necessarily a negro (ibid.: 508). "There are no negroes who are not persons of color; but there are persons of color who are not negroes" (ibid.). Because Act 87 of 1908 used the term *negro* rather than *person of color*, the court argued that the legislature's intention could not have been to extend the crime of interracial concubinage to persons of color who were not negroes. The court noted, among other things, that the author of the original bill had included a clause that enlarged the meaning of the word *negro* to include most persons of color, but that the legislature struck out that particular clause before the bill was passed. The clause specified "that a person who is as much as one thirty-second part-negro shall be, for the purpose of this act, a person of the negro race." Why then did the legislature strike out this particular clause? The court reasoned that it could only have been struck out because the act was not meant to apply to non-negro persons of color. "If the act was intended to apply to Mulattoes, quadroons, etc., the clause could do no harm, and there was absolutely no reason to strike it out. It could only tend to make the act more definite" (ibid.: 510). The court also dismissed a further suggestion that the clause was struck out because it was useless and unnecessary to include a definition of *negro*.

To say that the definition was wholly useless would be to lose sight of the fact that until the decision of this court in the case of Lee v. New Orleans and Great Northern Railroad Co., 125 La. 236, 51 South. 182, no one in this state—not the Governor, not any judge of any of the courts of the state—could have undertaken to say with any degree of authoritativeness what proportion of blood a person had to have in his veins in order to be classed as a person of color. The question had to come to this court, and a definition [one-sixteenth traceable negro blood] was adopted by this court only after study of the general jurisprudence upon the subject, and even then the definition first adopted was changed in consultation. To say, under these circumstances, that the reason why the definition which for the purpose of enlarging the ordinary dictionary meaning of the word "negro" the author of this bill had added to it was stricken out was that the definition was useless, mere surplusage, dead matter in the bill, is, in our opinion, to go dead against the plain truth of the matter. Had the definition not been stricken out, but remained in the bill, it would have saved this court much labor in the case of Lee v. N. Or. and G. N. R. Co., supra. We can come to no other conclusion than that the Legislature struck the definition out because the statute with the definition in it included mulattoes, quadroons, etc., whereas, short of the definition, it did not include them (ibid.: 510–511).

However, the state supreme court was soon to be proven wrong in its interpretation of the legislature's intention. The state legislature, which convened a month after the court's final decision on the Treadaway case, passed a bill extending the anticoncubinage statute to persons of color. Act 206 of 1910 was a nearly exact replica of the 1908 act, except that it substituted the phrase "person of the colored or black race" for the phrase "person of the negro or black race" which had appeared in the 1908 act. Justice Land had foreseen such a change in his dissenting opinion on the Treadaway case. He had argued that Act 87 of 1908 had been "intended as an additional legal barrier against the intermixing of the blood of the two races" (*State* v. *Treadaway*, p. 511).

> To hold that the term "negro race" includes only persons of unmixed African blood would defeat the plain purpose of the lawmaker. Under such a rigid construction, a person of African descent with any admixture whatever of white or non-negro blood would be immune from the operation of the anti-miscegenation statute of 1908, and would render its prohibition practically nugatory. . . .
>
> The anti-miscegenation act of 1908 has since its passage been uniformly construed and enforced as including negroes of mixed blood and a number of persons have been convicted, sentenced, and punished on that theory of the law. The case at bar is the first and only one in which this construction has been controverted. *Fortunately the General Assembly will convene next month, and will have an opportunity of expressing the legislative intent in no uncertain terms* (ibid.: 511–512; emphasis added).

The Treadaway case is crucial on several counts. It expresses the dilemma of the period of transition from a ternary system of classification to a binary one. It brings to the surface the express use of statutory law to prevent interracial consanguinity and its implications. And it brings out into the open the growing concern with interracial consanguinity. The Supreme Court of Louisiana was well aware of the changing ideological climate. It noted that, up to the session of 1908, the legislature had not deemed the time ripe for prohibiting concubinage even with the pure-blooded negro. "It is the growth and progress of ideas that has induced this legislation" (ibid.: 509). Although statutory law had always been used in Louisiana to prevent the social and economic implications of consanguinity from applying across social boundaries, the use of statutory law to prevent interracial concubinage signified a changing ideological climate that stressed purity of blood to a much greater degree than ever before.

The 1908 and 1910 acts condemned interracial concubinage, *whether open or secret.* Their purpose was to prevent continued interracial sexual relations. Concubinage itself had never been considered criminal, as long as the parties involved belonged to the same "race." Moreover, concubinage between persons of the same race did not incur any disabilities when it did not offend public morality—that is, when it remained secretive and discrete. When it was open and notorious, the law would limit a concubine's right to inherit from his or her lover, but this was its greatest sanction. The statutes passed against interracial concubinage were significantly harsher than any prior law dealing with concubinage itself. Interracial concubinage became a felony and a crime regardless of whether it was open or secret. The 1910 statute was tested on the latter point in 1917 in the case of *State* v. *Daniel* (141 La. 999, 75 So. 836). Walter Daniel was convicted under an indictment charging that he, being a man of the Caucasian, or white, race, did willfully and feloniously live together and cohabit with a woman of the colored, or black, race. In arguing its case affirming Daniel's conviction, the Louisiana Supreme Court stressed that secret as well as open interracial concubinage was felonious under the provisions of the 1910 act.

Further twentieth-century jurisprudence sought to clarify possible ambiguities in other aspects of antimiscegenation law. One of these concerned the meaning of *person of color.* People of non-Caucasian, non-Negro ancestry had been labeled *persons of color* throughout the nineteenth century. But to continue to call them persons of color in the twentieth century would mean that they would assume all legal disabilities intended only for those with African ancestry. The relabeling of Indians and Filipinos was part of the movement to clarify the intentions of anti-miscegenation statutes.

The Louisiana Supreme Court decision in the case of *Adele* v. *Beauregard* (1 Mart [O.S.] 184) in 1810 explicitly stated that American Indians were persons of color, and this classification was accepted as valid throughout the nineteenth century. This meant that until 1870 when antimiscegenation statutes were repealed by Reconstruction governments, marriages between Indians and whites were prohibited. When interracial marriages were again outlawed in 1894, Indians—still classified as persons of color—were again prohibited from marrying whites. This depended exclusively on their identification as persons of color. The first legal sign of a change in the classification of Indians came in the form of a 1920 statute (act 220; Louisiana Revised Statute 9:201) that treated the union of an Indian and a person of the "colored and black" race as miscegenetic and thereby nullified it completely. Indians were thereby described as noncolored for the first time in Louisiana's legal history. By the 1930s, we find the attorney general explicitly stating that marriage between white persons and Indians was not prohibited in Louisiana (cf. *Opinions Attorney General* 587 [1932–1934]; and Pascal 1962: 28). No cases have challenged the validity of white-Indian marriages in the last half century, and it is now generally thought that such marriages are valid (Pascal 1962: 28). The result has been a legal reclassification of Indians and confirmation of the interpretation that the 1910 act really applied only to persons of African ancestry.

Similar conclusions must be drawn from judicial decisions dealing with the racial classification of Filipinos in Louisiana. On January 21, 1946, Charles Stephen Villa filed a suit to annul his marriage to Josephine Lacoste on the ground that she was a Negro (*Villa* v. *Lacoste*, 35 So. 2d 419). He had concluded that she was Negro when he discovered that her birth certificate labeled her as *colored,* and he, it seems, equated *colored* with *negro*.

The defense conceded that Mrs. Catherine Lacoste, Josephine's mother, had registered her daughter and her grandchild as colored. But, the judicial opinion explained,

> that she did so under the erroneous belief that persons of Filipino extraction are colored, resulting from information given her at the office of the Recorder of Births, Marriages and Deaths and that, as a matter of fact, neither the defendant wife nor child is colored in the sense that they are Negroes or have any Negro blood in their veins. In support of this contention, numerous witnesses were produced and the District Judge, after hearing them testify, remarked at the close of the case: "The recordation of two of the persons involved in this suit as colored has been explained to my satisfaction and there is nothing in the evidence to indicate that there was ever any Negro blood in the family of either the plaintiff or the defendant. The only color involved at all is that of the Filipino" (35 So. 2d 420).

Genealogical research preceded the final court decision. The defendant's father, Leopold Lacoste, "is shown to be a Frenchman and this fact is not contested" (35 So. 2d 420–421). The defendant's mother was the issue of Mary Louise Caruso, a white woman, and Manuel Azago, a Philippine national. The court accepted the testimony of an eighty-six-year-old Filipino (Raymond Calibash) who stated that Azago came to the United States as a young man from the Philippines. Calibash called Azago, the defendant's mother's father, a "Blanco Filipino," literally Philippine white. Further inquiry revealed that the Registrar's Office had informed the defendant's mother when she registered the birth of her daughter and her grandchild "that if she was Filipino the persons she was registering should be recorded as 'colored'" (ibid.). It is interesting to compare the attitudes of the two deputy recorders in charge of recording the two respective births in question. The first birth certificate, dated January 9, 1913, was issued by P. Henry Lanauze, a white Creole who, according to his successor, "would always record Filipinos as 'colored' and . . . would not record them as Filipinos unless they insisted on being registered as white" (ibid.). The second birth certificate, dated July 23, 1941, was issued by Mr. Prudhomme, also a white Creole, who assumed there must have been strong reasons for registering the mother "colored" in the first place. If the child's mother is labeled colored, whatever the actual ancestry involved, the child must be labeled colored also. Mr. Lanauze was following the nineteenth-century practice of considering non-Negro, non-Caucasian persons colored, while Mr. Prudhomme's attitude was to question the reliability of testimony that there was indeed no Negro blood in the child's veins, given the later twentieth-century popular assumption that the term *colored* implied at least some admixture of Negro blood. In reaching its verdict, the Louisiana Supreme Court dealt with both men's approaches. It dismissed Mr. Prudhomme's assumptions for lack of evidence, and it described Mr. Lanauze's practice as erroneous. In so doing, the court denied the possibility that there may have been historical change.

THE CRITERION OF TRACEABILITY

The last four decades have been marked by an active struggle over racial classification. In 1938, in *Sunseri* v. *Cassagne* (191 La. 209, 185 So. 1—affirmed on rehearing in 1940, 195 La. 19, 196 So. 7)—the Louisiana Supreme Court proclaimed traceability of African ancestry to be the only requirement for definition of *colored*. In 1949, Naomi Drake assumed the post of supervisor and deputy registrar of vital statistics at the Louisiana Bureau of Vital Statistics, and she figures prominently in cases filed against the bureau through the mid-1960s.

Armed with the traceability criterion established by the court in 1938, she followed the practice of race-flagging,

pulling out a birth certificate that lists a baby as white but bears a name common to blacks. Such birth certificates are checked against a "race list" maintained by the Vital Records Office. . . .

If the name appears on the "race list," then a further study of genealogical records maintained by the Vital Records Office is conducted (a description given to the *New Orleans States Item,* June 5–16, 1978, by a Dr. Doris Thompson who had been assistant secretary of the State Department of Health and Human Resources, of which the Bureau is a part).

If the bureau determined through study of its genealogical records that the person in question had any African ancestors, the applicant was then informed that a certificate would be issued only if it declared the person to be colored. If the applicant refused to accept such a certificate, the bureau in turn refused to issue a certificate. There is evidence that between 1960 and 1965 a minimum of 4,700 applications for certified copies of birth certificates and a minimum of 1,100 applications for death certificates were held in abeyance by the bureau under the supervision of Naomi Drake (188 So. 2nd 94). Of course, not all of these were withheld because of disagreements over racial designations, but most presumably were.

As a result, during her tenure thirty-eight dockets of petitions for writs of mandamus were filed against the Bureau of Vital Statistics, the City of New Orleans, the State Board of Health, and individuals who served as registrars of vital statistics. Individuals petitioned the courts to force the bureau to change the racial labels that appeared on the birth or death certificates of members of their families. They presented evidence that purported to prove that these people were white despite the imputations of bureau genealogists. In each case, the bureau questioned the authenticity of much of the evidence adduced, or the nature of the evidence introduced during the proceedings. Plaintiff's job was to dispute the authenticity of the document(s), prove that (s)he was the child of a different marriage or of a sexual union resulting from a parent's remarriage or concubinage, or dispute the meaning of the specific social label that in the eyes of the bureau implied Negro ancestry.

Docket 335-465, filed January 11, 1955 (*Vealey Smith et al.* v.

Louisiana State Board of Health et al.) illustrates a successful use of the first strategy. Vealey Smith and his wife Susie Welch of Crowley, Louisiana, had three children, Lawrence J., Jessie Willard, and Elsie Oller, whose birth certificates contained a host of errors. The number of obvious mistakes in these certificates was clearly a factor in the plaintiff being granted all requests. Jessie Willard Smith's birth certificate, for instance, listed him as female, misspelled his mother's maiden name (Welsh where it should have read Welch), gave the wrong birth date (actually born December 8, 1922, not December 9), misnamed the child Jessie Willie, and designated his father and mother as "colored," whereas the petitioners claimed to be members of the white or Caucasian race. Laurence J. Smith's birth certificate contained a similar number of errors—specifying his sex as "fem and boy," misnaming him Louis, and labeling his parents colored. In the case of the third child, only the parents' race was mistaken. While legal actions of this sort often last several years before they are finally resolved, Judge W. B. Hamlin of the Civil District Court found this case obvious enough to render judgment in plaintiff's favor in only ten days.

Only partially successful in disputing the authenticity or correctness of personal documents were Joseph Billiot and his wife Arthemise Theriot of New Orleans (docket 340-209, filed on September 1, 1955). They had appraised the nearly insurmountable difficulty of obtaining a white legal identity and sought instead to change the racial designation of several lineally related members of their immediate family from colored to Indian. According to the plaintiff, her mother, Ernestine Theriot, was listed "through mistake, inadvertence and error . . . as 'colored'" on her 1906 certificate of death. A child, Ray Billiot, died on April 16, 1936, in Terrebonne Parish. "Through mistake, inadvertence and error," the certificate of death registered the decedent as "B." And on the birth certificate of their daughter Molly born February 2, 1935, Joseph Billiot and Arthemise Theriot themselves appear as "colored."

The relatives argued that all of their ascendants, except for her mother, were registered "as white persons or Indians," and that "they are direct descendants of the original Houma tribe of Indians, and that all of their anticedents [*sic*] were either pure blood Indians or in some cases their anticedents [*sic*] were married to white persons, either French or American, and that there is no Negro blood in any of their antecedents." To support their contentions, they submitted to the courts dozens of birth and death certificates of immediate lineal ancestors, descendants and collaterals. In addition, Billiot and his wife submitted their daughter Molly's high school diploma, which proved she had attended white schools all her life. On December 2, 1955, the attending judge granted the Billiot-Theriot family, and all thirty-eight kinsmen and affines named in the case, legal Indian status. The Bureau of Vital Statistics had been unable to produce a single vital record of any close relative labeled colored, Negro, mulatto, or any other such designation.

In a protracted case that matched the wits of Larry Lille Toledano and Naomi Drake (cf. dockets 395-651; 411-465; 428-393; and 161 So. 2d 339), Toledano sought to prove that the man who had acknowledged him as his child and who was married to his mother at the time of his birth was not his genitor. His *pater,* Chester Joseph Toledano, was legally colored; his mother's first husband, whom he claimed retrospectively as genitor, was white. For Toledano, the verdict was not wholly satisfactory, although the courts did rule that his birth certificate was to be corrected to identify him as white. It seems that Naomi Drake, not convinced by Toledano's arguments, decided to comply with the court's orders by crossing out the word colored and writing over it in red ink the word white. She also inserted "altered 6/14/62 by court order—N.O. Civil Dist. Court #395-651, Div. "C" signed May 4, 1962 Judge F. J. Cassibry." Dissatisfied with the manner in which the records were changed, Toledano then filed a rule for contempt on Naomi Drake and petitioned for a writ of mandamus ordering her to erase and completely obliterate the word *colored* from the face of the records. While the lower court acceded to his request, the appellate court concluded that total obliteration of the word colored from the birth certificate was not necessary. In a 1968 judgment on a similar case (*Cline* v. *City of New Orleans,* 207 So. 2d 856), the same appellate court, but with two out of three judges changed, criticized the earlier Toledano decision. "We might add," they wrote, "as an additional distinction that we entertain some doubt about the *ratio decidende* of the Toledano case" (207 So. 2d 959).

The 1962 Richards case is similar (cf. docket 406-345, *Sybil Marie Richards* v. *Mrs. Naomi Drake, Registrar, city of New Orleans Health Department*; cf. also docket 408-231, *Raleigh P. Richards, Jr. et al.* v. *Naomi Drake, Registrar, City of New Orleans Health Department*). Sybil Marie Richards was born August 24, 1960, in Orleans Parish to Raleigh Paul Richards, Jr., and Elizabeth Ann Curé. When Naomi Drake refused to register the child as white or Caucasian, the parents sued. On November 23, 1962, Judge René Viosca granted an injunction to keep Naomi Drake "from further changing or altering, or causing or permitting the change or the alteration of, all records in her possession relating to the plaintiff in this suit and to any person related to the said plaintiff in the direct ascending line during the pendency of this suit." Then in a series of motions filed over a period of more than five years, the family of the plaintiff and the Bureau of Vital Statistics discussed the child's genealogy in detail. From the records submitted to the court, I have been able to draw up a genealogical chart. (See Figure 2.1.)

The central problem in this case was to identify the individual who was Sybil Marie Richards's father's mother's father (FMF). Plaintiffs argued that Louise Jeanne's (SMR's FM) (GEN. IV) genitor was Fred Snider, a man of undisputed Caucasian ancestry, and not Louis J. Soyez, whom they admitted had "a traceable amount of Colored blood." Lydia Hendrickson (GEN. III) married Fred Schneider of Gretna on February 1, 1908. Casimir, Thelma and Edward (GEN. IV) were born in 1908,

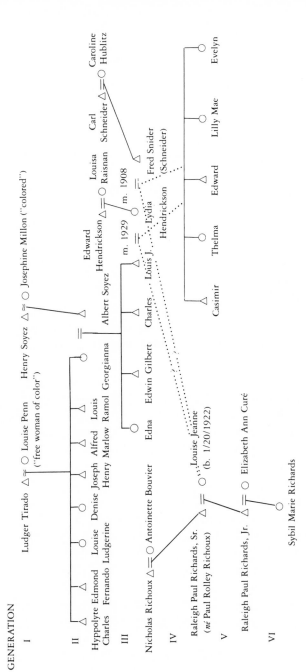

Figure 2.1 Sybil Marie Richards's Genealogy

1910, and 1911. All three were labeled white on their birth certificates. On January 20, 1922, a fourth child, Louise Jeanne, was born to Lydia Hendrickson. But this time Lydia registered the child as the illegitimate daughter of Louis Soyez, and not her husband's legitimate child. In fact, she registered the child with the Bureau of Vital Statistics under the name of Louise Soyez. Lydia may well not have known about Louis's Negro ancestry, since he registered all his children in the bureau as white. At some point, however, genealogical research at the bureau produced substantial documentation of Negro ancestry on the part of Louis J. Soyez. This included his own mother's death certificate, which listed her as "Col.," his father's mother's death certificate, which likewise labeled her "colored," his mother's siblings' birth records, which were listed in the old "colored"/"Negro" birth registry books, and documents to the effect that his mother's mother, Louise Penn, was "a free woman of color." This discovery led the bureau to change the racial designations on the birth certificates of Sybil Marie, Raleigh Richards, Jr., Louise Jeanne Soyez, Evelyn Soyez/Snider, Lilly Mae Soyez/Snider, and Louis Soyez from white to Negro. Because of the abundance of documentation produced by the bureau proving Louis Soyez had partial Negro ancestry, plaintiffs' only recourse to restitution of their white legal status was to challenge Lydia Hendrickson's declarations concerning the paternity of her fourth child.

Plaintiffs asked the court to disregard the mother's declarations in said birth certificate, and cited three cases (*Eloi* v. *Mader* [1841] 1 Rob. 581, 38 Ann. Dec. 192; *Tate* v. *Penne* [1829] 7 Mart. [N.S.] 553; *Feazel* v. *Feazel* [1953] 222 La. 113, 62 So. 2d 119) holding that the legitimacy of a child born in wedlock cannot be affected by the mother's declarations. The bureau's response stresses the ideology of purity of blood:

> We see that it is the hope of plaintiffs to prove that the true race of Louise Jeanne Soyez is white, merely by reason of the presumption of paternity under Louisiana Civil Code Article

184. Respondent has no interest whatsoever insofar as the rights of Louise Jeanne Soyez to inherit from Fred Snider are very dubious, inasmuch as her birth was, beyond doubt, concealed from Fred Snider. . . .

Nevertheless, the right of Louise Jeanne Soyez to inherit from Fred Snider is not at issue before this Court in herein proceedings. . . .

The only issue before this Court at this time is what is the true and actual race of Louise Jeanne Soyez, Raleigh P. Richards, Jr. and Sybil Marie Richards, and since race is a natural fact which necessarily follows from the actual relationship of a child to his actual parents, the relationship of parents to child cannot be presumed *de jure et de jure* and the public interest demands that evidence to rebut any presumption of Article 184 of the Civil Code of Louisiana could and would be used as an instrument of fraud, misrepresentation and deception to show the race of a person to be something other than which it actually is.

The case dragged on until 1968 when a motion of dismissal was signed by the officiating judge. The plaintiff told the court that Naomi Drake's successor in office had complied with his request, so there was no longer any reason to sue. But during the course of the case, the bureau made it clear that its concept of race was based on the notion of purity of blood, and that it considered any legal attempts to define *Negro* arbitrary and unnatural.

February 28, 1963, memorandum:

It is the position of respondent that the Legislature of this State may enact legislation, which, by way of presumption, may create legal rights, duties and obligations, such as the right to inherit from the presumed father, or to demand damages for the death of the deceased presumed father, or to demand support from the presumed father (Louisiana Civil Code Article 184), but vigorously denies that the Legislature has the authority to change the race of an individual from that which it actually is to that which it actually is not by way of presumption, for such legislation would be arbitrary, capricious and unreasonable;

would have no foundation in fact or reason and would give to the Legislature the power to do the impossible. The Legislature can no more change the race of an individual from white to Negro or from Negro to white, than it can change day to night or night to day.

Naomi Drake's conception of the job of supervisor and deputy registrar of the Bureau of Vital Statistics of the City of New Orleans was so much at odds with the changing political climate of the fifties and sixties that in the end it brought on her dismissal (188 So. 2d 92). In a letter addressed to her dated March 18, 1965, Dr. Rodney Jung, director of the Board of Health, spelled out the reasons for her discharge:

1. Constant harassment to members of the Board and to the Director of Health by irate citizens complaining of your failure to assist them in obtaining the necessary certificates they have requested.

2. Frequent complaints in writing from attorneys and the public alike complaining of your failure to assist them in obtaining the necessary certificates they have requested.

3. On November 5, 1958, a meeting was held with you, myself and the then Director of Health, the late Dr. Walter P. Gardiner, wherein "certain practices pertaining to bad public relations were discussed at great length." In his letter to you Dr. Gardiner also stated, "The continuance of such practices shall invoke appropriate disciplinary action." *Bad public relations* apparently seem still to exist.

4. Your apparent lack of leadership and the manner with which you address your fellow employees.

5. Reprimanding employees before fellow workers and the public, rather than in the privacy of your office.

6. Lack of courtesy and tact by making such statements to a citizen as, "All of the people born in White Castle, La. are *half breeds.*"

7. Rate of turnover of employees under your supervision because of your attitude and treatment of them as can be attested to

by numerous letters to this office and the City Civil Service Department (emphasis added).

Upon dismissal, Naomi Drake initiated legal action to obtain reinstatement to her former position, which the lower court and later the appellate court denied her. Seven hundred ninety-four pages of testimony fully substantiating the charge of insubordination accompany the case. Two letters from Dr. Jung, dated August 19, 1964, and March 12, 1965, instructed her "to issue certified copies of birth and death certificates, on request, *to persons qualified under the provisions of R.S. 40: 158.* . . . This means that in the future certified copies are not to be withheld because of the incompleteness or suspicions of inaccuracy of the original record" (188 So. 2nd 94).

The fact is, however, that the practice of race-flagging and withholding certificates continued long after Naomi Drake's departure from her post. We have no way of estimating the number of applications for birth or death certificates withheld since the mid-sixties (this information is now considered confidential and is carefully guarded by clerks and bureaucrats), but other indices are telling. Twelve mandamus proceedings against the bureau have been initiated since Drake's official departure. Also on May 26, 1977, Wayne Parker, at the time registrar of vital statistics, admitted to me in an interview that in 1977 the bureau employed two full-time clerk investigators to handle only cases concerned with racial designation, and that the bureau spent some six thousand man-hours in 1976 exclusively on race cases. Parker estimated that between sixty and a hundred surnames were regularly flagged by the bureau and checked in a special file room against fairly extensive genealogies kept by the bureau on the many branches of these families. Thompson (cf. *New Orleans States Item,* June 5-16, 1978) estimated that 250 names of "white" families with partially black ancestry were kept at the bureau.

But the job was clearly made more difficult when the Louisiana state legislature passed Act 46, entitled "Designation of race by public officials," in 1970. That act stated: "In signifying race, a person having one thirty-second or less of Negro blood shall not be deemed, described or designated by any public official in the state of Louisiana as 'colored,' a 'mulatto,' a 'black,' a 'negro,' a 'griffe,' an 'Afro-American,' a 'quadroon,' a 'mestizo,' a 'colored person' or 'a person of color'" (La. Rev. Stat. Ann. 42: 267—Supp. 23A of 1975).

The new law demanded a mathematical determination of a person's racial makeup. To do so required making certain assumptions about the use of social labels and the process of intergenerational transmission, which the courts simply could not accept as factual. For instance, the bureau assumed that *mulatto* always meant precisely half-Negro, *quadroon* one-quarter Negro, *octoroon* one-eighth Negro, and *Negro* or *African* meant 100 percent Negro. Using these ideal equivalences and assuming that always half a person's "racial traits" are transmitted to his children in the blood, the bureau came up with the following figures. In *Thomas* v. *Louisiana State Board of Health* (278 So. 2d 915; La. App. 1973), the Board of Health argued that Ms. Thomas "had" 5/32 "Negro blood," and her children 2.5/32 "Negro blood." In *Messina* v. *Ciaccio* (290 So. 2d 339; La. App. 1974), they claimed the child was 3/32 Negro. In *State ex rel. Plaia* v. *Louisiana State Board of Health* (275 So. 2d 201; La. App. 1973), the registrar determined that Elizabeth Maria Plaia, age five, had 5.75/32 "Negro blood," and in *Ward* v. *Director of the Bureau of Vital Statistics, Louisiana State Health Department* (docket #74-2349, section "H," United States District Court, Eastern District of Louisiana 1975), the bureau contended that Lisa Marie Anthony had precisely 3.375/32 "Negro blood."

In response to a letter of inquiry dated September 26, 1975, from a member of the staff of the Hastings Constitutional Law Quarterly, legal counsel for the Louisiana Board of Health, which administers the Bureau of Vital Statistics, argued that "Act 46 of 1970 has presented an almost impossible situation as far as keeping accurate statistics as to race in the State of Louisiana and it appears that the courts either will not or do not want to understand the unconstitutional structure of Act 46 of 1970, which is vague and indefinite and furnishes no definition or guidelines for the use of the terms contained therein" (Davis 1976: 206). But the bureau persevered.

Its efforts are particularly noteworthy in its case against Plaia. (See Figure 2.2.) First the registrar determined that Frank Joseph Plaia's ancestors were indisputably white, as there was no evidence anywhere to the contrary. The bureau, then, traced the child's maternal line back seven generations. References in the *Clarion Herald Newspaper* in June 1970 (volume 8, no. 17) and in a few other such publications to the Metoyer family of the Cane River area described Marie Thérèse (GEN. I) as a "native of Africa." The registrar equated this with "100% African blood." Jean Baptiste Metoyer (GEN. III) was listed in one document placed in evidence as a freeman of color and in the 1850 census as "mulatto." But since his mother's race was unknown (which led the registrar to assume that she was white, the unmarked category), and only one of his paternal grandparents was "Negro," the bureau decided he was one-fourth Negro. Census records identified Suzette Anty (GEN. III) as "mulatto"; for the registrar she was one-half Negro. Marie Julia Metoyer (GEN. IV) appears in the 1870 and 1880 censuses as "mulatto," but was labeled "white" on her death certificate; the registrar made her out to be three-eighths Negro. Clay Llorens (GEN. IV), Harriet Prudhomme (GEN. IV), Firmin Christophe (GEN. III), Marie Frances Mailleur (GEN. III), Alfred Demery (GEN. IV), and Elizabeth Watts (GEN. IV) appear as "mulattoes" on U.S. censuses between 1850 and 1880. The bureau assumes they are all exactly half-Negro. Clothilde Llorens (GEN. V) was "white" on her death certificate, Louise Demery (GEN. V) "French" and "colored" simultaneously, also on her death certificate, and Robert Lee Demery (GEN. VI) "white" at his deathbed. Atha Lucy Christophe (GEN. VI) is without racial designation on all records except her marriage certificate, which lists both her and

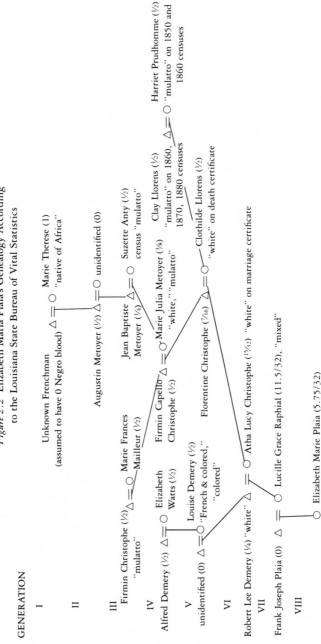

Figure 2.2 Elizabeth Maria Plaia's Genealogy According to the Louisiana State Bureau of Vital Statistics

her husband as "white." Lucille Grace Raphial's (GEN. VII) siblings are variously labeled "French," "mulatto," and "colored," while she herself was registered as "mixed." Atha Lucy Christophe's (GEN. VI) three nephews and nieces are labeled "white" in the state registrar's office.

The multiple and often seemingly contradictory labels were totally ignored in the registrar's mathematical calculations. Especially problematic is the use of the term *mulatto*. As the Louisiana Court of Appeals acknowledged in rendering its judgment on the case in 1973, U.S. censuses did not provide many alternatives for racial identification. This meant that the term *mulatto* was often applied loosely. The late nineteenth-century census records allowed only five options: white, black, mulatto, Chinese, or Indian. "When the census taker filled in that part of the form he certainly did not intend the entry of mulatto to mean that the person was half black because it would then follow that anyone who was anything less than one-half Negro would have been placed on the census record as white, a conclusion which hardly seems realistic" (275 So. 2d 204). Limited lexical options meant that the term *mulatto* was used to denote anyone who did not appear all white *or* all black. It rested primarily on phenotype. As the judges argued, "it is a fair conclusion that some of those so listed on the census reports had as little as 1/16 Negro blood and certainly many did not have as much as 1/2 Negro blood" (275 So. 2d 204).

Figure 2.3 summarizes the bureau's reasoning in its case against Lisa Marie Anthony. Evidence for Negro ancestry, with one exception, antedates the Civil War. The bureau's assumptions in this case seem even more arbitrary than in the Plaia suit (cf. Bennett 1976). For instance, the most recent document suggesting Negro ancestry is the 1937 death certificate of Ancel Baham (GEN. IV), the girl's father's mother's mother's father, which identified him as "C," shorthand for colored. Though in earlier cases the registrar had equated *colored* with *mulatto* and interpreted both to mean half Negro blood, here for some unexplained reason he counted Ancel Baham as "100% Negro."

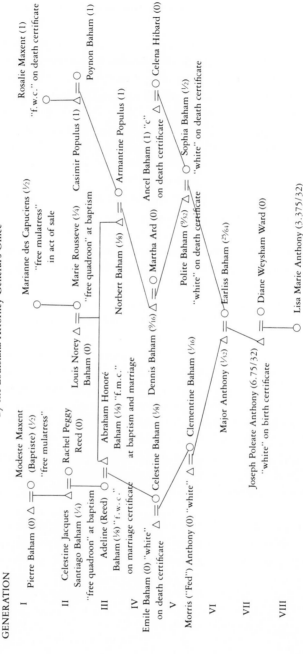

Figure 2.3 Lisa Marie Anthony's Genealogy Prepared
by the Louisiana Attorney General's Office

Likewise, he assumed that Rosalie Maxent (GEN. I) was "full-blooded Negro," when in two available documents—her 1843 death certificate and an 1830 inter vivos donation—she is simply labeled as a "free woman of color." The same is true for Abraham Honoré Baham (GEN. III) and Adeline (Reed) Baham (GEN. III). An act of sale of land described Marianne des Capuciens (GEN. I) as a "mulatresse libre"; a baptismal certificate referred to her daughter Marie Rousseve as "quarterona libre"; and Celestine Jacques Santiago Baham's baptismal certificate named him "quarteron libre" and his mother Modeste "mulata libre." The state registrar equated these lexical items with one-half, one-fourth, one-fourth, and one-half Negro blood respectively. Heavy reliance on these questionable assumptions, in the end, lost the case for the Bureau of Vital Statistics.

RATIONALIZING LAW

What is most revealing in the post-1970 period is the bureau's persistent objection to the premises of Act 46. Fundamental criticism of the act was so strong that it led counsel for the Board of Health to agree to a joint stipulation cosigned by counsel for the plaintiffs. This Joint Stipulation of Counsel, dated March 20, 1975, overtly questioned the constitutionality of Act 46 and employed a language acceptable to both defendant and plaintiff. But, of course, the two counsels were diametrically opposed in their reasons for signing the document, the defendant arguing that the law should not interfere with "the facts of biology" and the plaintiff contending that the alleged "facts of biology" were so ambiguous as to render any racial classification capricious, arbitrary, and necessarily invidious.

March 20, 1975—joint stipulation of counsel, cosigned by John D'Angelo and James Screen:

I. The one thirty-second (1/32nd) fraction contained in Act 46 of 1970 (La. R. S. 42: 267) was arbitrarily picked by the

Legislature; that there were no studies or hearings in arriving at said fraction; that there was no scientific medical, genetical, or other reasonable basis for choosing the one thirty-second fraction;

II. That the legislature provided no mode of computation to the fractional amount specified in Act 46 of 1970, nor did they furnish any guides as to the meaning of words in said act;

III. That the State of Louisiana promulgated rules and regulations to enforce Act 46 of 1970 and compliance with the said rules and regulations is mandatory upon the Registrar of Vital Statistics and requires positive action on his part;

IV. That under Act 46 of 1970, the rules and regulations promulgated to enforce that act, the Registrar of Vital Statistics has the power to withhold or change a birth certificate of anyone having a percentage of negro blood exceeding one 32nd (1/32nd);

V. The Act 46 of 1970 and the rules and regulations connection [*sic*] therewith for enforcement, have been and are being used against Lisa Marie Anthony and those persons similarly situated.

Self-consciously the lawyers raised questions about the role of law in the definition of identities. Is it not arbitrary and capricious? Is identity, in fact, not determined by nature? If the law has the power to grant or to withhold the right of self-identification to individual citizens, on what basis does it do so?

The Phipps case raised the issues again. When Lee Frazier, who wrote the 1983 law, explained that the Louisiana legislature was moved to act "to reflect modern thinking," his reference was to changes in scientific understanding of race. His phrasing implied that the 1983 statute was *more* in tune with nature than previous such laws because it accords with current thinking on the nature of race. In this sense, it is still nature—or, more precisely, his image of nature—that determines racial identity. Law, in his view, intervenes to legitimate *natural* processes of differentiation, not to supersede them. It presupposes; it does not create, despite the fact that the act of legislation itself is inherently creation by fiat. The contradiction is reproduced in the provisions it introduces to replace the 1/32 barrier. The new law would allow parents to designate the race of their children as they wish (*New York Times,* June 26, 1983, sect. E, p. 41)— clearly an act of positive law. At the same time, it uses the phrase "the preponderance of [evidence]" to set the conditions under which it will allow citizens to make changes in their birth certificates: "Changes in birth records can be made on 'the preponderance of' rather than 'overwhelming evidence'" (*New York Times,* ibid.). Talk of evidence evokes once again an image of nature determining racial identity.

The specter of contradiction, or at least of inconsistency, runs through a second dimension of the Phipps case as well. Susie Phipps's attorneys invoked the language of justice to plead her case. The Associated Press focused on fairness in its opening remarks on the case (cf. *Durham Morning Herald,* Wednesday, September 15, 1982, p. 3): "State lawyers used statements from relatives Tuesday to dispute the claim of a woman who says she has been *unfairly* classified as black because one of her ancestors was an 18th century slave" (emphasis added). The December 3 *People* magazine introduced the story with the sentence, "Given the simple life she'd led, Susie Phipps, 48, had never needed formal proof of her identity." Overwhelmingly, Susie Phipps was presented as a simple woman confronting a powerful social institution beyond her control. But here the law played two seemingly contradictory roles: as the institution or the agent of the institution limiting her freedom to choose what she was, and as the institution or mechanism through which she could appeal for the right to choose. To put it more generally, it is as if the individual were pitted against society, and sought recourse through the very legal system that caused the trouble in the first place. The legal system becomes at once counsel and prosecution, the agent of society at large and the only hope for redress.

Here the domain of law appears elusive, even evasive. It appears to reflect nature and to distort it, to be arbitrary as well as motivated, to represent society at the same time that it grants individuals freedom from society.

In the case of Louisiana, a curious contradiction emerges. Legal disputes over race are nearly always *naturalized*. The details of the nature of race are disputed, but some general premises are clearly shared. There is, for one, a shared perception of the social significance of race in Louisiana. There is, in addition, at the very least a shared willingness to argue over the validity of racial classification in terms of the *nature* of race. To put it differently, there is a willingness to recognize nature as the architect of racial distinctions, and man simply as the foreman who interprets nature's design. The interpretations may be couched in terms of blood or of genes, of physical appearance or of ancestry. It may stress the preponderance of genes, the uniqueness of each person's genetic makeup, or the continued transmission of even a single gene. But in the final analysis, parties to the dispute seek to subordinate the understanding of identity to the processes of nature.

Legislation follows suit. Laws are changed in order to conform to images of nature. Laws are rationalized in terms of a perception of nature. Laws are challenged on the basis of interpretations of nature. Each side denies the arbitrariness of its own claim by couching it in terms of nature. Each side proclaims the arbitrariness of its opponents' claims by contrasting them to its view of nature. This is a common premise, part of public opinion or even a cultural logic. The irony is that it produces on each side an apparent reluctance to admit to political, or even cultural, bases to the legal positions they support.

Herein lies the contradiction. To the extent that there is in the legal process an element of power politics, each time racial identity is demarcated by law we hear the voice of a sector or group of the larger society. To the extent that nature is invoked as a basis of the law, we hear the denial of power politics as an element of law. To the extent that there is in the legal process an element of public opinion, each time racial identity is demarcated by law we hear the voice of a broad sector of the public. To the extent that nature is invoked as a basis of the law, we hear the denial of public opinion as an element of law. It is as if the historical pattern documented in this chapter were implicitly considered too manipulative to be true.

Chapter 3

THE PROPERTIES OF BLOOD

The history of changing legal definitions of racial identities has an unbelievable ring to it: legislatures, not genes, determining boundaries; individuals finding themselves "white" one day and "colored" the next; scientism serving the interests of a legacy of racism. But is this, as the saying goes, just a matter of semantics?

Boehm (1980: 20) has recently argued that natural definitions are "special semantic (sometimes even metasemantic) statements made by natives about the meanings of their own meanings," and that they function both as descriptions and explanations "made by natives for our edification in the same mode as they are made for the benefit of other natives." The suggestion is that definitions, as descriptions, presumably reflect a high degree of awareness of usage and permutations of the terms in question and that, as explanations, they reflect attempts to find order in a disorderly usage.

The legal determination of racial identities in Louisiana is, however, complicated by the tendency I discussed in Chapter 2 to naturalize definitions of identity. A serious problem of consciousness enters the equation, and in the process definitions become prescriptive, rather than descriptive.

The classic problem is the relationship of racial identity to socioeconomic class. The tendency to naturalize racial identities promotes the view that race is determined independently of class. And yet a persistent body of Louisiana family and property laws points in the opposite direction.

Bans on interracial marriage, efforts to limit the incidence of interracial cohabitation, clauses that deny nonwhite children the right to seek acknowledgment of paternity from their white natural fathers, and the establishment of categories of illegitimate children with unequal rights to inheritance all amount to legal efforts historically to ensure that relationship by "blood" did not entail equality of status or through equality of status equal access to property. The implication, of course, is that without laws to the contrary, consanguinity implies both a sharing of social identity and a sharing of the spoils.

A curious phenomenon emerges whereby identity is thought to be regulated by nature but to be indexical of class. A chain of assumptions links marriage with consanguinity, consanguinity with equal status, and equal status with equal access to property. The legal record makes it very clear that definitions of identity are, in fact, chains of propositions leading to *and* reflecting entitlements and disenfranchisements. The many calculated attempts to prevent "blood" from *necessarily* implying and entailing class would obviously not have been deemed necessary if definitions of identity were just a matter of semantics. I concentrate here on the attempts to regulate consanguinity by regulating marriage and the attempts to restrict the flow of property across category lines. The issue is the linking by law of racial and class identities.

THE QUESTION OF MARRIAGE

Bans on certain kinds of marriage are highly visible forms of manipulating the entailments of controversial identities. At one level the case is simple. Interracial marriages were prohibited in Louisiana between 1807 and 1972, except for a period during Reconstruction (1870 to 1894) when the legislature made them temporarily legal (La. Civil Code [1.48] 1808; La. Civil Code, art. 95 [1825]; La. Civil Code, art. 94 [1870], as amended by La. Acts 1894, No. 54; La. Civil Code Ann. art. 94 [Supp. 1; 1975]). Separation was an obvious goal, and domination, on the part of the white population, the instrument that made it possible. And yet, at the level of how such marriages were conceptualized in the law, the conceptual and institutional struggle is more obvious.

Louisiana law distinguishes between impediments to marriage that can be removed under certain circumstances and those that can never be, by law. The distinction determines which marriages contracted illegally must be nullified and which do not have to be.

The first category consists of those marriages conceived and encoded in the law as pure anathema. Article 93 of the 1870 Code (still applicable today) illustrates the strength of the absolute form of the marriage prohibition: "Persons legally married are, until the dissolution of marriage incapable of contracting another, under the penalties established by the laws of this State." The Louisiana Supreme Court decision of 1860 in the case of *Summerlin* v. *Livingston* (15 La. Ann. 519) provided early support for the notion that bigamous marriages were absolutely null in the state of Louisiana, and later cases have confirmed and perpetuated the ban (cf. *Succession of Prieto,* 165 La. 710, 115 So. 911 [1928]; and *State* v. *Donzi,* 133 La. 925, 63 So. 405 [1913]). The perceived immorality of nonmonogamous marriages in Western European societies lends strength to this prohibition, and the potential for incurring serious difficulties in the administration of cases of inheritance and succession reinforces the institutional "need" for a strong prohibition against bigamy. The argument is that "the integrity of the family"— both its morality and its estate—warrants the absolute prohibition of bigamy.

Likewise, the legal prohibition of certain types of incestuous marriages falls into this first category. The civil law of Louisiana has always prohibited marriage between ascendants and descendants in the direct line, whether "legitimate" or "natural." So strong is the prohibition against legalizing sexual relations between persons lineally related by blood that the codes have always made it clear that the law does not, for this purpose, distinguish between legitimate and illegitimate descendants.

But there are proscribed marriages that are not, by law, grounds for absolute nullification. These include marriage to persons of insufficient age and marriage to persons to whom one is related by legal adoption. In these cases, individuals get the chance to decide for themselves whether or not to have their marriage annulled on either of these grounds (Pascal 1962).

There are even cases of marriage types that have been legally shifted from one category to another. Adultery and marriage to nonlineal relatives are the most prominent examples. The former was, until recently, in the first category of absolute grounds for nullification. Article 161 of the 1870 Civil Code stated that "in case of divorce, on account of adultery, the guilty party can never hereafter contract matrimony with his or her accomplice in adultery, under the penalty of nullity of the new marriage." In 1958, however, the legislature began to bend to more contemporary views of marriage and divorce, and ratified all marriages contracted before 1958 in contravention of the provision against adultery.

In the case of marriage to nonlineal relatives, the law has had a long history of shifting boundaries and categories. The Civil Code project of 1804 (article 161), for example, prohibited marriage between persons connected by marriage in the same direct line, in other words, marriage between step-kin. The 1808 project of the code eliminated this prohibition. The 1804 project, article 162, prohibited marriage between brother and sister (legitimate or natural), and "between those connected by marriage in the same degree" (the step-kin provision), but it did not specify whether or not half-siblings were included. The 1808, 1825, and 1870 articles dealing with incestuous marriages dropped the step-kin provision but extended the definition of incest to include half-siblings.

In addition, article 163 of the 1804 project of the code, as well as corresponding articles in subsequent codes, prohibited marriage between uncle and niece and between aunt and nephew. But no criminal statute specified punishment for incestuous marriages of this type until recently. The first criminal trial for incest of this sort, held in 1898 (*State* v. *Guiton,* 51 La. 155, 24 So. 784), established a precedent and seems to have led the legislature to pass an appropriate criminal statute. The case was made without recourse to criminal statutes.

Then there is the even more involved question of first-cousin marriages, which were legal in Louisiana throughout the nineteenth century. In 1900, in a move that was apparently unpopular, the state legislature amended article 95 of the revised Civil Code of 1870 to include first cousins: "Art. 95 (as amended in 1900): Among collateral relations, marriage is prohibited between Brother and Sister, whether of the whole or the half blood, whether legitimate or illegitimate, between the Uncle and the Niece, the Aunt and the Nephew and also between First Cousins." Of this move, legal expert Saunders wrote in 1925,

> the sentiment of the people in this state seemed to be very strongly against the law—it was one of those rules which are legislated contrary to the general desires and trend of habit of the people; it was therefore a matter of public notoriety in 1904 that that law had been very generally disregarded, and that numerous efforts to evade prohibition had been made. All of the States surrounding Louisiana permitted marriages between first cousins, and it was said that in over 100 cases the parties left Louisiana to go to an adjoining State to marry relying on the rule that the validity of a contract is determined by the law of the place where it is entered into, and that if valid in the state where it is made it will be treated as valid everywhere—so that in 1904 the legislature re-enacted for a third time the law prohibiting the marriage of cousins, but declaring valid the marriages that had occurred prior thereto. It was shown to the legislature that a great many lawyers had advised their clients who came to them for advice on this matter that the marriage would be valid if the parties withdrew to another State and there married and then

came back. Now in order to put an end to any uncertainty on this point, in 1904 the legislature re-enacted the statute and at the same time declared that if persons, both or either of whom were domiciled in this state, and were first cousins, went to another State to Marry and then returned, the marriage should be declared invalid; and in 1906 the legislature again took the matter up and made such marriages a felony (Saunders 1925: 26–27).

Legislation against first-cousin marriages brought hardship to many. First-cousin marriages had been popular, even customary, in parts of Louisiana since the eighteenth century. Genealogies of both white and colored Creole families frequently include first-cousin marriages, and they are strongly in evidence in the genealogical records of aristocratic planter families, some of whom still argue today that it is better to marry a close cousin than to marry someone of much lower social status (cf., e.g., De la Vergne family papers and Bringier family papers in the Trist Wood Collection).

The state legislature has then, not surprisingly, periodically acknowledged the persistence of this practice by granting ex post facto dispensations for marriage between first cousins. From time to time since the passing of the 1900 amendment to the Civil Code prohibiting marriages between first cousins, the code has been amended to ratify all marriages of persons domiciled in Louisiana, who are related within the prohibited collateral degree of consanguinity, so long as the marriages were in existence before the passage of the prohibiting amendment and were contracted in a jurisdiction in which they were permissible (La. Acts 1938, No. 426; La. Acts 1950, No. 242).

The ban on interracial marriages has, by contrast, always been *absolutely* null and void (except when temporarily repealed during Reconstruction). It has always appeared in the code article (94) that deals with incestuous relations of the first order, that is, between lineally related consanguineal relatives, and never in the articles (93 and 95) that deal with adultery and incestuous relations of the second order (i.e., among collateral kin). The juxtaposition of miscegenation and incest of the first order in the same code article seems awkward but is telling: "Marriage between persons related to each other in the direct ascending or descending line is prohibited. This prohibition is not confined to legitimate children, it extends also to children born out of marriage. Marriage between white persons and persons of color is prohibited, and the celebration of all such marriages is forbidden and such celebration carries with it no effect and is null and void." The association of miscegenation with the type of incestuous relationship considered least acceptable reveals the intended strength of the legal prohibition against miscegenation.

PATERNITY

Louisiana law, however, has further attempted to obstruct the chain of implicational assumptions in the area of paternity and inheritance. By legislating against Caucasian-Negro marriages, the legislature ensured that the offspring of interracial unions would necessarily be illegitimate. But this was not enough to ensure that the property of white families would not pass on to the population of color.

The distinction that Louisiana civil law draws between illegitimate children who could ultimately be legitimated by following certain specified procedures and those who could never be provides some legal recourse to white families. Children whose parents are incapable of contracting marriage to each other fall into the latter category. These hardcore bastards are, because of their permanently illegitimate status, legally entitled to receive from their mothers and their mothers' ascendants only what the civil law calls "alimony." Recent judicial decisions have interpreted this to mean food, clothing, lodging, and some sort of training (possibly college) that would allow them to earn their own living. Legally they have no rights of inheritance from either father or mother, or from the family estates of either parent, as evident in Article 920 (revised Civil Code of 1870; identical in the 1825 code, and essentially the same also for the 1808 project of the Code, article 46; and the Code Napoleon Article 762): "Bastard, adulterous or incestuous children shall not enjoy the right of inheriting the estates of their natural father or mother, in any of the cases above mentioned, the law allowing them nothing more than a mere alimony." What Article 920 did not explicitly say was that the children of miscegenetic unions also fell into this category. This omission makes Article 920 ambiguous and unreliable as a way of keeping white property from passing into colored hands. It would apply to the colored children of any white married man, but not necessarily to the colored children of unmarried whites. Consequently, other safeguards were built directly into the legal system.

A partial solution was to limit the right of a colored person to prove that his father was white. This had major legal consequences. For an illegitimate child to acquire any rights to inherit from his genitor, his genitor first has to acknowledge him as his child. Paternal acknowledgment makes an illegitimate child a "natural child" and enables him to inherit part of his father's estate. To deny illegitimate colored children the right to establish their white paternity, or to seek paternal acknowledgment, is to make it nearly impossible for them to inherit from him. Only the father's voluntary acknowledgment would grant them the status of "natural children."

Explicit racial concerns made this provision of Louisiana law significantly different from one that already existed in French law denying illegitimate children the right to prove paternal descent. It had long been customary in France to grant illegitimate children greater access to their mother and her property than to their father and his property (cf. Brinton 1936). This extended to their right to prove descent. Article 340 of the 1804

Code Napoleon denied illegitimate children the right to prove paternal descent, while Article 341 of the same code granted them the right to prove maternal descent. Although the 1804 Code Napoleon was used as a partial model for the Louisiana Civil Code (cf. Dargo 1975), the 1808 project of the Louisiana Civil Code drew this distinction *only* for the children of miscegenetic unions, thus adopting only a modified version of French statutes.

The intention of Louisiana lawmakers was explicit in 1808: "Article 30—Illegitimate children who have not been legally acknowledged [in the manner described earlier in the code], may be allowed to prove their paternal descent, provided they be free and white." And it was even clearer in the 1825 Code. Article 226 (reproducing article 30 of 1808) added the following: "Free illegitimate children of colour, may also be allowed to prove their descent from a father of colour only."

Even the right of white persons voluntarily to acknowledge their colored children, when they have no legitimate white children of their own, has been challenged over the years. In *Compton* v. *Prescott* (12 Rob. 56) in 1845, collateral kinsmen of Leonard B. Compton called this right into question. In his holographic will, Compton had donated a sizeable portion of his estate to his colored concubine and his two colored illegitimate children. The plaintiffs argued that the children were entitled only to alimony, because they were children of a man and a woman incapable by law of contracting marriage with each other. In their opinion, these children had no more right to inherit any part of Compton's estate than did children of incestuous or adulterous unions. Like the latter, the plaintiffs argued, Compton's children could not be legally acknowledged by him, and without legal acknowledgment they had no right to inherit any part of his estate.

The Supreme Court of Louisiana essentially ruled against them, noting that there was a provision in the code that allowed white men to acknowledge their colored children by a specific notarial act, even though they could not do so by marriage to the children's mother. Because this right was not granted to the parents of incestuous or adulterous bastards, the court concluded that the "illegitimate colored children [of a white man] are not on the same footing with adulterous bastards" (12 Rob. 72). In making its decision, however, the Louisiana Supreme Court had to overrule a common interpretation of the statutes on which the plaintiffs had rested their case.

In *Casanave* v. *Bingaman* in 1869 (21 La. Ann. 435), counsel for the plaintiff again argued that white men could not legally acknowledge their children of color. He stated in his brief:

That the decedent was a free man of color, the son of Mary Ellen Williams, a free woman of color, and the said A. L. Bingaman being a white man, labors under a twofold disability in the matter of the acknowledgement of paternity, because the laws of Louisiana forbid a white man from legitimating his colored children, and because A. L. Bingaman was incompetent to marry Mary E. Williams, the mother, at the time of the conception of the son, and hence could not acknowledge him as his natural child (21 La. Ann. 436).

Although the plaintiff's interpretation of the Code did not accord with the interpretation established by the courts in *Compton* v. *Prescott* and quoted in the court's decision in this 1869 case, it seems to have been a popular one. In *Casanave* v. *Bingaman,* the plaintiff's case was made even weaker by the existence of a notarial act dated July 13, 1865, by which the defendant, A. L. Bingaman, had formally acknowledged the decedent as his natural son (21 La. Ann. 436). But the plaintiffs still insisted that acknowledgment of colored children by whites ran counter to the basic principles of Louisiana law.

In the *Succession of Mélasie Hébert* (33 La. Ann. 1099) in 1881, the two arguments again appeared in court. Here was one of only a few known legal cases where a white woman (Mélasie

Hébert) was a colored man's concubine and where, correspondingly, the issue was maternal, rather than paternal, acknowledgment of the child. The case had deep emotional overtones. In the words of the Appellate Court, "the case appears to have been as warmly contested in the lower court as it was here; but the grounds for respective resistance are more easily ascertained from the course of the proceedings than from the pleadings" (33 La. Ann. 1101).

Two opposing parties fought for the succession of Mélasie Hébert: her acknowledged natural daughter, Emelia Hébert, and Mélasie's collateral kin. The collateral kin contended that Emelia was a "colored person, the illegitimate and unlawful fruit of the connections of the deceased, who was a white woman, with a man of African blood" (ibid.: 103); that Emelia was never acknowledged by her mother either by notarial act or in birth or baptismal records; that her mother was insane; and that tne law prohibited the acknowledgment of children of interracial unions. The purpose of their argument, however, is clear in section 12 of the brief presented by C. Debaillon, who represented the collateral kin—"there was an absolute necessity in this State to discourage the amalgamation of the white and colored race, which did not exist in France 6 An. 161, Old Code 95" (33 La. Ann. 1100).

Emelia, on the other hand, denied that she was a person of color. Her presumption here was interesting. She argued that the status of a child depended upon that of the mother, and she extended the notion of status both to civil or legal status and to racial identity—"the child of a free woman is free, and the child of a white woman is white." But the court rejected her reasoning. The presumption of social equivalence with the mother did not, by virtue of the cultural logic described earlier, extend to racial identity. There was no proof that the mother was insane, although she was deaf and dumb. One wonders, in fact, if her collateral kinsmen judged her to be insane because she had sexual relations with a colored man, and used the convenient fact that she was deaf and dumb to argue that she was insane. But the court was not convinced and ruled that Emelia was entitled under article 230 of the 1825 Code to make proof of her *maternal* descent, whatever her own color. This was easily established in court. Mélasie's sister testified that she was the midwife who helped Mélasie give birth to Emelia and that she had known and followed the child from her birth to the days of the testimony in court. Moreover, Emelia's baptismal record shows Mélasie to be the mother, though Mélasie did not herself sign the record. The courts, taking into account the mother's disability, accepted these various proofs of maternal acknowledgment and deemed Emelia to be Mélasie's acknowledged illegitimate child. The plaintiffs lost the case but not without first making a powerful emotional argument.

In 1903 the Louisiana Supreme Court became very particular about the manner in which white men were allowed to acknowledge their colored children, although it implied that such acknowledgments were still legal in the state. J. P. Vance died in May 1902, leaving in his will most of his property to a woman named Eliza James (*Succession of Vance*, 110 La. 760; 34 So. 767). "I do hereby make this my last will. I give to Dr. Tom Vance my Plain Dealing property. I want Eliza James to have the remainder of my real estate and to hold absolutely. I appoint Dr. Tom Vance my sole executor of my will." He left no legitimate children. But his brothers, sisters, and nephew filed an opposition to the will in which they challenged the bequest made to Eliza James. They declared her a free woman of color, the bastard daughter of the deceased, born of a colored mother in 1862, and as such incapable of receiving anything from the deceased by donation *mortis causa* (as opposed to a donation made while parents are still alive, called *inter vivos*). (34 So. 767). The courts ruled in their favor. It was shown to the satisfaction of the state Supreme Court that Eliza James was the daughter of the deceased, and this determined limits to her rights to receive the donation made in Vance's will. She would have been entitled to a part of his estate if she had been acknowledged by him. But the court was able to come up with only one witness who heard Vance *once* refer to Eliza as his daughter, and this, it argued, did not constitute sufficient proof of acknowledgment. "A mere reference by a man one time, in casual conversation, to a child as his is not that proof of acknowledgement which makes him or her what the law describes as a natural child. If calling a child his offspring be relied on to establish legal acknowledgement (supposing it permissible for a father to acknowledge a child that way), the proof should be that the father was in the habit of so calling the child when speaking of it, or did so in habitual conversation with others" (ibid.). Eliza was declared a bastard, officially unacknowledged by her white father, and thus ineligible to receive any part of the bequest granted her by her father's will.

In 1910, the Louisiana Supreme Court issued an opinion on the *Succession of Davis* (126 La. 178; 52 So. 266) that suggests that the question of acknowledgment was still not resolved. In this case, George Gamble, the colored illegitimate son of Virginia R. Davis (a slave freed by the Emancipation Proclamation), contested his mother's will, in which she granted her white consort, Frank Walker, her sizeable estate consisting of twenty lots of ground, household furniture, and several hundred dollars in money. The Civil District Court of New Orleans ruled in favor of the son, but Walker appealed and the Louisiana Supreme Court reversed the lower court's decision.

The lower court, based on evidence that the deceased had named her son and acknowledged him to her friends and acquaintances as her son, determined that George Gamble was the natural or acknowledged illegitimate child of the decedent. Because she had no legitimate descendants, this fact entitled him to inherit the greater part of her estate. But the Louisiana Supreme Court challenged the lower court's opinion that Davis had acknowledged Gamble as her son. It rested its case on the 1831 statute (March 24, p. 86) that natural children were the issue of parents who "might at the time of conception have contracted marriage." In bringing this forth, the court ignored the fact that the time of conception involved here was 1865, when according to the 1864 state constitution the parents were free to contract marriage. But more importantly, the court returned to the popular nineteenth-century interpretation of the code that made the possibility of legal acknowledgment contingent on the possibility of legal marriage. This was clearly a new interpretation. It was not the case of a white man acknowledging his colored child, but rather of a colored woman acknowledging her colored child. By earlier judicial interpretation, it would have fallen under statutes dealing with the acknowledgment of colored children by their colored parents—a situation where strict and specific procedures were not considered necessary. Evidence of Virginia Davis's habitual reference to George Gamble as her son would have been sufficient to deem him her natural child. But now the court ruled otherwise, and argued that Gamble was incapable of inheriting from her, since she had not legitimated him during Reconstruction when such legitimation would have been permitted. Earlier judicial interpretation would have ruled such legitimation unnecessary. The Louisiana Supreme Court's conclusion in this case reflected popular challenges to the notion that whites were entitled to acknowledge their colored children much more than the traditional judicial interpretation. Hence the law prohibiting the acknowledgment of children whose parents were incapable of contracting marriage at the time of conception is applicable to this case. By denying Gamble the status of "natural child" of the deceased, the courts enabled a white man to inherit a colored family's estate. One wonders if this consequence of judicial decision did not play a major part in the judges' deliberations leading to the decision.

Three well-known challenges to the right of whites to acknowledge their colored children followed within a few years of this decision, in 1913, 1919, and 1923. In all three, legitimate collateral kinsmen of deceased persons argued that such acknowledgments were not valid in Louisiana, and that the illegitimate colored children of the deceased had no right to inherit any part of the deceased's estate. In the *Succession of Yoist* (61 So. 384), collateral kinsmen disputed the validity of Yoist's will, in which he named his children by Eudora Bergeron, his colored concubine, as his universal legatees. They argued that the act by which the children claimed to have been acknowledged and legitimated by him was not valid in Louisiana. In the *Succession of Segura* (63 So. 640), Segura's collateral kin claimed that acknowledgment of colored children by a white man by notarial act was no longer legally possible in the state. In *Murdock* v. *Potter* (155 La. 145; 99 So. 18), the sister of the deceased, a woman of color, argued that the deceased's son was incapable of achieving the status of a natural child, because he was the illegitimate child of a white man and a colored woman.

In resolving these cases, however, the Supreme Court of Louisiana returned to its more traditional interpretation of the Civil Code. In *Murdock* v. *Potter,* it reviewed its earlier decisions and commented on the *Succession of Davis.*

> It is true that, in the *Succession of Davis,* 126 La. 178, 52 So. 266, the opinion rendered is susceptible of being interpreted as giving to Act 54 of 1894 the effect of preventing the acknowledgment of children, conceived before the passage of the act, when one of the parents is white and the other colored, at least when the case is considered with the *Succession of Hebert,* cited supra, upon which it is made to partly rest, but, in so far as there may be any conflict between it (the *Davis* Case) and the views herein expressed, the *Davis* Case must be considered as overruled (99 So. 21).

It held that the antimiscegenation act of 1894 had not repealed the 1870 codal provision permitting a white man to acknowledge *and* legitimate his colored illegitimate children, whatever the laws at the time the children are conceived. Act 68 of 1870 corresponded to the lifting of the prohibition against interracial marriages. In at least two of the three cases that followed the *Succession of Davis,* the plaintiffs assumed that the 1894 antimiscegenation act applied to acknowledgment and notarial acts of legitimation as well. But the Louisiana Supreme Court found the 1894 act not specific enough on matters of acknowledgment or legitimation to warrant such an interpretation. Thus, it was legal for John Yoist to acknowledge and legitimate his children conceived and born between 1870 and 1894, but it was also legal for Joseph Segura to acknowledge and legitimate his three children conceived after 1894. Only twice since 1923 have the higher courts of Louisiana entertained the question of interracial acknowledgment, once in 1928 (*Tyson et al.* v. *Raines,* 165 La. 625, 115 So. 803) and once in 1957 (*Goins* v. *Gates et al.,* 93 So. 2d 307); and in both cases they have upheld the state Supreme Court's interpretation in the *Yoist, Segura,* and *Murdock* cases.

It is not, however, altogether surprising that there have been so few challenges in recent years to the traditional judicial interpretation on the question of interracial acknowledgments. After all, the laws passed in the first two decades of this century prohibiting interracial concubinage and interracial cohabitation did their part in limiting the extent of interracial sexual unions.

Moreover, succession law itself has provided additional safeguards against the transfer of white families' estates to colored relatives. Throughout the history of the state of Louisiana, Louisiana law has prescribed that a natural child—that is, an illegitimate child who has been duly acknowledged—is called to the legal succession of his natural *father* only when the father has left no other relatives, however distant. On the other hand, the same child is called to the legal succession of his natural mother if she has left no legitimate children or descendants. The natural child in these circumstances inherits from his mother to the exclusion of all other relatives. This differentiation did not exist in the 1804 Code Napoleon.

Code Napoleon, article 756, sentence 1—
Natural children can not inherit; the law grants them rights on the property of their deceased father or mother only when they have been legally acknowledged.

Article 757—the right of the natural child to the property of his deceased father or mother is regulated as follows:

If the father or the mother has left lawful descendants, this right amounts to a third of the hereditary portion that the natural child would have had if he were legitimate: it amounts to a half when the father or mother leaves no descendants but only ascendants or brothers or sisters; and to three fourths when the father or mother leaves neither descendants, ascendants nor brothers or sisters.

Article 758—The natural child has a right to the whole of the property when the father or mother has left no relations of a degree capable of inheriting.

By comparison, Louisiana law draws a clear distinction. Article 918, first paragraph, of the revised Civil Code of 1870 (equals article 912 of the 1825 code, and article 44 of the 1808 project of the code) states: "Natural children are called to the legal succession of their natural mother, when they have been duly acknowledged by her, if she has left no lawful children or descendants, *to the exclusion of her father and mother and other ascendants or collaterals of lawful kindred*" (emphasis added). And article 919, first paragraph, of the revised Civil Code of 1870 (equal to article 913 of the 1825 code, and article 45 of the 1808 project of the code) reads: "Natural children are called to the inheritance of their natural father, who has duly acknowledged them, *when he has left no descendants nor ascendants, nor collateral relations, nor surviving wife, and to the exclusion only of the State*" (emphasis added).

These differences are not limited to cases of intestate succession. The capacity of the natural parent to donate property to his or her natural child is also limited by the codes. If there exist legitimate children or descendants, a natural child cannot receive from either mother or father, either when the parents are alive (*inter vivos*) or by will (*mortis causa*), anything "beyond what is strictly necessary to procure them sustenance, or an occupation or profession which may maintain them" (article 1483,

Revised Civil Code 1870). But differences between the capacities of a natural mother and a natural father to dispose of their property arise when there are no legitimate children or descendants. In such a case, the natural mother may donate the *entire* amount of her succession to her natural children, whether *inter vivos* or *mortis causa* (article 1484, 1870 code); but the natural father may donate only up to one-fourth of his property to such children if he leaves legitimate ascendants or legitimate brothers or sisters, or descendants from such brothers and sisters, or up to one-third, if he leaves only more remote collateral relations (article 1486 of the revised code of 1870).

Although these code articles do not openly differentiate rights to inherit by race or color, they effectively protect the estate of white families from being passed on to colored relatives. Relationships between white males and colored females (the practice of *placage*) were common, whereas relations between white females and colored males were relatively rare. Thus, statutory provisions brought about a de facto separation of the properties of white and colored branches of Louisiana families, although they could not ensure a perfect separation.

An 1873 and an 1899 succession case put these laws in perspective. On September 20, 1858, a widower by the name of James S. Morgan made an *inter vivos* donation before the recorder of New Orleans to two minor children he acknowledged as his daughters (*Fowler, Morgan et al.* v. *Morgan*, 25 La. Ann. 206). The property, a lot with "improvements" (probably a house), was appraised at $5,000. H. V. Babin accepted the donation on behalf of the minors. But collateral kinsmen contended that the donation was null "because the donees being illegitimate colored children, can receive only what is necessary to procure their sustenance or an occupation or profession, under the provisions of article 1470 of the Code of 1825 [then in effect] and that the donation being one of real estate in fee simple is not susceptible of redonation as contemplated by the second clause of said article, and is therefore not a settlement of the alimony, but is in violation of the letter and spirit of the said article and absolutely null" (25 La. Ann. 207). The plaintiffs tried to argue that Morgan's daughters were hardcore bastards, ineligible to inherit, or to receive donations beyond mere sustenance. They were unwilling to yield even a small part of his estate to their colored kinsmen. But the statutes protected them from any great loss of real estate by limiting a man's right to donate to his illegitimate children. In this case, the court determined that $5,000 equaled a quarter of Morgan's estate. Sizeable as it may have seemed at the time, it was only a quarter of his total property.

The plaintiffs did try to use an additional argument to prevent the transfer of property. They argued that Ellen Morgan, the defendant, and her children were technically slaves when the donation was made, and that as slaves they were incapable of receiving property by any act of donation. The allegation convinced the Fifth Judicial Court, but it did not convince the appellate court. Upon further investigation it was established that the donees were *statu liberae,* slaves who had been granted freedom at some future time. This made Morgan's children more like free people of color than like slaves, and under the provisions of article 193 of the 1825 code, "the slave who has acquired the right of being free at a future time, is from that time capable of receiving by testament or donation. Property given or devised to him must be preserved for him, in order to be delivered to him in kind, when his emancipation shall take place. In the meantime it must be administered by a curator" (25 La. Ann. 208).

As the donees were *statu liberae,* and not simply slaves, and as they were acknowledged by their father who donated to them no more than the allowed quarter of his estate, the higher court had to reverse the lower court's ruling. It did so reluctantly, even though the statutes severely limited the man's right to donate property to his only children. "We can see no circumstances in this case which have defeated the rights of the children of the defendant, *whatever may be the moral view of the question"* (emphasis added).

The *Succession of Fortier* (926 So. 554) illustrates the importance of racial identity in matters of succession. It concerns the right of one person of color to inherit from another, and is therefore not interracial. But the lengthy judicial opinion on this case shows how central racial identity is to succession law in Louisiana.

The facts are as follows. Angela Fortier, widow of Placide Bienvenu, died intestate in New Orleans on April 8, 1896. On May 27, 1898, Delphine Fortier filed a petition in the civil district court asserting that she was the niece and only surviving heir of the deceased. By a judgment of the probate court on November 13, 1898, Delphine inherited her aunt's entire estate. But on February 9, 1899, the attorney general filed a motion on behalf of the state to appeal the lower court's ruling. The question the state supreme court would eventually answer was whether the natural child of a natural brother of the deceased could inherit from her.

Angela Fortier and Gustave Fortier were two of seven children of a white man, Jean Michel Fortier, then director of the Bank of Louisiana, and a free woman of color, Marguerite Henriette Milon. Gustave Fortier in turn lived in open concubinage with a free woman of color named Caroline Delzay. Of this union, Delphine was born. Delphine proved to be Angela Fortier's only surviving consanguineal relative. Of the seven children of Jean Michel Fortier, only the deceased had ever married, and of the seven only Gustave had fathered a child. Article 917 of the 1825 code, still in effect at that time, provided for the following resolution of the case. "If the father and mother of the natural child died before him," it states, "the estate of such a natural child shall pass to his natural brothers and sisters, or to their descendants." Counsel for the state insisted that the word *descendants* here applied only to legitimate relations, but the court rejected that interpretation, as "the language of the article did not justify that interpretation" (26 So. 562). Counsel for the state also tried to get the court to declare invalid an unrecorded religious marriage between Delphine's parents two or three days before Gustave Fortier's death in 1862. Counsel argued, mistakenly, that Gustave was a white man. The importance of racial identity in this case is evident in the court's evaluation of the fact that Gustave was not white.

> The father of Gustave Fortier being a white man, and his mother a woman of color, he was necessarily a person of mixed blood,—one-half colored and one-half white,—and, consequently, not a white man. There was, therefore, no prohibition in law against his being married to Caroline Delzay, a free person of color. For the same reason Angela Fortier was a person of mixed blood, and there was no prohibition in law against her inheriting the estate of her brother Gustave. The same is equally true of Delphine,—she being the issue of the union between Gustave Fortier, a person of mixed blood, and Caroline Delzay, a free person of color. On this theory, and upon the evidence detailed in support thereof, all doubts and difficulties in this case have been resolved in favor of the validity of the marriage of Gustave Fortier and Caroline Delzay, and relieve it from the imputation of any illegality which has been suggested by the attorney general. There is certainly no prohibition in the law which has been referred to—and there is none of which we are aware—against the marriage of free persons of color inter se, or between free persons of color and persons of mixed blood. Our conclusion is that the marriage between Gustave Fortier and Caroline Delzay must be given its full effect, as having legitimated Delphine Fortier as the issue thereof, to the extent, at least, of enabling her to inherit from her natural aunt, Angela Fortier, even if that were necessary (26 So. 567).

The court argued for the validity of Gustave's marriage, although it did not think it really necessary to consider Delphine to be the legitimate daughter of Gustave Fortier in order to deem her Angela's heir.

Had Gustave been white, his marriage to Caroline Delzay would have been invalidated, as it took place before the repeal of Louisiana's antimiscegenation laws during Reconstruction. Had Gustave been white, he would most probably also have been legitimate. And according to article 921, "the law does not grant any right of inheritance to natural children to the estate of the legitimate relations of their father or mother." Thus, had Gustave been white and legitimate, Delphine could not have inherited any part of her aunt's estate. Had Gustave and Angela Fortier been white but illegitimate, it is unclear whether Delphine could have inherited from Angela. The court would have had to place greater emphasis on the issue of whether an illegitimate unacknowledged child can inherit from his or her natural father's natural collateral relatives. It is possible but doubtful that the final judgment of the court would have been the same as in the actual case described.

In more recent years, legal discrimination against illegitimate offspring has come under the scrutiny of the United States Supreme Court, but with mixed results. The Court has, in fact, issued somewhat contradictory decisions since the late 1960s. In 1968, the Court invalidated Louisiana's limitation of recoveries for wrongful death to relatives (*Levy* v. *Louisiana,* 391 U.S. 68; *Glona* v. *American Guarantee and Liab. Ins. Co.,* 391 U.S. 73). These decisions obviously challenged the constitutionality of Louisiana's treatment of illegitimacy. Yet in 1971 (cf. *Labine* v. *Vincent,* 401 U.S. 532) the Court upheld Louisiana's discriminatory succession laws (cf. Pascal 1971). Mr. Vincent, a resident of Louisiana, died intestate leaving no legitimate children or descendants. He did leave a nine-year-old natural child and some collateral relatives. By Louisiana law, Vincent's collateral relatives stood to inherit the estate to the exclusion of his natural child. A suit was instituted for the benefit of the child. After several appeals, the case reached the U.S. Supreme Court, where four of the nine justices thought the controversial statute unconstitutional. The majority, however, upheld the statute—a decision meant to discourage illegitimacy and maintain the stability of land titles. The Supreme Court's decision in *Labine* v. *Vincent* kept Louisiana's illegitimacy laws alive, for at least a while.

On April 26, 1977, the Supreme Court handed down two further rulings that may well affect Louisiana's succession laws. In a five-to-four decision in the case of *Trimble* v. *Gordon* (docket number 75-5952), the Court ruled that it is unconstitutional for states to bar illegitimate children from inheriting the intestate succession of their father. The ruling specifically struck down an Illinois statute that allowed illegitimate children to inherit from their mother, but not their father, in case of intestacy and yet allowed legitimate children to inherit from either parent. This 1977 ruling contrasted sharply with the *Labine* 1971 decision. But the Court was quick to point out some dissimilarities in the statutes in question. The Louisiana law was favored, because it at least entitles the illegitimate child to support (alimony) from the estate of the deceased—a right not granted by Illinois' statutory counterpart. On the other hand, there are certain inescapable similarities between these Illinois and Louisiana statutes, a fact acknowledged by dissenting as well as concurring justices. The four dissenters issued a brief joint statement indicating that they, like the Illinois Supreme Court, found "this case constitutionally indistinguishable from *Labine* v. *Vincent*" (*New York Times,* April 27, 1977, sect. A, p. 17). The five concurring justices added a footnote to the majority opinion: "to the extent that our analysis in this case differs from that in *Labine* the most recent analysis controls" (ibid.). There was thus some question again as to the constitutionality of Louisiana's succession laws.

To complicate the matter, however, the United States Supreme Court handed down another decision on that same day, April 26, 1977, an apparently contradictory decision. Here— *Fiallo* v. *Bell* (docket number 75-6297)—the majority of the Court voted to uphold immigration laws that discriminate against illegitimate children. These provisions basically prevent illegitimate children and their fathers from getting the special immigration preference that is given to legitimate children and parents of U.S. citizens or permanent U.S. residents. The decision in this case may well reflect the Court's flexibility in questions such as these, when it is clear that there are compelling state interests in the matter. The Court argued that Congress has broad powers to regulate immigration, that many distinctions are made and categories distinguished, and that the provisions on illegitimate children are "just one of many" such distinctions. Clearly so long as the Supreme Court continues to hand down partially contradictory decisions, the Louisiana "system" can survive the constitutional challenge, at least in part.

INDIRECT INHERITANCE

Judges and legislators have long been aware of the possibility of indirect inheritance and have done their part to limit both their frequency and their effect. For judges, this has meant uncovering disguised sales and donations; for legislators, limiting the right of concubines to inherit from each other and the right of whites to adopt their illegitimate children. I examine here three mid-nineteenth-century cases that illustrate the various stratagems by which white men sought to transfer property to their colored children.

The first, *Robinett et al.* v. *Verdun's Vendees* (914 La. 542), dated March 1840, was an attempt by the heirs of Alexander Verdun to cancel and annul various sales of tracts of land that Verdun had made to Jean Baptiste Gregoire and six or seven other colored persons alleged to be his illegitimate children. Verdun's heirs alleged that these sales were really disguised donations to his colored children, and were as a result fraudulent. The defense denied that the persons to whom the sales were made were the illegitimate bastard children of the deceased, but evidence was adduced, and admitted in court, showing that they were indeed his children. This evidence changed the nature of the case. The question became whether these bastard children could then receive from Verdun's succession the quarter of his estate that the law allowed acknowledged illegitimate children to inherit. The court argued that the defendants, though proven in court to be Verdun's illegitimate children, had never been duly acknowledged by him and were, therefore, incapable of inheriting from him. The color question was openly dealt with in the court's written opinion.

> It appears to us, also, very clear, that the object of the law, Louisiana Code, article 226, is to exclude illegitimate colored children from any right in the estate of their white natural father, by whom they have not been duly acknowledged, and that they can only set up such right, when their father is a man of color. . . .
>
> On the merits of the case, we are of opinion that, the laws that allow to natural colored children from a white father, the right of claiming alimony from his heirs, and even to receive a part of his inheritance in certain cases, by donations inter vivos or mortis causa, when they have been duly acknowledged, have denied them the capacity of receiving anything from him, when they have not been acknowledged. *Were it otherwise, the object of the law would be easily evaded,* and it would suffice to avoid making a direct legal written acknowledgment, to give to that class of our population, not only equal, but more extensive rights and capacities than are allowed to our white citizens; for, although known to the world and openly declared as the illegitimate issue of a white man, *they would be considered as strangers to the family in the legal sense of the word,* and as such would become capable, to the whole extent of the law, of receiving from their white father, donations inter vivos and mortis causa, *to the prejudice and even exclusion of his legal heirs.* This our laws have never contemplated (emphasis added).

The question of disguised donations was present in both reasons the court gave for ruling in favor of the plaintiffs:

> (1) children of color (from a white person) are not allowed to prove their paternal descent when they have not been legally

acknowledged; but this may be shown by proof against them, by the adverse party, in order to annul a sale made to them as a disguised and simulated donation to incapable persons.

(2) children of color (from a white person) unacknowledged, cannot inherit or receive by donation inter vivos or mortis causa, even one fourth of the ancestor's estate, and, if by a disguised sale or donation, an attempt is made to give them a greater amount of property than can be legally disposed of, it is not reducible to the disposable portion, but absolutely null.

Compton v. *Prescott*, 1845, mentioned earlier in connection with the question of paternal acknowledgment, shows clearly that the deceased used every available means to transmit property to his colored family. Compton died early in 1841, leaving no ascendants or legitimate descendants. The testimony, however, established that he had been living in open and notorious concubinage with a "mulatress" named Fanchon who was emancipated in April 1825, and that he had several children by her, two of whom, Scipio and Loretta, were named in his will as his children. On May 14, 1830, and December 27, 1837, Compton acknowledged these two children in front of a notary public and two witnesses, as prescribed by law. To ensure the transmission of property to them, Compton made a series of disguised donations in the form of sales of land to his concubine and his children. On April 25, 1838, Compton sold to a Mr. Kelso a tract of land situated on the Red River, which Kelso proceeded to sell to Fanchon, Compton's concubine. The record showed this latter sale to be really a donation; the amount of money transacted in the sale was negligible. On January 2, 1840, B. C. Martin and wife donated a tract of land below Alexandria to Scipio and Loretta, the deceased's children. Again the record shows that this was intended as a disguised donation from the deceased to his natural children. Similarly, on June 15, 1840, P. B. Compton donated to Scipio and Loretta "at the instance of the deceased," who paid for the land, a tract of ninety-nine acres. The deceased also made two direct donations: on

May 17, 1830, he gave two of his children another piece of land on Bayou Robert; and at an unspecified date he gave Fanchon a note of hand for $5,000.

In his will, moreover, he bequeathed to Scipio and Loretta his plantation on Bayou Robert, the slaves attached to said plantation, and the sum of $10,000 apiece—so "that they shall have one-fourth in value of my estate" (12 Rob. 60). He bequeathed "to the free woman of color Fanchon [without calling her his concubine] all my household and kitchen furniture of all descriptions whatever; also one saddle horse, and my carriage, pair of horses, two patent gold watches, stock of cattle, etc." (ibid.). And finally, he made a disguised *mortis causa* donation of $20,000 to Aaron Prescott, Compton's friend and neighbor, intended for his two colored children, as is clear from a letter that Compton wrote to Prescott on March 5, 1840.

After examining the facts, the court invalidated all of the disguised donations, as it had in *Robinett* v. *Verdun*, but it ruled that Scipio and Loretta were still entitled to one-fourth of Compton's estate because they had been legally acknowledged by him. This case illustrated the need for overlapping legal safeguards, since it became clear that the antimiscegenation statute alone could not prevent the transmission of a white man's estate to his colored children.

In *Badillo* v. *Tio* (New Orleans, February 1851; 6 La. Ann. 129), Marie L. Badillo et al., the collateral heirs at law of Augustin Macarty, argued that the defendant Francisco Tio, named as legatee of Macarty's estate, was "a mere intermediary, interposed for the benefit of the following persons: Céleste Perrault, the concubine of the testator; Patrice Macarty, her natural son by the testator; Joséphine Macarty, the natural daughter of the testator, by Victoria Wiltz, his first concubine, and herself the concubine of the defendant [Francisco Tio]; and finally, the natural children of the defendant and Joséphine" (6 La. Ann. 130).

The problem here was to prove that the defendant, Francisco

Tio, was not a bona fide legatee. The court's written opinion on this matter is a revealing social commentary.

> The defendant is not shown to have had any social or business relations with him [the deceased]. Their position in life, education and habits of thought were too dissimilar to induce the belief that much sympathy could exist between them; and we can discover no apparent motive for making the bequest, except that the defendant lived with a woman whom Macarty had some reason to believe was his daughter, and that he was besides the confidential friend and agent of Céleste Perrault. We have come to the conclusion, that nothing prevented him from making a donation to Joséphine. But he was not, probably, aware of this, and may have been induced to select the defendant as the instrument to be used for the transmission of his property in fraudem legis. It is not to be believed that Macarty failed to provide for Céleste Perrault, who, with her son, engrossed all his affections; or that if the dispositions of the will had been intended to be real, he would not have given her all that the law authorized her to receive. According to the ideas and manners of his time, Céleste was, in his eyes, what a kind and dutiful wife would be in ours; and his omission to provide for her is unaccountable, on any principle of human action. These circumstances raise a violent presumption, that the defendant was not the real object of the testator's bounty (6 La. Ann. 133).

On the basis of this judgment, the Court of Appeals invalidated Macarty's will. The attempted transmission of property from a white man to his colored family, however indirect the inheritance, went against the very intent of Louisiana law.

The legislature did its part by severely limiting the capacity of concubines to donate to each other. According to article 1481 (of the revised code of 1870), "those who have lived together in open concubinage are respectively incapable of making to each other, whether *inter vivos* or *mortis causa,* any donation of immovables; and if they make a donation of movables, it cannot exceed one-tenth part of the whole value of their estate." This is why Compton did not describe Fanchon as the mother of his children, and why Walker in the *Succession of Davis* tried to prove that he had never lived in concubinage with Virginia Davis.

In 1808, drafters of the project of the Louisiana Civil Code abolished adoptions. The Code Napoleon of 1804 had permitted them:

> Article 343—Adoption is only permitted to persons of either sex, above the age of fifty years, and who at the period of adoption shall have neither children nor legitimate descendants, and who shall be at least fifteen years older than the individuals whom they propose to adopt.
>
> Article 350—The party adopted shall acquire no right of succession to the property of relatives of the party adopting; but he shall enjoy the same rights with regard to the succession of the party adopting as one possessed by a child born in marriage, even though there should be other children of this latter description, born since the adoption.

But in article 35 of the 1808 project of the Louisiana code, its drafters made it clear that "adoption which was authorized by the laws heretofore in force, shall be and is hereby abolished."

With the abolition of adoption, Louisiana joined the common-law states of the United States that did not allow legal adoptions. It is quite possible, although undeterminable, that Louisiana abolished adoptions as a result of pressure from common-law states, and that fear of the implications of miscegenation was not the primary motive. Still, by abolishing adoption legislators could prevent white men from resorting to adoption as a means of transmitting property to their illegitimate colored children. From 1808 until 1864, when Louisiana passed its first adoption law, adoption was possible only through special legislative action. A special act of the legislature was necessary to sanction specific petitions for dispensation from the anti-adoption law (Backer 1930: 5). By the time the revised Civil

Code was adopted in 1870, specific provisions regarding illegitimate children were included in the statutes.

Revised Civil Code of 1870, article 214 (same as article 214 of the proposed revision of 1869; it is analogous to article 117 of the state constitution of 1864, to Acts 1864-1865, No. 48, as amended by Acts of 1867, No. 17, and Acts 1868, No. 64 [RS §§2322-2328]):

Any person may adopt another as his child, *except those illegitimate children whom the law prohibits from acknowledging;* but such adoption shall not interfere with the right of forced heirs.[1]

Because the 1870 code permitted interracial marriages, this provision acted only against the children of incestuous and adulterous unions. Thus, from 1870 to 1894 (when miscegenation was not outlawed), interracial adoptions were permitted. During this twenty-four-year period, a white man could legally marry a colored woman, thereby automatically legitimating his colored children and enabling them to inherit from him.

With the passing of the antimiscegenation statute in 1894, jurisprudential interpretation of the adoption law banned interracial adoptions. It is clear in the 1910 case, *Hodges' Heirs* v. *Kell et al.* (125 La. 87; 51 So. 77), that the judges were ruling in favor of the defendants only because they were conceived before 1894, when interracial adoptions were unquestionably legal, and that they were no longer considered legal.

John E. Hodges had died in the parish of Madison on July 16, 1906, leaving an estate worth $15,000 to $20,000. In a will dated April 10, 1906, Hodges bequeathed his estate to Eliza Kline, Cornelia Johnson (wife of Charlie Johnson), John Edward Hodges, Jr., Bertha Winbush, Lucinda Gant (wife of Mat Gant), Katie Hodges, Willie Hodges, and Blandina Hodges. Collateral kinsmen of the deceased challenged the validity of the will, alleging that "Eliza Kline was a negro woman of African blood," that Hodges lived with her at his domicile in Madison "in open and notorious concubinage and adultery for thirty years," and that the other persons named in Hodges' will "are, each and all, illegitimate children and bastard offspring of the said John Edward Hodges, deceased, begotten by him and born from the body of said Eliza Kline, in concubinage, and had never been legitimated by the said John Edward Hodges, deceased, and that under the laws of the state their position, at best, is that of illegitimate or natural children, who cannot inherit from their natural father, and can only take, if at all, one-fourth of his estate under a valid donation inter vivos or mortis causa."

But there was also evidence that on October 22, 1898, four years after the new antimiscegenation act was passed, the deceased had legally adopted two of his aforementioned illegitimate children. Was the adoption legally valid? It is true that, at the time of the adoption, Hodges could not legally have married the mother of these children, nor therefore could he have legitimated them by contracting such a marriage. But at the time the children were conceived, such a marriage would have been legal. The issue was of great consequence since the adoption act, if valid, would keep collateral kin from inheriting any part of the estate. The court in the end gave preference to time of conception over time of adoption and ruled the act of adoption valid. It based its ruling on code article 214 of 1870 on adoption, which prevented a person from adopting only "those illegitimate children whom the law prohibits him from acknowledging," and on code article 200, which specified that one could acknowledge and legitimate one's illegitimate children so long as there was no impediment to one's marriage to the children's mother at the time the children were conceived. Thus, Hodges could technically acknowledge, legitimate, and adopt his own children and thereby turn them into his legitimate, forced heirs in spite of the color bar.

By 1932, the statute openly banned interracial adoptions. Adoptions were permitted, "except such child as may have in him or her the blood of another race" (Bernard 1944). Likewise, legislators writing the 1942 act believed "that it was necessary [to prohibit interracial adoptions] because of the Codal provision on miscegenation, and, because of interracial relationships, wishing to avoid a frank statement of the intent of the provision, that is, to limit its application to the Negroes" (ibid.: 86). Thus, as long as antimiscegenation statutes were on the books, a white man was legally incapable of adopting a colored child, and through adoption of transmitting his estate to such a child.

The law ironically worked against both white and colored families. In 1956, for example, in *Green v. The City of New Orleans* (Department of Public Health; 88 So. 2d 76), a Negro couple filed suit against the Bureau of Vital Statistics to force the bureau to change the racial label on the birth certificate of the infant girl they wanted to adopt. Unless the girl's official racial identity were changed from white to colored, the couple would be incapable of adopting her.

On November 2, 1950, a white woman named Ruby Henley Preuc had given birth to Jacqueline Ann Henley at the Charity Hospital of New Orleans. Because the mother was white, the hospital recorded her newborn daughter also as white and forwarded this record to the Bureau of Vital Statistics. Three weeks after the birth, Ruby Preuc took the child to the home of her sister, Mrs. Harold McBride. On October 11, 1952, Ruby Preuc died of a brain tumor at the Home for Incurables, where she had been confined since shortly after the birth of her child. She never revealed the identity of the child's father. On August 1, 1952, Mrs. McBride requested the Department of Welfare to accept the child, "as she felt that it was a Negro and she could no longer permit her to remain in her home, since the neighbors were beginning to comment about the medium brown color of the child's skin" (88 So. 2d 76). To facilitate the proceedings, the Juvenile Court of New Orleans declared that the child had been technically abandoned. Then, on October 1, 1952, she was placed in a Negro foster home, and her foster parents now sought to adopt her.

Suspicions that the girl had "Negro blood" arose in two connections: her mother had been employed as a barmaid in a Negro saloon, and there was some suspicion that she associated with Negroes outside work; and the child was "darker" than the rest of the members of the McBride family—"she didn't fit in my family, she was too dark" (ibid.: 78). The courts refused to accept these presumptions as evidence of Negro ancestry, but it partially accepted the judgment of Dr. Arden King, a Tulane University anthropologist, who relied on the girl's phenotype alone in evaluating her "racial" identity. Dr. King stated that on the basis of the girl's phenotype it seemed quite possible, even probable, that the girl had some Negro ancestry, but he explained that he could not scientifically ascertain this beyond the shadow of a doubt. Asked if he could "say positively that there was some degree of Negro blood less than one-fourth, no matter how small," he responded, "you ask me to not be scientific, and I can not. I won't go beyond saying extremely probable" (ibid.: 79). But the court decided, based on earlier recent jurisprudence (*State ex rel. Treadaway* v. *Louisiana State Board of Health*, on rehearing, Louisiana App. 1952, 56 So. 2d 249; *Villa* v. *Lacoste*, 213 La. 654, 35 So. 2d 419; *Sunseri* v. *Cassagne*, 191 La. 209; 185 So. 1), that extreme probability was not enough. "The general rule that a civil case need not be proven beyond a reasonable doubt is conceded, but we know of no case wherein the courts have applied this general rule when the purpose was to change the race of a person as disclosed in a birth or death certificate" (88 So. 2d 80). The Court of Appeals concluded that there was insufficient evidence to prove beyond any doubt that the girl was at least partly Negro, and blocked adoption proceedings. Although many people had serious doubts that the girl was "pure Caucasian," the court rested its entire case on the fact that there was some slight doubt that the girl "had Negro blood" in her.

The decision had unfortunate social consequences, as dissenting Judge Janvier predicted it would have. It effectively prevented Green's adoption of the girl, and it could eventually also prevent her from marrying. She was to grow up in a Negro foster home, attend Negro schools, have Negro friends, associate socially almost exclusively with Negroes, but be unable to marry a Negro because she was legally white.

The case seems absurd at first glance—a kind of role reversal of what we have seen so far. Plaintiff wants to be declared black, not white. The courts seek proof, beyond any reasonable doubt, that the girl has African ancestry. In practically every other case, the object is to prove that one does not have African ancestry. And yet the decision "makes sense."

The courts reinforce the perception that it is not up to individuals to determine their racial identity, approach their role as seekers of *biological truth,* and decide cases not with regard to the best interests of those individuals concerned but rather in terms of a body of laws designed to prevent people from drawing their *own* conclusions about the implications of particular "blood lines."

A kind of paranoia seeps through these statutes, directly or indirectly, limiting nonwhite access to property held by whites. Individually, the various legal areas explored in this chapter point to empowerment of some and disenfranchisement of others. But not until we study the full set of family and estate laws do we get a glimpse of what amounts to an unstated conspiracy.

The problem, I am arguing, stems from the existence of widespread assumptions about the properties of blood—that identity is determined by blood; that blood ties, lineally and collaterally, carry social and economic rights and obligations; and that both racial identity and class membership are determined by blood. Clearly both the restrictive statutes on marriage, paternity, inheritance and adoption *and* the individual attempts over the years to circumvent those restrictions hinge on such asumptions. The point is that property is not just a corollary of racial classification; it is also a criterion of it.

Part II

THE POLITICAL ECONOMY OF LABELING

Chapter 4

SHAPING A CREOLE IDENTITY

Who and what then are the Creoles? In *State ex rel. Cousin* v. *Louisiana State Board of Health* (138 So. 2d 829), the Louisiana State Court of Appeals was forced to examine discordant views of the meaning of *Creole*. Taylor Cousin, born October 18, 1906, in St. Tammany Parish, had initiated a mandamus proceeding against the Louisiana State Board of Health. Cousin described how he had asked the State Board of Health to issue him a delayed birth certificate showing him to be white, and to issue his sister, Beatrice Cousin, a corrected birth certificate showing her also to be white. The State Board of Health had refused to grant him the request, arguing that there was on file genealogical information "proving" that Taylor Cousin was "a member of the colored race." Among the evidence presented on behalf of the State Board of Health was Taylor Cousin's mother's certificate of death, which listed her as "creole." The State Board of Health interpreted this to mean nonwhite, and seemed fairly certain that at least in this particular case the term implied some admixture of "Negro blood." Examining this particular piece of evidence, the Court of Appeals evaluated the uses of the term as follows:

America Marie Cousin, relator's mother, must also come in for discussion. Her death certificate shows her race as "creole," this information having been given by the physician who presumably attended her.

All informed persons in this area and in every area of the United States, and particularly in the South, who are familiar with the term "creole" should know that the term does not to any extent evidence any percentage whatever of Negro blood.

We think it well known that when a person is called a "creole," this evidences an absence of any Negro blood, and the word is usually applied to one born of French or Spanish descent or a mixture thereof. In Webster's New Century Dictionary in the definition of the word "creole," the following meaning is applied to it:

". . . in Louisiana and elsewhere, a person born in the region but of French ancestry: in general, a person born in a place but of foreign ancestry, as distinguished from the aborigines and half-breeds. . . ."

We direct particular attention to the word "creole" as used to distinguish those who are not of Negro blood as is stated in the above quotation from Webster's New Century Dictionary.

However, we know that among uninformed persons sometimes the word is incorrectly used to designate a person of partial Negro blood, and we have no doubt at all that in the particular case in which the death of relator's mother was registered as "creole," the word "creole" was used by the registrar to evidence doubt as to her race. Certainly, he would not use the word "creole" to designate relator's mother as being white!

The court first argued that Creoles were pure Caucasian, then stated that there was "no doubt at all" that the registrar was not sure whether America Marie Cousin, the relator's mother, was white. Obviously the court's decision did not rest on the supposedly correct meaning of the term *Creole*. Additional evidence had been introduced in the trial to undermine Cousin's case. A brother and a daughter had birth certificates in which they were listed as colored. If one brother was colored then she, his full sister, could not possibly be white. The Court of Appeals concluded that the physician who registered America Marie Cousin as Creole had simply followed the "erroneous" though common practice of the "misinformed."

The court's view was obviously manipulative. It acknowledged lack of uniformity in the use of *Creole,* but described it as a problem in the distribution of knowledge. The "correct" use was that of the "informed"; the "incorrect" use was a practice of the "uninformed." That someone classified as Creole by a state or parish official also had some Negro ancestry did not lead the court to question its own criteria of terminological correctness, by which only pure Caucasians were truly Creoles. Instead of questioning its own judgment, it challenged the judgment of others. It saw nothing wrong with its own definition; the mistake was in classifying a specific individual as Creole when there was a suspicion she had some Negro ancestry. Indeed, Cousin's case itself rested wholly on the court *not* recognizing that there was any other usage, "correct" or "incorrect." Had the court not taken the allegedly "incorrect" usage into account, it would have had to conclude from Cousin's mother's death certificate that she was "white."

The questions are numerous and puzzling. What is it about Creole identity that leads the court to invoke linguistic patterns of usage to determine the person's racial identity? On what basis does the court reject public opinion, or at least a large sector of it, to privilege the interests of a particular class? And why should the actual text of the decision make such a point of clarifying the meaning of *Creole* when it only needed the final paragraph to justify its interpretation? There is a central question here: how is it possible for there to be no clear consensus about the racial identity of the Creole population in a state as persistent as Louisiana in defining its racial structure? The partial answer that I explore in this chapter is that the racial question only emerged in the context of sharpening racial polarization over the past century.

THE INITIAL LABELING

The earliest uses of the term *Creole* for which we have written evidence are descriptions of individual settlers in the baptismal, marriage, and death registers of the Catholic church in Mobile and New Orleans, the two main outposts of the fledgling French colony on the Gulf Coast. A death entry dated May 23, 1745, for a man named Robert Talon, described him as the "first Creole in this colony" (WPA records, available at the Howard-Tilton Memorial Library; also De Ville 1968). Talon's story is credible. Records from the Basilica of the Immaculate Conception at Mobile dated June 15, 1717, show the birth of a child "*née* Marie Margarite de Jean colon habitant de l'isle dauphine and Marg. Prau," and name Robert Talon as *parrain* (godfather). Talon had to have been at least seven years old, the age of reason in the Catholic church, to be eligible to serve as godfather. More likely he was in his teens. Thus, he would have been born around 1700, when the first European settlements along the Mississippi Gulf Coast were established (Biloxi by a group of Canadian explorers in 1699 and Mobile in 1704).

Not having the actual records of Robert Talon's birth or baptism means that we simply cannot document whether *Creole* was, in fact, used then either to describe or refer to the newborn child. But there are numerous examples of early uses of the term in the first baptismal book kept in New Orleans from 1731 to 1733 and in the marriage register of the Basilica of the Immaculate Conception in Mobile, covering the period from 1726 to 1830. For example, on February 18, 1732, Jean Baptiste Alexandre, son of Jean Alexandre of Normandy and Marie Marguerite Dufrere of Paris, married Françoise Hyppolite Baudin, daughter of Nicolas Baudin *dit* Miragain de Tour and Françoise Paillet (Bailly) of Louins. The groom was described as *creole de cette colonie* and the bride as *creole* (St. Louis Cathedral Archives, Mobile records: 76). When Laurent Courade Wiltz, a Swiss soldier, married Marie Anne Colon on May 30, 1733, the entry described her as *creole de cette paroisse* (ibid.: 12a). Baptiste Alexandre was born May 10, 1734, to Jean Baptiste Alexandre and Françoise "Hypolite Bodin" mentioned above. Again they are referred to as *creoles*. A September 7, 1754, entry registers the death of Marie Anne Daniau, *Creole of Mobile,* and daughter of Jean Girard.

During this early period, however, *creole* is rarely capitalized and often alternates with *native,* as in the register of marriage of Pierre Rochon to Catherine Peaux on April 14, 1738, which lists them both as natives of Mobile. In fact, *creole* is but one of many social labels used in these early records. As brief as these baptismal, marriage, and death entries were, they still conveyed information about the person's social status in the community. The records frequently mention occupations of the inscribed males. Françoise "Hyppolithe"'s godfather was "Sr Olivier advocat" (December 9, 1716, Mobile). Gabriel's owner and godmother's husband was a Mr Saussier "marchand du Ft. Louis" (April 7, 1708); Jean's, Charlotte's, Louis's and Marie's owner was a Mr. De Bienvenu, "commandant general de la province" (April 5, 1732). Likewise, the word *esclave* appears frequently, as do the terms *sauvage* (wild, referring to unincorporated Amerindians), *nègre libre* (free Negro), *negresse, mulatress, negrion* (young black boy) and *negritte* (young black girl). The earliest registry of funerals for New Orleans contains 301 entries for this short period in the 1730s. Forty are labeled *nègre* or *negresse;* eight are *sauvage;* an eight-day-old child born July 30, 1732, is called *mulatress,* and 252 are unmarked, implying they are Europeans or children of Europeans in the colony.

Creole was used to describe the first generation of children of European settlers along the Gulf Coast, but it carried little political meaning or significant social connotation for the first few decades of colonial settlement. In fact, Jean-Bernard Bossu (1962) probably unconsciously implied that when he classified the residents of New Orleans into four types and did not include *creole* in his typology. His account of *Travels in the Interior of North America, 1751-1762,* probably the earliest published reference to Creoles in Louisiana proper, merely states on July 1, 1751, that "There are four types of inhabitants [in New Orleans]: Europeans, Indians, Africans or Negroes, and half bloods, born of Europeans and savages native to the country. Those born of French fathers and French, or European, mothers are called Creoles. They are generally brave, tall, and well-built and have a natural inclination toward the arts and sciences" (1962: 32). Similar remarks have been attributed to then-governor of Louisiana, the Marquis de Vaudreuil, a native of French Canada. In an official dispatch dated 1749, he regretted that there were not more Creoles, that "they are the best men to fight the Indians" (Gayarré 1886). The first generation of native-born settlers was barely beginning to reach maturity.

The 1750s and 1760s witnessed continued casual usage of *Creole*. Records of the Superior Council of Louisiana, locus of French colonial government, include references to creoles, but show little evidence of an exclusive (or allegedly exclusive) political faction or social group labeled *creole* (Cabildo records; Howard-Tilton Memorial Library, Archives). Although historians and writers of later periods (e.g., Gayarré 1885; Fortier 1892; King 1921; Herrin 1952) generally assumed that the term was accorded as much social significance in the mid-eighteenth century as it was in most of the nineteenth and early twentieth centuries, manuscripts and official documents of this period do not support that assumption. Even for the 1760s, when the colonial status of Louisiana was in question and turmoil and dissent characterized the fledgling community in southern Louisiana, there is little evidence that there was any serious conflict or tension between the creoles and the noncreoles.

The setting was a dispute between France and Spain. Louisiana had proved to be an economic and fiscal burden during the half-century of its existence (Rodríguez Casado 1942). So in 1762 Louis XV of France donated the colony of Louisiana to his cousin, Charles III of Spain, and proclaimed his extravagant gesture as consolation for Spain's loss of Florida during the Seven Years' War. But Spain was not quick to bite. From 1762 to 1768, Louisiana belonged at once to both and to neither. The absence of mercantilistic economic policies and well-defined political regulations made the area a kind of no-man's land or duty-free port. Its economy flourished for the first time since its colonial birth. When in 1768 the Spanish government finally agreed to take formal possession of the territory, the residents of southern Louisiana were less than ecstatic. They viewed the arrival of Governor Antonio de Ulloa with resentment, even overt hostility. With him came the mercantilistic policy of the Spanish Crown and a different, somewhat unfamiliar, body of legislation. Louisianians revolted and expelled Ulloa shortly after his arrival. They rallied behind the French flag as symbol of their French culture. The fact that a number of them were native-born was insignificant compared to their desire to oppose the Spanish takeover. Native-born and nonnative-born residents of the colony together wrote letters, denunciations and declarations opposing the imposition of Spanish government and Spanish law upon the colony. They begged France not to relinquish its rights over the territory of Louisiana and thereby abandon them. They preferred to flounder about in temporary anarchy, or illusions of independence, rather than submit to the Spanish Crown. In the many official letters, declarations, and documents concerning the 1768 uprising and the period immediately preceding it, residents of Louisiana described themselves as the "inhabitants and merchants of the province of Louisiana," with never a word about their Creole identity (cf. appendices in Rodríguez Casado 1942; manuscript collections of French Superior Council and Actas del Cabildo). They portrayed their act as an affirmation of Louisiana's French identity—French as opposed to Spanish, not Creole versus French or Creole versus Spanish.

One cannot help but wonder if economic motives were not more salient than the rebels made them out to be. During the chaotic years of the middle of the decade, Louisiana enjoyed a process of economic deregulation that intensified competition between local businesses and traveling entrepreneurs, and greatly expanded the realm of economic activity. Had the opportunity really existed for France to repossess its Gulf Coast colony, would the newly liberated colonial residents of southern

Louisiana have really welcomed French colonial government anew? Although the question is hypothetical, it does help to put in perspective the larger question raised here of the social and political meanings of *Creole* at that time.

Demographic conditions were not irrelevant. The O'Reilly census of 1769 taken shortly after the second Spanish attempt to take possession of the colony showed a grand total of 3,190 individuals in New Orleans. Of these, 1,288 were slaves, 99 were *gens de couleur libre,* and 1,803 were white and free (O'Reilly Census, Archives of Louisiana; also cited in Wood 1938: 14–15). Barely the size of a large village, with probably no more than one thousand free adults, only a minority of whom would have been native-born by this time, New Orleans was not exactly ripe for serious internal divisions. Nor had there been, during the first half-century of its settlement, any significant competition for land or a degree of economic prosperity worth fighting for. Land abounded; it was labor that was in short supply. To encourage colonization and thereby secure political and economic claims to the territory henceforth, the Spanish Crown adopted a policy of facilitating the private ownership of land (Arena 1954; Actas del Cabildo; dispatches of Spanish Governors at Howard-Tilton Memorial Library). One could secure a land grant from the Spanish government by performing military or civil service for the Crown or by becoming a settler. Full ownership hinged on compliance with conditions set forth by the Crown to insure settlement and economic expansion. Settlers were to build levees wherever their land bordered on the Mississippi River, keep public roads in good repair, and clear a specified amount of land within three years of obtaining the grant (Arena 1954: 19).

The Spanish period of Louisiana history (1768–1803) saw a series of interrelated processes begin to take shape. The population grew significantly; the land became more and more privately owned; Anglo-Americans pushed westward toward the Mississippi River; and sugarcane cultivation suddenly became very profitable. Competition increased at all levels, and a Creole/American opposition was born. The Spanish government's efforts to populate the territory with loyal settlers was successful, unlike earlier French attempts. Of course, not all was by simple design of the Spanish Crown. External circumstances suddenly left thousands of European peasants able and willing to move to new territories in the Americas. With a little initiative, part of the migratory flow was diverted to southern Louisiana.

The Acadian settlers are a case in point. Thousands of French settlers were expelled from Acadia by the British at the end of the Seven Year's War (popularly known in this country as the French and Indian War, 1756–1763) when Canada passed from French to English hands. Returning to France as landless farmers offered little comfort and security. After short stays in France, large numbers of Acadian settlers moved to southern Louisiana between 1765 and 1790. Spanish governors, it is said, encouraged their immigration because they were (or were thought to be) hardened to frontier life, independent and uncomplaining, even politically disinterested (cf. Dargo 1975: 8). Between May and December 1785 alone, some sixteen hundred Acadian exiles arrived in southern Louisiana (Voorhies 1973; Kniffen 1968: 127; Dufour 1968: 33–35; Clark 1970: 52). Few remained in New Orleans itself, going instead to the area between New Orleans and Baton Rouge (now the parishes of St. James and Ascension), along the bayous Teche and Lafourche south and southwest of New Orleans, on the Vermillion River, at Point Coupee and at Avoyelles. Although they were more rural than urban, their presence solidified the Latin Europeans' position in the territory.

In 1788, the Spanish Crown relocated some fifteen hundred Canary Islanders to Louisiana in an effort to bolster the legitimacy and popularity of the Spanish language. Most Isleños, as they came to be called, settled south of New Orleans along the Mississippi River, an area extremely underpopulated before their arrival. By 1810, just under a thousand Isleños could be identified in this region (Kniffen 1968; Clark 1970). Many became hunters and trappers, some small farmers, some river merchants.

Contrasting sharply with these rural peasant immigrants were men and women of prominence and education who exiled themselves in southern Louisiana in the last fifteen to twenty years of Spanish rule. Both the social restrictions of the Bourbon period and the ideological excesses of the French Revolution unleashed waves of political refugees. The most significant of these waves was the entry of several thousand refugees from Haiti between 1789, when the slave revolution began, and about 1810, when there remained little doubt of the permanence of a free black state in Haiti. The influence of this group of people on southern Louisiana was marked then and is still felt now. They came from an island that excelled in sugar production, had long had large labor-intensive plantations, had been settled much longer than Louisiana, and hence boasted a socially established Creole sector. It had such a skewed racial imbalance before the 1789 revolution that there were insufficient whites to go around as plantation owners and, as a result, a sizeable number of *gens de couleur* of mixed Caucasian-Negroid ancestry joined ranks with the white elites both in Haiti before the revolution and in exile thereafter. Because these people did regularly call themselves Creoles, even identified themselves in print as *créoles de St. Domingue* (Creole de St. Domingue 1959), a growing, influential sector of the population of southern Louisiana in the latter years of Spanish governance imbued sociopolitical connotations into the meaning of *Creole* in the colony. Practically all the refugees from St. Domingue (Haiti) qualified as creoles, regardless of physical appearance or the racial characteristics of all their ancestors.

But the growing significance of the term *Creole* in Louisiana in the latter years of the eighteenth century and the first few decades of the nineteenth only partly derives from the Haitian refugees' self-identification as Creoles. Spanish land-tenure policies fostered the distribution of titles to land and the parceling of colonial territory. To a large extent they laid the groundwork for the formation of a landed aristocracy that would relinquish its social status and political power only under real duress. Spanish land laws in effect created two classes of landowners: small farmers or peasants with medium to small grants of land, who would produce food crops for the domestic colonial market and who were for the most part later to become the "poor whites" of the antebellum and postbellum South (Buck 1925; Jackson 1935; Shugg 1939); and estate owners who acquired their land as a result of special service to the Crown, social contact with the colonial governors and administrators, and special legal provisions that favored initiative, drive, and social position. The founder of each new settlement, according to Spanish law, received a quarter of the total settlement land, not counting the public domain attached to the settlement. The law prescribed a quarter, but governors could enlarge the grant by adding land adjacent to, but technically outside, the settlement. Thus, for example, Baron de Carondelet, governor of Louisiana, made a grant of 208,344 arpents of land[1] on January 1, 1795, to the Marquis de Maison Rouge when he applied for a permit to establish a settlement in the Ouchita District near Fort Miro (Arena 1954: 25). This land stretched some thirty leagues along the Ouchita River. In addition, under the provisions of the *Recopilación de Indias* (Code of the Indies) promulgated during the early stages of colonization of the New World but still in force during the period of Spanish rule in Louisiana, all land was to be divided according to the status of the grantee. *Escuderos* (gentlemen, literally shield-carriers) were entitled to large grants known as *caballerías,* while *peones* (laborers or peasants, literally those on foot) were allowed smaller grants called *peonías* (Recopilación, Libro IV, Titulo XII, Ley I). Ideally, the *caballero* would also be a nobleman, but in case he was not, a separate law almost automatically remedied the misfortune. It provided for the ennoblement of the recipient, his children, and his legitimate descendants: "que los pobladores principales y sus hijos y descendientes legítimos sean hijosdalgo en las Indias" (Recopilación, Libro IV, Título VI, Ley VI).[2] Thus, Spanish laws legitimated the differentiation of rights to land in the New World by identifying meritocracies and creating aristocracies.

The effects of such a system of land grants upon colonial Louisiana at the close of the eighteenth century cannot be overestimated. It helped bring about social and economic stratification in colonial Louisiana and led the way to the creation of a self-styled aristocracy. The differentiation would be compounded with economic prosperity.

With the end of Spanish mercantilism in 1789 and the introduction by Etienne de Boré in 1795/96 of a breed of sugarcane that could withstand the hardships of cultivation in the marshy soil and inclement weather of southern Louisiana, there was an explosion of economic activity in the territory (Gray 1941; Clark 1970; Cabildo records, Carondelet papers). Until then Louisiana had had a mixed economy: some cattle, some tobacco growing, and some indigo cultivation. Within a few years it became for all practical purposes a monocrop export economy. The same external forces of demand for sugar that facilitated Cuba's movement towards monocultivation in the latter part of the eighteenth century (Knight 1970; Hagelberg 1974) prodded Etienne de Boré to experiment with different breeds of sugarcane in New Orleans; and the same change in Spanish policy that released colonial merchants to trade directly with regions and countries other than Spain also increased commercial and agricultural competition, accelerated economic growth, and let supply and demand determine prices and volumes of production (Clark 1970). Suddenly land accrued in value and people with economic power gained social standing. Those who had managed to procure sizeable land grants during the earlier decades of the Spanish period found themselves suddenly at great advantage, as both the Spanish Crown and the first American governor of Louisiana realized around the turn of the century. On October 22, 1798, the Crown removed land-granting powers from colonial governors, for the reason that they tended to make unusually large grants. There is evidence of incipient misgivings by the Crown about the social and political consequences of its land-granting policies (Arena 1954: 59; Morales papers). Cabildo positions became seats for the landed aristocracy. Of the eleven posts within the cabildo, six—the posts of *regidores perpetuos*—were actually bought and sold. Land and sugar had finally combined to wield considerable power.

In 1806, Governor William C. Claiborne made similar observations in a private letter to Thomas Jefferson. Amazement, curiosity, and awe all have their turn in his remarks. He wrote:

Other planters followed the example of M. de Boré, and the cane will doubtless be very soon cultivated in every part of this territory where the climate permits. The facility with which sugar planters amass wealth is almost incredible. . . . It is not uncommon with 220 working hands to make from ten to fourteen thousand dollars; and there are several planters whose field negroes do not exceed forty who make more than twenty thousand dollars a year. . . . The sugar planters raise a sufficiency of corn for their own use; nor do those citizens who reside near New Orleans neglect their gardens. I think Colonel Macarty told me that his daily receipts from the markets were equal to nine dollars.

. . . Yesterday I dined with Mr. Destrehan; he is esteemed the best sugar planter in the territory and is perhaps the wealthiest; his sugars bring him in near thirty thousand dollars per annum and his rents in the city, six thousand. But he is nevertheless an economist; everything around him has the air of simplicity; his table is good but by no means luxuriantly served. He is much attached to retirement; and the education of his children (ten in number) and the improvement of his estate constitute at present his primary cares.

M. Destrehan (de Boré's brother-in-law) is certainly a man of
sense, but has strong prejudices and although they may be
founded in error it is not in the power of man to remove them.
He continues in the opinion that Congress has not been just to
the ceded territory; but is nevertheless an admirer of the American government (Rowland 1917, vol. 3: 61).

To add to the spirit of newfound prosperity, the United States
and Spain signed a treaty in 1795 that allowed Anglo-Americans
to deposit goods and merchandise in New Orleans, free of government charges, while awaiting transfer from riverboats to
oceangoing vessels. Joseph X. D. de Pontalba, a prominent
resident of New Orleans, foresaw much of the imminent growth
and diversification of southern Louisiana: "The country is going
to become one of the most prosperous in the world. . . . The
population will increase in an incredible manner, property will
double in value, and our city will resemble Philadelphia in the
diversity of nations who will live here" (translated and cited by
Priestly 1929: 275). Indeed the difference in port traffic between 1794 and 1798 was staggering. Oceangoing vessels increased from 31 to 78; river craft, from 23 to 110; and outward-
bound boats from 26 to 66 (Canning 1917: 311). Growing port
traffic signalled greater contact with Anglo-Americans. The
American frontier had reached the Mississippi River. English
speakers were settling the northern parts of the Louisiana territory, and the river had become the main commercial artery of
the vast basin. With the opening of this "duty-free" port and the
discovery of a gold mine in sugar cultivation, the gradual "invasion" of formerly Latin Louisiana by Anglo-Americans began.

The stage was set for a politicization of Creole identity.
Roughly three generations had experienced colonial life. The
native-born population, free and slave, white and colored, had
grown in size. It is indeed for this period, 1779 to be precise,
that we find the earliest uses of the term *creole* in reference to
colored individuals in local Louisiana documents (St. Louis Ca-

thedral Archives, baptismal records 1779). Modern-day conceptions about the Creoles are so strongly dichotomized that
even the eminent colored Creole historian Charles B. Roussève
fell into the trap of assuming that Creole was a racial term even
then. Of one baptismal entry, he wrote: "In the archives of the
St. Louis Cathedral the very first appearance of the word 'creole'
is found in the baptismal record, dated 1779, of a slave from
Jamaica, referred to as 'negre creole.' In a later entry in these
archives a person first designated as 'Marie mulatress' is referred
to in the body of the record as 'une creole'" (Roussève 1937:
22–24).

We know, of course, that the term had been in use long before
1779, and I suspect that we may yet find an earlier entry in some
official document where creole refers to a free-colored Louisianian or to a locally born black slave. Still, the term did not carry
any special political or social connotations at this time. Nowhere is this more obvious than in the hundreds of pages of
letters, documents, lists, proclamations, and statements that
form part of the Favrot Collection at the Special Collections Division of the Tulane University Library. In none of the manuscripts from the 1790s to 1803, in Spanish or in French, do the
terms criollo or creole appear. There are numerous references to
Americans, frequent mention of nègres, mulatos, and gentes de
color, but no creole references. A handwritten memorandum by
Pedro Favrot, dated June 1795, outlines nine "needed reforms"
for New Orleans. In it there are thirty references to different
types of social identities, but nowhere is there any mention of
creoles.

Neither Spanish rule nor the arrival of Acadian and Canary
Island settlers led to the formation of a self-identified Creole
group in the colony. Foreign-born and native-born shared the
task of governance, maintenance, protection, and economic development. Most native-born had foreign-born parents, and
most foreign-born had, or were soon to have, locally born children. There was no split between generations. Nor was there,

contrary to earlier expectations, a significant break between the Spanish and the French in the colony, or between people of Spanish parentage and the children or grandchildren of French settlers. I have not found any record of French/Spanish riots, violence, duels, or overt political antagonism after the initial opposition to Spanish rule in 1768 and the Spanish government's decision to execute the instigators. The only indication of separatism between the French and the Spanish during this period is that there were separate French-language and Spanish-language schools. Bishop Luis de Peñalvert y Cárdenas wrote of the Ursulines near the turn of the nineteenth century: "The nuns are so intensely French that they refuse to receive Spanish subjects ignorant of French and shed tears for being obliged to make their spiritual exercises in Spanish books" (cited in Riley 1936: 617). They did not object to Spanish children per se, simply to their speaking only Spanish.

But there were few such individuals in New Orleans after the early years. The records show that many Spanish merchants and settlers married women of French birth or parentage. Of the five Spanish governors (1769–1803; see Appendix), the first three—Unzaga, Bernardo de Galvez, and Estevan Miró—married local French-speaking women. The fourth, the Barón de Carondelet, of French origin himself, was committed enough to the French language to found *Le Moniteur de la Luisiane,* the colony's first newspaper, which was published in French. Gayoso de Lemos, the last Spanish governor, was only in office a short period of time. Likewise, other prominent Spanish residents of southern Louisiana—the Gayarrés, the Boulignys, the Almonesters—married local French-speaking women (de la Vergne family papers, genealogical folders). French speakers occupied high civilian and military positions in government, even soon after the 1768 uprising. Pierre François Marie Olivier de Vezin, for example, road and bridge inspector for the French colony since 1749, was appointed to a seat in the Spanish cabildo in 1769 (Augustin-Wogan-Labranche family papers, folder 7). Jacques Beauregard (referred to in Spanish documents as Santiago Beauregard) served as attorney general of Louisiana in 1771 (Cabildo lists, Favrot papers).

In two lists of officers of the Regiment of Infantry of Louisiana dated January 26, 1797, and October 12, 1803, there is no evidence of systematic discrimination of one group by another. Table 4.1 summarizes the distribution of Frenchmen and Spaniards in the units in 1797 and 1803. Of the two men ranked as colonel in 1797, one came from a Spanish family and the other

Table 4.1
Officers of the Regiment of Infantry of Louisiana, by National Origin

	Spanish	French	Other
(a) 1797			
Colonels	2	2	
Lieutenant colonels	1	5	
Captains	7	14	2
Lieutenants	12	15	
Sublieutenants	22	8	2
	44	44	4
(b) 1803			
Colonels	0	2	
Lieutenant colonels	1	5	1
Captains	9	9	1
Lieutenants	14	5	2
Sublieutenants	22	10	1
Sergeants	23	1	
Cadets	7	12	2
	66	44	7

was of French descent. The man in charge of the regiment in 1803 (a lieutenant colonel) was a Spaniard of English ancestry, but the two colonels of the unit were Louisianians of French descent. In the middle ranks, the French had an edge, even though Louisiana was at the time a colony of Spain. In the lower ranks, the Spaniards dominated, but almost two-thirds of the regiment's cadets were of French descent.

THE POLITICIZATION OF CREOLE IDENTITY

Economic prosperity and the sale of Louisiana to the United States late in 1803 altered the relationship of the colonial population with the newcomers. The movement of Anglo-Americans into southern Louisiana, which began in the mid-1790s, intensified with the sale of Louisiana to the Americans. French speakers outnumbered English speakers in New Orleans by about seven to one at the beginning of the decade but only by three to one towards its end. So fast was the English-speaking population growing that contemporary French and English commentators both tended to overestimate their respective numbers. The Frenchman Berquin-Duvallon, who visited Louisiana in 1802, thought that English speakers outnumbered French speakers. He went so far as to say that the English outnumbered the Americans (Berquin-Duvallon, 1806 translation: 48). John Gurley, one of the new Anglo-American land registrars, wrote to Gideon Granger on July 14, 1804, that he thought there were already equal numbers of French and Americans in New Orleans, and he added that "if the increase of American population should continue for three years to come to equal what it has been for the last nine months they must inevitably constitute a large majority" (Jefferson papers, Library of Congress). More moderate in his overestimation was businessman Vincent Nolte, resident of New Orleans in 1806 and 1807, who guessed that the French (white and colored) constituted three-fifths of the total number of inhabitants and that the Spanish, Americans, and Germans constituted the remaining 40 percent (Nolte 1854: 86; Dargo 1975: 9–11, 180–181). Actually the growing tension between French and English speakers in southern Louisiana deluded these observers into assuming near demographic equality between the groups. The 1805 city directory lists 1,400 white heads of families, and not even 200 of these had recognizable non-French or at least nongallicized names (1805 census, Special Collections Division of the Howard-Tilton Memorial Library at Tulane). One could perhaps add a couple of hundred transient Americans who might have gone unrecorded in this census.

Barely two weeks after the delivery of the territory of Louisiana to the United States, French- and English-speaking military officers created a disturbance at a public ball in New Orleans. It began as an argument over whether French or English dances should be placed first. Governor Claiborne reported to Secretary of State James Madison that it was symptomatic of "a political tendency" (Rowland 1917, vol. 1: 331). Other brawls followed. Claiborne again wrote to Madison on January 31, 1804, "I fear you will suppose that I am wanting in respect in calling your attention to the Balls of New Orleans, but I do assure you Sir, that they occupy much of the Public mind, and from them have proceeded the greatest embarrassments which have heretofore attended my administration" (ibid.: 355). Following a major riot that erupted on January 22, 1804, over the playing of an English country dance, and that led to several controversial arrests, the city council established regulations intended to contain these manifestations of growing tension (Records of the City Council I(1): 26–28). But conflict ensued.

In mid-June, Captain James Sterrett reported to his friend Nathaniel Evans at Fort Adams, Mississippi,

a Company of Mulatoes paraded at the Governor's to receive a stand of Colours that His Excellency was pleased to present them with—His guard were placed round the Square to keep off the mob and one of Michlenberg's men struck a French man (that crowded on him) with his gun. The French man enter'd a Complaint and this day we are to try the Soldier—the other Soldiers Swear hard in favor of their mess mate—and the French Men Swear equally hard against him—some of those little *Frog eaters* will get themselves into trouble, I foresee (June 23, 1804, Sterret to Evans *in* Nathaniel Evans Papers, LSU).

On Bastille Day, Americans tried to break up French festivities (Rowland 1917, vol. 2: 249). On October 12, 1804, the *Louisiana Gazette* openly lamented persons "trying to create animosity between Creoles and Americans." A personal feud in mid-October triggered another violent outbreak (Claiborne to Madison, October 19, 1804, in Rowland 1917, vol. 2: 367; Captain Sterrett to Nathaniel Evans, October 22, 1804, in Nathaniel Evans Papers, LSU). On November 9, 1804, the *Louisiana Gazette* printed an article by a man called Laelius defending the United States and Governor Claiborne "against Creole attitudes." It was followed by heated responses on January 11 and January 15, 1805. On December 17, Sterrett again wrote,

Nothing very important here. Now and then a battle—a few days ago Mr. Abner L. Duncan had a dispute with a French att.y. The dispute became warm[.] Mr. D. took the French-mans Stick from him and was So *impolite* as to knock him down—The French-man is no less a personage than Chevalier De Moyet—he came from France in the *suits* of Mon.sr Lussatt [Laussatt] the Colonial prefect, and did think on this Occasion that his rank etc. etc. was too great to risque a Single Combat with Mr. D. and ran (bleeding in all his glory) to Judge Prevost and made his complaint[.] The Judge of Course had to call up Mr. D. for insulting the Majesty of the law and now the business is before court—so we fight our battles (Sterret to Evans, December 17, 1804, *in* Nathaniel Evans papers).

The population of New Orleans doubled between 1805 and 1810. Additions came from the north and the east but also from

St. Domingue via Cuba. The Franco-Hispanic population continued to outnumber the Anglophones. Anti-American sentiment tended to unite *l'ancienne population*, now increasingly self-identified as Creole. Together they fought successfully to retain Civil Law as the law of Louisiana, to retain the teaching of French in the public schools, and to dominate both regional and local government (Dargo 1975; City Archives WPA Project 1940 #665-64-3-112). Up to 1840, ten of the twelve mayors of New Orleans were Creole (cf. WPA project, City Archives). An equally disproportionate number of assistants to the mayors, recorders, city attorneys, treasurers, commissioners, and aldermen during this period also were Creole. This was true even of those who served under Mayor John Watkins (1805–1807) and Mayor James Mather (1807–1812), the two non-Creole mayors of the period.

Louisiana became a state of the United States in 1812. Of the fifteen governors who served between 1812 and 1860, nine qualified as members of *l'ancienne population*, the Creole sector, or the French-speaking community. Six were born in southern Louisiana of French-speaking parents; one, Henry Thibodaux (1824), arrived in Louisiana in 1794, son of French Canadians; one, Pierre Derbigny (1828–1829), was said to be a Frenchman of noble birth who went to St. Domingue after the French Revolution, then to various cities of the United States before coming to New Orleans; and one, Joseph M. Walker (1850–1853), was born in New Orleans of a French-speaking mother and an English father. (See Appendix.)

On January 22, 1819, Benjamin Latrobe entered the following remarks in his diary: "There are in fact three societies here: 1. the French; 2. the Americans, and 3. the mixed. . . . the French and Creoles are universally of good healthy color, fair" (Latrobe 1951: 32–34). And on April 14 of the same year he remarked that "the Creoles are now more reconciled to American jurisprudence and to the administration of justice by juries" (Latrobe 1951: 127; Stone 1968). The Duke of Saxe-Weimar-Eisenach mentioned the Creoles in his account of travels through

Louisiana: "The aversion of the French Creoles to the Americans is noticeable" (Saxe-Weimar-Eisenach 1828: 70). Apparently the Washington's Birthday public ball was not well attended in 1826 despite lowered admission prices and other added inducements.

Explicit references to Creoles in manuscripts and in print seem to increase in the late 1820s and 1830s. Many appear in letters from overseers and supervisors of the St. Gème estate in New Orleans to St. Gème himself in France over several decades. Jean Boze, for example, on September 4, 1829, gave St. Gème a description of that summer's yellow fever epidemic and its casualties. Then he added: "Il est aussi mort plusieurs Creoles, de St. Domingue, et des ses colons, ainsi que des Creoles de la Louisiane et autres, mais de maladie de nature ordinaire" (St. Gème Collection, 1829 manuscript).[3] On June 25, 1830, he described some of the incidents of ongoing electoral campaigns. One was a duel between a Mr. Gibson, publisher of the newspaper *Argus* and supporter of A. B. Roman for governor, and Felix Labatut, who wrote an article in *L'Abeille* supporting the candidacy of his brother-in-law, A. Beauvais. Pistols were chosen for the first round (Boze commented, "si familières aux americains!"),[4] swords for the second. Another duel took place on June 22, 1830, "entre deux jeunes Creoles par suite de coups donnés en société."[5] Also earlier that same month an American attacked the self-identified Creole candidate Roman. Exhibiting some of the dilemmas of *l'ancienne population* at this time, Jean Boze found it necessary to criticize a person he considered Creole although he acknowledged the need for public unity among Creoles.

Mon précedent Bulletin vous a dit que Mr Marvin americain instituteur avait donné des coups de Baton au candidat Mr A. B. Roman le 6 du courant a la Bourse, qui n'avait point Rougè de le livrer a la justice au lieu d'en demander satisfaction. Le 18-C^t le jury qui avait été nommé le jugeat coupable, et alors la cour criminelle le condamna a 100= d'amende et 2 mois de prison s'il faut en croire les on dit!

Ce malheureux est depuis son enfance extropié de ses pieds, qu'il ne peut tenir son equilibre que par le secours d'un baton, *Et cet arrogant et orgueilleux Creole*—n'eut pas honte de le fouetter sur le grand chemin a sa sortie de son service avec l'assistance de plusieurs de ses camarades lesquels, sous le pretexte de mepris se refusèrent de lui faire raison d'une insulte aussi humiliante, néanmoins cette victime ne jugeat pas a propos a sa rentrée en ville d'aller porter ses plaintes a un tribunal, En se réservant de son venger a la prémière rencontre et qui eut son execution dans le lieu public deja lité, dont la nouvelle lui a fait perdre beaucoup de votans disposés en sa faveur, pour faire esperer qu'il n'aura pas la majorité des suffrages dans l'election des gouverneur, a moins d'en vouloir un a l'epreuve de la Bastonnade [emphasis added]![6]

The 1820s, '30s and '40s were years of growing difficulties for the old French-speaking population. To maintain their political and social status, a semblance of unity was essential, and criticism of the sort Boze voiced of A. B. Roman was increasingly confined to inner circles of family and friends. Self-identified Creoles began to lose their numerical dominance in southern and middle Louisiana. The total population of New Orleans went from 27,176 in 1820 to 46,082 in 1830, and to 102,193 in 1840. (See Table 4.2.) With the St. Domingue refugee movement completed and no known wave of immigration from French-speaking regions or colonies into southern Louisiana at this time, most of the immigrants must have identified themselves as non-French and non-Creole. Clearly they were mostly white. The colored sector of the New Orleans population, both slave and free, grew only 64.4 percent from 1830 to 1840, whereas the white population more than doubled (a growth of 121.8 percent). Irish and German immigrants were among the new arrivals, but the "invasion" was essentially Anglo-American (Tregle 1952).

Table 4.2
The New Orleans Population of Color: 1721–1970

Census Year	Total pop. of New Orleans	Pop. of color	% Colored of total	Free-colored	% of colored	Slave	% of colored
1721[a]	472	173	36.7				
1732[a]	893	258	28.9				
1769[b]	3,190	1,387	43.5	99	7.1	1,288	92.9
1778[c]	3,659	1,507	41.2	353	23.4	1,154	76.6
1785[d]	5,028	2,194	43.6	563	25.7	1,631	74.3
1791[e]	4,816	2,751	57.1	1,147	41.7	1,604	58.3
1803[f]	8,056	4,110	51.0	1,335	32.5	2,775	67.5
1805[g]	8,475	4,671	55.1	1,566	33.5	3,105	66.5
1810[h]	17,242	10,911	63.3	4,950	45.4	5,961	54.6
1820	27,176	13,592	50.0	6,237	45.9	7,355	54.1
1830	46,082	25,953	56.3	11,477	44.2	14,476	55.8
1840	102,193	42,670	41.8	19,222	45.0	23,448	55.0
1850	116,375	28,029	24.1	9,961	35.5	18,068	64.5
1860	168,675	24,074	14.3	10,689	44.4	13,385	55.6
1870	191,418	50,456	26.4				
1880	216,090	57,617	26.7				

1890	242,039	64,491	26.6
1900	287,104	77,714	27.1
1910	339,075	89,262	26.3
1920	387,219	100,930	26.1
1930	458,762	129,632	28.3
1940	494,537	149,034	30.1
1950	570,445	181,775	31.9
1960	627,525	233,514	37.2
1970	591,502	267,339	45.2
	(city proper)		
	1,045,809	323,973	40.0
	(SMSA)		

Notes:

[a]See Beer 1911: 92.

[b]See the O'Reilly Census, cited frequently (cf. Wood 1938).

[c]See Wingfield 1961 (Table I, *n* 4). He cites documents in *Archives of the Indies*, Seville, 1717–1820, prepared by the U.S. Survey of Federal Archives, document 42,70A.

[d]See Berquin-Duvallon (1803), translated by John Davis in 1806, p. 136 of 1806 ed.

[e]See Wood 1938.

[f]See Berquin-Duvallon (1806 ed.), p. 33.

[g]See the New Orleans City Council 1805 census, published in 1936.

[h]U.S. Bureau of the Census, census years 1810–1970.

The growing Creole/American opposition was reflected in settlement patterns. As the population more than doubled, many self-identified Creole families moved east of the French Quarter along the river into an area known as the Faubourg Marigny (Toledano et al. 1974; Notarial Archives, New Orleans). The Americans, on the whole, moved west of the French Quarter along the river into the Faubourg St. Mary. By 1836, these residential patterns were so marked that the Americans proposed a division of the city of New Orleans into separate municipalities, which would give them the self-governance and political participation that they did not enjoy under Creole administrations. The growing power of Anglo-Americans in southern Louisiana became evident with the state legislature's approval of the American plan.

Three municipalities were created. The first included the old French Quarter and its extension north to Lake Pontchartrain; the second corresponded roughly to Faubourg St. Mary; the third to the Faubourg Marigny and expanding Creole Sector (Louisiana Session Laws 1836: 28–37).[7] New Orleans itself would continue to have a single mayor for the entire city and a general council in charge of common problems such as wharfage rates and relief for the poor, but each municipality would have its own board of aldermen, presided over by a recorder, or police court judge. Although the Creoles on the whole had not supported separation, initially at least it seemed to present no extra tension or add much to the Creole/American rivalry.

By the 1840s, however, marked economic differences between the municipalities aggravated the Creole/American conflict and heightened Creole consciousness. The first and third municipalities experienced serious economic recessions, while the second clearly prospered. The "American sector" had notably better transportation facilities, well-kept wharves, a superior public school system, fire engines, market houses that made $70,000 a year (amounting to half the interest on the city debt), and a beautiful municipal hall (*New Orleans Daily Orleanian,* October 18, 1850; *New Orleans Daily Crescent,* February 9,

1850). In the first and third municipalities, bankruptcy was an increasingly distinct possibility. By 1847, the second municipality had ten daily newspapers; the first had one, and the third none. On April 8, 1850, at the instigation of New Orleans Creole representatives to the state legislature, the city held a plebiscite to decide whether or not to reconsolidate the three municipalities. Strong opposition to the plan by voters in the American sector sent it down to defeat (*New Orleans Daily Picayune*, April 9–25, 1850). Reconsolidation would have meant loss of considerable power to the Americans. The self-identified Creoles, the Germans, and the Irish immigrants who occupied the first and third municipalities might well have outnumbered the American community of the Faubourg St. Mary (*New Orleans Daily Crescent*, March 26, 1850; *New Orleans Daily Orleanian*, January 30, 1852). When the adjacent community of Lafayette proposed annexation of their independent municipality to New Orleans, the Americans changed their minds and began to support consolidation (*New Orleans Daily Delta*, April 11, 1851; *New Orleans Daily Crescent*, January 8, 1852; cf. also Briede 1937: 91). Lafayette was primarily an extension of the Faubourg St. Mary, overwhelmingly "American." By combining the second municipality and Lafayette, the Americans would wield considerable power. Hence, the Creoles began to oppose consolidation (cf. Soulé 1955).

Within this atmosphere of intense competition and fear of defeat, Creole self-identification became more vocal. Boze wrote at length about an incident between Felix Labatut and "deux officiers de la garrison militaire americaine," which ended in a duel and in which the Creole/American opposition loomed large (St. Gème Collection, folder 180, January 19, 1832). On August 9, 1835, he outlined perceptions of this heightening social dichotomization in no uncertain terms:

> Mr. Caldwell ancien comedien au theatre americain et aujourd'hui l'entrepreneur pour l'eclairage du Ejoz. Postule mais en vain la place de maire quoi qu'il desire profiter de la division

qui regne *Entre les Créoles* [in large letters], *les étrangers francais*, et *la population americaine*, par ce qu'elle ne peut offrir que des avantages en faveur des nationnaux legitimes pour occuper le temps tous les emplois lucratifs, car ils gagnent chaque jour du terrain sur les créoles *a* quoique notre nouveau gouverneur ait deja manifesté son impartialité a cet egard. Ce qui donne des louanges a sa sage conduite.

On espere toujours que Mr Denis Prieur Créole sera encore continué dans sa place de maire qu'il a toujours exercée honorablement que l'on se soutiendra pour le llève [*sic*] de nouveau au jour d'election prochaine pour ne pas risquer de rencontrer un citoyen de moin de capacité (August 9, 1835, Boze to St. Gème; emphasis added).[8]

The 1836 duel between J. B. Giquel and A. R. Brooks was also seen in Creole/American terms (de la Vergne Collection, correspondence September 2–5, 1836). Giquel was a prominent self-identified Creole; Brooks, a member of the Washington Guards. In the duel, Brooks was killed and Giquel charged with murder. Judge Reval held him without bail, but then Judge Joachim Bermudez, also a prominent and powerful Creole, released him on $15,000 bond. On the night of September 5, 1836, an angry mob attacked the residence of Judge Bermudez. In the attack, three mobsters were killed though Bermudez himself remained unharmed. In one of those ironies of mid-nineteenth-century Louisiana, it was Captain Hozey of the Washington Guards themselves who then offered the judge official round-the-clock protection and brought an end to the bloody incident. Individuals could sidestep the intense rivalry, but the masses had their hearts elsewhere (Klein 1940: 156–157).

Adding to Creole self-consciousness, A. Lussan wrote a play in 1836/37 entitled *La famille creole* and had it staged at Le théâtre français de la Nouvelle Orleans beginning February 28, 1837. The libretto was printed in New Orleans itself in 1837, so it may have been widely distributed (LSU archives). In it, the protagonists are described as "anciens colons de St. Domingue,

réfugiés à la Nlle. Orleans" and as "créoles." The action takes
place both in New Orleans and in Paris. There is little mention
of Anglo-Americans or of social conditions in New Orleans itself, but there is constant reaffirmation of the Creoles' cultural
tie to France.

That same year Hains Boussuge of the Creole community
founded a biweekly magazine oriented towards the arts. It was
entitled *Louisiana Creole; gazette des salons, des arts et des modes,*
and it began in its first issue with the following description of
Louisiana Creole women:

> Si l'art n'existe qu'à certaines conditions, la poésie au contraire
> est partout. . . . Le mot femme est le secret de l'art. Ce mot
> magique, puissance cabalistique, l'Abracadabra, l'Abracalan du
> poète, est au fond de toutes les tentatives intellectuelles. A l'âge
> des rêves enchantés il est le synonyme de gloire de l'espérance.
> C'est à tort qu'on représente la poésie sous la forme d'un
> ange. . . . La Créole, c'est une houri moins le Coran, une Sul-
> tane pour la beauté mais moins le sérail; une fille de Smyrne ou
> de Georgie, qui ne vous répond pas, Allah est grand Mahomet
> est son prophète! quand vous lui dites bonjour; C'est un ange aux
> ailes de feu . . . mais qui parle français. On dirait à lire les poètes
> qu'ils sont tous nés sur les bords du Mississippi. Ils peignent
> d'après l'original, alors même qu'ils ne croient faire que des por-
> traits de fantaisie: les chimères de là-bas sont des réalites ici: ici,
> elles ont leur nom de famille et leur extrait de baptême; Cet idéal
> chéri qu'il poursuivent à travers les nécessités de la vie, au grand
> galop de leur pensée, ils l'atteindraient surement à l'aide des
> navires.[9]

Again a romantic portrayal of the Creole and of Creole life, this
was quite in keeping with contemporary French cultural
tradition.

To many of those quoted above the typical Creole, at least the
ideal Creole, was a descendant of colonial French settlers in Louisiana; but it was not necessary for someone to be a white descendant of colonial French settlers in Louisiana in order to be con-

sidered Creole. The term had always been used in Louisiana to signify local birth and foreign parentage. By traditional definition then in use, children of black or racially mixed parents and children of Anglo-Americans qualified as Creole. Evidence of this usage is plentiful. For example, in 1812 the first session of the first legislature of the state of Louisiana approved the formation of a corps of volunteers manned by Louisiana's free men of color. The Act of Incorporation specified that the colored militiamen were "to be chosen from among the Creoles, and from among such as shall have paid a State tax" (Acts Passed 1812: 72). The idea for the formation of this militia corps goes back to 1804, to a letter of petition from fifty-five free men of color to Governor Claiborne (Carter 1940: 174). But for years it had been opposed by *anciens Louisianais* and by Anglo-Americans. Records show strong objections to the formation of a colored militia corps; interestingly, though, they do not contain objections to the use of the term *Creole* to refer to a sector of the state's colored population.

Likewise, in one of Boze's letters to St. Gème in France dated February 1831, he used the term quite casually several times. A Madame Veuve noïlle ou noye, he wrote, died on the nineteenth, and a "Madame Veuve Pierre Canué" on the twenty-second. The first he described as

agée d'une 70aine d'années *creole Louisianaise,* matelassiere de son etat a la rue Condé proche de l'encoignure de celle S^t philippe et des bains public, capitaliste de plusieurs maisons dans ce voisinage. Elle avait aussi quelques moyens En numeraire, dont ses deux garçons qui ne l'avaient point respectée, dit on, de son vivant profiteront a loisir de son heritage (St. Gème Collection, folder 168, February 1831 letter, p. 1; emphasis added).[10]

Of the second, he wrote:

il est aussi mort Ma^dame Ve Pierre Canué *ancienne creole louisianaise et de couleur,* qui etait riche proprietaire de plusieurs belles maisons en ville et d'une habitation a la metairie. C'etait une femme dit on très respectable pour se meriter d'etre regrettée (St. Gème Collection, folder 168, February 1831 letter, p. 2; emphasis added).[11]

In addition, Boze recounted marital problems between a man and his wife, both with French names, and described the wife's adulterous courtier as "un beau Garçon Creole de S[t] domingue issu d'une famille respectable et jeune encore" (ibid.).[12] On the fourth page of the letter, he made a generalization about the Creoles in which, as throughout this antebellum period, no racial distinction is made. He wrote:

> Les aimables Creoles tant par intrigue que par protection, sont parvenus a occuper aujourd'hui presque tous emplois honorables de ce gouvernement, comme aussi les charges les plus lucratives, dont leur administration se trouvant plus severe que celle de leurs prédecesseurs hommes de dehors, qu'on les Regrettes En ayant été plus traitables dans leur fonction pour percevoir les impots attachés a l'industrie de l'infortuné (St. Gème Collection, folder 168, February 1831 letter, p. 4; emphasis added).[13]

The irrelevance of "race" to identification of self or others as Creoles is evident also in wills and land sales of the period. We find whites identifying themselves as Creole, we find persons of color identifying themselves as creole, and we find no argument about either usage. Pierre Favre Hazeur, noted in the archives as a free man of color, described himself in his 1843 will as "creolle de la Nouvelle Orleans"; Louis Hellene, also noted as free man of color by notary public L. T. Caire on February 15, 1827, described himself as follows: "I am named Louis Hellene, son of Helene Porée, f.c.l., and a father of which I am ignorant of the name. I am creolle of New Orleans and aged about fifty years" (Evans 1974: 26). And Pauline Steven Macarty dictated to Octave de Armas on August 10, 1852, that she was about seventy years old, lived on Customs Street between Derbigny and Roman, had no living relatives or heirs, owned her house, and was "créole de la Louisiane" (Notarial archives, filed January 15, 1861). An article in the *New Orleans Daily Picayune*, July 15, 1859, referred to the "'creole colored people,' as they style themselves," and an essay on the "Education of the Colored Population of Louisiana" in the July 1866 issue of *Harper's New Monthly Magazine* (33: 246) discussed the "colored Creoles." I have been unable to find any printed or handwritten evidence of objections by white Creoles to the use of *Creole* to signify members of the colored communities of southern Louisiana.

Equating *creole* with *native* did create a classificatory problem, however. A person of Anglo-American parentage or ancestry but born in Louisiana would also qualify as a Creole, but to accept such a person as a creole would be to subvert the increasingly significant Creole/American dichotomy and its social, economic, and political significance. A number of travelers' accounts and newspaper references attest to the possibility of using Creole to refer to children of Anglo-Americans.

Harriet Martineau reported in her *Retrospect of Western Travel* (1838, vol. 2: 136), "Creole means native. French and American creoles are natives of French and American extraction." In 1841, J. H. Ingraham in the preface to his novel *The Quadroone; or, St. Michael's Day* tells his readers: "The term Creole will be used throughout the work in its simple Louisiana acceptation, *viz.* as the synonyme of native. The children of northern parents, if born in Louisiana, are 'Creoles'" (1: ix). And Benjamin Norman, in *Norman's New Orleans and Environs* (1845) wrote: "Creoles are those who are born here . . . without reference to the birthplace of their parents" (ibid.: 73). The *New Orleans Mercantile Advertiser* (quoted in the *New Orleans Bee*, September 2, 1833) referred to J. B. Dawson as "creole of Louisiana . . . a native of the parish in which he resides, the district of Florida," though Dawson had no genealogical connection to French or Spanish colonial settlers of the region and no known social or political ties to that sector of the population (Tregle 1952: 24).

And in 1834 Isaac Johnson, a leader of the so-called Florida "American" political faction, told Edward Douglas White, "I am a creole. . . . I had considered myself a Creole in the ordinary acceptation of the term," that is, as native-born (*New Orleans Mercantile Advertiser*, July 1, 1834).

Sociopolitical reality, however, was at odds with the inherent logic of such statements. As years went by and more and more Anglo-Americans gave birth to children in Louisiana, more children of Anglo-Americans technically had the right to call themselves Creole. In underpopulated and unsuccessful Louisiana of the eighteenth century, this would not have mattered much. But the classificatory dilemma followed rather than preceded the explosion of commercial and political rivalry between French-speaking families and English-speaking newcomers. These Anglo-American, Louisiana-born children were born into the Creole/American conflict. Although usage allowed it, few children of Anglo-American parents seem to have identified themselves openly as Creole. Classification as Creole had social-cultural connotations that were incompatible with classification as American. In general, though not universally, persons identified as Creole spoke French and identified with French culture. So it was something of an anomaly to hear an American referred to as Creole.

As locally born Anglo-Americans grew more and more visible and sociopolitical tension between French and English speakers mounted, the meaning of *Creole* began to shift. Cultural attributes of the descendants of French and Spanish colonial settlers who had been calling themselves Creole for a number of generations became criteria of Creole identity. Language became crucial, and social customs were frequently mentioned and compared. Southern Louisiana society was polarized into Creoles and Americans. Classification as Creole or as American soon became, for sociopolitical purposes, more significant than classification by economic status. *Gens de couleur* were not excluded from the Creole category (cf. Lanusse 1845; Desdunes 1911)—nor were descendants of Acadian settlers in southern and southwestern Louisiana. The press regularly counted areas of heavy Acadian settlement in its enumeration of Creole parishes (e.g., *New Orleans Louisiana Advertiser*, March 4, 1834).

In Harriet Martineau's account of New Orleans customs, drawing comparisons between social customs of the two groups seemed to be a favorite pastime. "The division between the American and French factions," she wrote, "is visible even in the drawing room. The French complain that the Americans will not speak French; will not meet their neighbors even half way in accommodation of speech. The Americans ridicule the toilet practices of the French ladies; their liberal use of rouge and pearl powder" (Martineau 1838: 272). Francis and Theresa Pulzskys described how the Creoles thought the Americans were wicked "because they do not attach any great importance to the commandment of honoring father and mother; for sons seldom consult their parents when they marry, and even the daughters choose for themselves" (Pulzskys 1853: 95).

Towards the end of the antebellum period, a number of objects and organizations took Creole for a name. This, I argue here, is part of the process of culturalizing sociopolitical differences. Creole ice cream made from local ice made its first appearance in New Orleans (*New Orleans Daily Picayune*, January 15, 1852, p. 1). A group of colored singers performed at the local German Volksfest under the name of the Creole Serenaders (*Deutsche Zeitung*, May 9, 1858, p. 3). The Ladies Southern Equestrian convention was held at the Creole course on March 30, 1859 (*Deutsche Zeitung*, March 22, 1859, p. 2; *Deutsche Zeitung*, April 1, 1859, p. 2). Announcements of trotting races at the Creole course between members of the Creole Club appeared in the *Daily Crescent* and the *Daily Times Delta* in February and March of 1861.[11] On October 26 an article appeared in the *Daily Delta* describing the so-called Creole market.

The culturalization of sociopolitical differences rested on the assumption that distinct cultural boundaries existed between the Creoles and the Americans. Ironically, the evidence already pointed in the opposite direction by the 1840s and 1850s. The

Creoles continued to speak French and the Americans English, but more and more Creoles began to speak at least some English and more Americans interspersed their speech with words and phrases of French. More subtle changes also made their gradual appearance.

Mardi Gras is perhaps the best example. Thought to be a typically Creole legacy, it was far from an exclusively French tradition. Americans played an increasingly influential role during the first half of the nineteenth century. The day itself had always been marked by festive celebrations of various sorts throughout the French and Spanish colonial periods (Kmen 1961; Superior Council records; Cabildo documents). But all the evidence suggests that these festivities were generally informal, often spontaneous, and never systematic. Public dances called *bals* were often held on such occasions, but there was nothing very special about them. Balls occurred frequently in New Orleans. By 1805 there were fifteen public ballrooms in the city; by 1815 another fifteen had opened up; by 1835 more than twenty more had entered the scene; and between 1836 and 1841 alone more than thirty new ones made their appearance (Kmen 1961: 7). Clearly it was a booming business. It was not unusual by the 1820s for ballrooms to schedule at least two or three regular *bals* a week during the winter and to fill the rest of the week with subscription balls and benefit balls (ibid.: 8). The five or six weeks before Mardi Gras served as popular excuses for public and private dances, but so did St. Joseph's Day, Christmas, Bastille Day, and a host of less fixed holidays. Masked balls were also common, and children would often wear masks on Mardi Gras day itself. The elements were all there, but not the organized form that Mardi Gras celebrations were to take in the late 1830s, '40s, and '50s, and in which the Americans increasingly participated.

In 1831, an Anglo-American from Pennsylvania founded a social club in Mobile whose New Year's Eve parades with torches and floats served as models seven years later for New Orleans Mardi Gras parades. "Some young Creole gentlemen," it is said,

"returning from their studies in Paris . . . decided to form a
street procession of maskers in imitation of the Carnival of Ven-
ice and the Mardi Gras celebrations in Paris and Southern Europe (Nott 1927: February 13; also personal communication).
Inspiration from abroad was clearly preferable, hence the presumption that the novelty had had its roots in civilized Europe
rather than in neighboring Mobile. But the Mobile novelty did
not go unnoticed in New Orleans proper. The *Louisiana Creole,*
the *Commercial Bulletin,* and the *Daily Picayune* all noted the
parade as novelty in New Orleans in 1838.

> The beautiful and joyous cavalcade! How it wound its ways at
> full speed, through a sea of curious and gaping faces! . . . All
> honor to the joyous. It was wonderful and provided even more
> than it had promised. And if the spectacle in the street was a
> curious one, that presented by the balconies of the city was admi-
> rable (*Louisiana Creole,* March 4, 1838; translated by G. W.
> Nott in Nott 1931: February 15).

> The European custom of celebrating the last day of the Car-
> nival by a proession of masqued figures through the public
> streets was introduced here yesterday, very much to the amuse-
> ment of our citizens (*Commercial Bulletin,* February 28, 1838).

> A large number of Creole gentlemen of the first respectability,
> went to no little expense with their preparations. In the pro-
> cession were several carriages superbly ornamented—bands of
> music, horses richly caparisoned—personations of knights, cav-
> aliers, heroes, demigods, chanticleers, punchinellos, and c, and
> c, all mounted (*Daily Picayune,* February 28, 1838).

The innovation, like the balls themselves, was seen as a product
of French Creole culture. So strong was the cultural association
that participating Anglo-Americans were either ignored or
resented.

The records show great excitement citywide during the 1839
Mardi Gras festivities. The *Abeille* claims a thousand *bals* were
held between January 6 and Mardi Gras day itself, and it is hard

to imagine all of these dances occurring only in the Creole community. Moreover, accounts of Mardi Gras activities during the 1840s and early 1850s depict masses of spectators, many scoundrels and agitators among them, watching the parade. The city as a whole seems to have participated, not just the French Creoles. By the mid-fifties, several newspapers led by the *Abeille* denounced these public Mardi Gras festivities. They had become, the papers argued, increasingly disreputable. Predictably, the Creoles blamed licentiousness on the Americans, and the Americans blamed it on the Creoles (*Abeille* and *Daily Delta*, February issues 1855, 1856). Then came the great surprise. Just when the newspapers began to predict the end of Mardi Gras, a new form of Mardi Gras activity entered the scene, and a group of Americans, not Creoles, were responsible for the change. Six Anglo-Americans had conceived the idea of founding a private men's social club, similar to one already in existence in Mobile, that would instill order and pageantry into New Orleans Mardi Gras celebrations. The Mystic Krewe of Comus was thus born in February 1857 (Miceli 1964: 10–15).

Contrasting markedly with events of earlier Mardi Gras, the Comus parade, tableau, and ball were organized, orderly, and pretentiously exclusive. The club's membership was limited to 100. The ball was by invitation only, each member entitled to ten invitations, one per couple. The exclusiveness of it all did not trouble the Creoles, as they themselves openly spoke of the advantages of a closed society.[15] But they deeply resented the fact that Anglo-Americans should steal attention away from the Creoles in a custom that many felt epitomized the cultural essence of their Creole identity. All six men who attended the organizational meeting of Comus, after all, were Anglo-American; and of the nineteen founding members of Comus's social front, the Pickwick Club, eighteen were Anglo-American and one was "foreign French." The French language press's coverage of the event is indicative of Creole resentment. The *Abeille* admitted that the pageantry had been "brilliant," but it suggested the krewe's real intention had been to celebrate Washington's Birthday. Why else, it asked, would Comus parade through uptown streets rather than in the French Quarter (*Abeille,* February 25, 1857)? The February 25 *Daily Creole* described it as "unusually flowr-y" and suggested that this was sure evidence that Mardi Gras had fallen into wrong hands. The *Daily Orleanian* did not cover the event but on February 25 described in great detail and with the utmost flair the other balls held that night. The Creoles were most unappreciative of the turn of events. This was after all the period of intense culturalization of social labels.

Political events of the mid- and late 1850s both reflect and absorb the significance of the polarity. On the surface, at least, New Orleans followed the national trend. Political parties crystallized. Whigs and Democrats vied for power. Beneath the surface, however, there continued to be mostly Creoles and Americans, the Creoles generally posing as Democrats, the Americans as Whigs or Know-Nothings. On February 13, 1852, the state legislature reconsolidated the three New Orleans municipalities and, with the passing of a supplementary act, added the adjacent town of Lafayette. Municipal and aldermanic elections of the fifties strongly reflected the Creole/American split (Soulé 1955). So strong was the ingrained opposition that both the *New Orleans Daily Crescent* and the *Abeille* questioned the real independence of the Independent Reform movement of 1852. Although it supposedly consisted of Whigs as well as Democrats and sought to free the city from "the baneful effect" of party politics, the Independent Reform movement fooled no one. Members of the movement were labeled "aristocratic" or Creole and were accused of being Democrats (*New Orleans Daily Crescent,* March 19, May 24, May 26, 1852; *New Orleans Abeille,* March 12–20, 1852). In 1854, however, the American press did support the Independent Reform party, and immediately the Creoles identified the movement as the Know-Nothing (Native American) party in disguise. As in all party politics, there was no perfect split between the Creoles and the Americans, but there was a clear tendency to identify community with party.

The experiences of Charles Gayarré tell much of this story.

Table 4.3

Indices of the Economic Power of Creoles and Americans
in Louisiana in 1859/60

	Creoles	*Americans*
Holders of at least 50 slaves in the sugar parishes	201	290
Holders of 100 or more slaves in the sugar parishes	68	145
Sugar-producing plantations in sugar parishes	181	254
Plantations producing 300 or more hogsheads of sugar	65	161
Cotton-producing plantations in the sugar-cotton area	39	116
Plantations producing 300 or more bales of cotton	0	77
Parishes in which Creole slave-holdings outnumber American ones and vice versa	7 (all but one in the South)	15
Of the 15 largest slaveholders	1	14
Of the 12 largest sugar producers	1	11
Of the 12 largest cotton producers	0	12

Source: Data represented on this table come from the 1860 census of Louisiana. For identification of planters as Creoles or Americans I relied on Joseph Karl Menn's 1964 master's thesis entitled, "The Large Slaveholders of Louisiana in 1860." On p. 83, *n* 4, he explains his methods and his limitations. I quote: By "Creole" is meant persons of French, Spanish, or Germanic background who were born in Louisiana. "American" designates natives of the rest of the United States resident in Louisiana and persons born in Louisiana of Anglo-American parentage. A relatively small number of individuals born outside of the United States of 1860 (they were about equally divided between natives of France or a German state and natives of the British Isles) have not been considered in the calculations, though a few of them may have been inadvertently included because their birthplaces were not known; in such cases the name of the slaveholder was the single criterion on which he could be judged Creole or "American." In a few cases it was very difficult to determine whether a large slaveholder was Creole or "American" and a few incorrect judgments were no doubt made, but the element of error in the figures arrived at is certainly slight. The handful of cases in which one partner was a Creole and the other an "American" have been excluded from these calculations.

Although Catholic and a Creole, he became a member of the Independent Reform party of New Orleans in the mid-fifties, one of only a few Creoles in the movement at the time. He became active enough in the movement to be elected delegate to the national convention of the Know-Nothing party, but he was refused admission to the national convention because he was Catholic. When word got back to Louisiana, the movement lost all popularity in Creole circles. The Creoles could not—would not—align themselves, even as individuals, with a party that was so blatantly against part of their cultural identity (Overdyke 1933). They supported John Lewis for mayor in 1854, but he was a Democrat and a friend.

Politically speaking, the late 1850s and early 1860s proved disastrous for the Creoles. Table 4.3 summarizes indices of economic status for Creoles and Americans just before the Civil War and reveals the extent to which the Creoles had already lost power and status by 1860. Thus, they presented candidates, campaigned actively, and contested several elections but in the end lost most seats in government after 1854. Their relative numbers had dwindled significantly. The population explosion of the thirty years prior to the Civil War had finally eroded their strength in numbers. There was no way they could keep up with the number of Anglo-Americans, Irishmen, and Germans simply by natural growth. They retained some of their economic power in southern Louisiana by holding on to profitable plantations, but they could retain neither their numerical strength nor their political power. As the class structure shifted, however, so did the "racial" identity of the Creoles.

Chapter 5

RACIAL POLARIZATION

Questions were asked about Creoles' racial identity. References were made to physiognomy and to "blood." Some Anglo-Americans argued that all Creoles were white, while others strongly insinuated that they all had a "touch of the tarbrush." The first view is illustrated in A. Oakey Hall's 1851 description of Creoles, which stressed the so-called "French physiognomy."

> The parlors of Monsieur De————'s plantation mansion were comfortably filled with the Creole beauty and fashion of the parishes of St. Bernard and Plaquemine; planter's families, with a small addition of city friends. . . . The complexion of the rooms was decidedly French, and yet with a dash of American feature and manner just sufficient to suggest a contrast. . . . You see the full black eye; the raven lustre and classic weight of hair, and the well-chiseled nose and gracefully met lips (1851: 122–123).

I will simply illustrate the other view with an 1856 novel by James Peacocke, a local physician. A visiting Northerner remarks,

> "I admire that peculiar rich tint, it shows a warm, and generous blood. She is a Creole, is she not?"
> "'A Creole!' laughed the doctor [a local descendant of French colonists]. You Northern people always commit an error about that. You think a Creole is a Mulatto, but of a very light color?"
> "Yes, certainly, is it not so?"
> "No, a Creole is a mere term taken from the Spanish, meaning a native descended from European ancestors"(pp. 90–91).

And later in Peacocke's novel, a young Northerner writing to a friend in New Orleans said: "I was thinking of you, and the pretty Southern girls, and says I [speaking to his landlady] 'Creole,' if you please, ma'am. "'Creole, sir?' says she, as sharp as a broken vinegar bottle. 'What do you mean by talking about them *niggers* here?'" (p. 184).

The close of the Civil War further aggravated the question of classification. White Creoles found themselves out of power, economically decimated, and a numerical minority. Colored Creoles found themselves in power but suddenly legally indistinguishable from the masses of freed slaves. The social identity of both was seriously in question.

The abolition of slavery, the polarization of North and South over the issue of slavery, the economic disarray of the immediate postbellum years, the enfranchisement of the numerically dominant colored population, and its recruitment into Northern carpetbagger administrations all served to create racial polarization. With the abolition of slavery, the legal distinction that had always existed in Louisiana between the slave and the free-colored disappeared. Whereas three legally defined social strata had existed in antebellum society, only one was legally recognized in the immediate postwar years. The law had provided a framework for social classification. Now it removed it. At the same time, bitterness and resentment towards the North deepened, along with resentment towards the freed slaves for whom the North had at least in part fought the Civil War. The North was made responsible for economic destruction, social disorganization, and street violence, but it was the freed slave who suffered for it. Since freed slaves were all colored or black,[1] the entire black population suffered. To add insult to injury, carpetbagger administrations actively recruited the newly enfranchised to serve and support local and state governments. Few freed slaves had the education or self-confidence to accede to these newly available posts. Of the 86,913 registered Negro voters in Louisiana in 1870, 76,612 were illiterate. By contrast, an estimated 90 percent of New Orleans free-colored population in 1860 was literate and many were well-educated (Roussève

1937: 110; oral genealogical histories). They account for practically all the registered Negro voters who were literate. Understandably they, and not the recently emancipated slaves, assumed most of the leadership roles available to the colored population during Reconstruction.

L'Union was founded in 1862 (after New Orleans's fall to the Northern army) by a group of wealthy free men of color seeking a forum for civil rights. Its editor, Paul Trevigne, was a prominent Creole, and it rarely appeared in anything but French. When *L'Union* closed down in 1864 after arousing angry reactions from whites, a Creole—Dr. Louis Charles Roudanez—founded the *New Orleans Tribune*. Jean Charles Houzeau, a Belgian, was hired as editor.

Among the top political leaders, only Oscar J. Dunn had ever been a slave (Perkins 1943: 105–107; Campbell 1971: 14).[2] The *Anglo-African,* a Northern Negro paper, described the 1865 Louisiana Republican convention as packed and controlled by "a very small clique" of free men of color of French extraction (*New Orleans Tribune,* March 7–10, 1865). The *Tribune* vehemently denied the charge but never published a full list of the names of the delegates to the convention (Campbell 1971: 26). Half the Louisiana delegates to the 1867 Constitutional Convention were colored. Of these, twenty-eight were *gens de couleur* (Creole), seventeen were ex-slaves from various Southern states, including Louisiana, and at least four were well-educated colored Northerners (Campbell 1971: 61). Among the colored delegates, the *gens de couleur* were in the clear majority.

The visibility of these Creole *gens de couleur* in political life served further to dichotomize racial distinctions. The colored Creole population was clearly split on the question of political participation and its foreseen consequences. A vocal and influential group actively participated; but an apparently larger and quieter group kept apart. Numerous articles in the *Tribune* exhorted colored Creoles to abandon their traditional separatism. The very first issue pictured the Creoles as natural, aristocratic leaders but insisted that they had to abandon their self-imposed isolation from the Negro masses in order to attain goals shared by all people of color. On July 21, 1864, one Creole contributor wrote: "Our future is indissolubly bound up with that of the negro . . . and we have resolved . . . to rise or fall with them. We have no rights which we can reckon safe while the same are denied to the fieldhands on the sugar plantations." Still, an independent group of *gens de couleur* petitioned the legislature in 1865 for limited suffrage for blacks. The issue came up in the Constitutional Convention of 1864, which had considered extending suffrage to Negro soldiers, Negro taxpayers, and intelligent free men of color. There the measure was defeated, but the state legislature was given the power to grant limited suffrage to such groups at a later time, if and when it so wished. The 1865 petition was one such attempt to gain separate legal rights for colored Creoles.[3]

There were indeed two realities during this period. As white politicians, Republicans and Democrats alike, criticized the *gens de couleur* in leadership positions for "trying to impose Negro supremacy in Louisiana," the *gens de couleur* retorted that it was precisely that white attitude that could force colored men to adopt overt racism (*New Orleans Tribune,* April, May, June, October, and November issues, 1867). The exchanges index the widening polarity. On the other hand, colored Creoles and non-Creole blacks were far from united. Many Creoles refused to participate in politics; those who did were frequently criticized by non-Creole blacks who feared that the Creoles would institutionalize themselves into a kind of oligarchy (*New Orleans Tribune,* May 21, 26, 29; July 20, 1867).

Rivalry between white Creoles and white Americans in the meantime lost momentum. Both groups increasingly perceived the entire colored population as a common enemy, and temporarily subordinated the Creole/American opposition for the sake of fighting together for white supremacy. Particularly expressive of this white perception is the formation in 1873 of a *Parti Blanc*

or White League. The French *Le Carillon,* "organe des populations franco-louisianais," claimed to have proposed the idea,
although the English-speaking press immediately picked it up
enthusiastically. Its overt goals were to return white supremacy
to Louisiana, though the task required more than the simple
reassertion of white power in government. There had to be a
psychological-cultural campaign to transform the antebellum
system of racial classification in Louisiana, which was ternary
(white/colored/Negro), into a binary one (white/Negro).

Le Carillon presented the complex idea to its French-speaking
readers on July 13, 1873:

"D'un coté ou de l'autre"

Ce que veulent les fils de la Louisiane, le moment de le dire est
venu: Il faut etre BLANC OU NOIR, que chacun se décide.
Deux races sont en présence: l'une supérieure, l'autre inférieure
. . . leur séparation est nécessaire *absolument.* Séparons donc, et
dès aujourd'hui, en deux Partis bien tranchés: le PARTI BLANC
et le PARTI NOIR. La position alors sera nette: La Louisiane
blanche ou la Louisiane noire. Le Carillon arbore le drapeau des
blancs, avec la conviction profonde que ce n'est que sous ses plis
que l'on peut sauver la Louisiane.[4]

The idea spread like wildfire throughout Louisiana. On September 14, 1874, fighting broke out in the Canal Street area of New
Orleans between some five hundred Metropolitan Policemen,
many of whom were black, and some three hundred to four
hundred members of the White League. Twenty-one White
Leaguers and eleven Metropolitan Policemen died in the shoot-
out, which lasted fifteen minutes. The White Leaguers won and
named the incident the Battle for White Supremacy. The next
day White Leaguers took over the statehouse, the former St.
Louis Hotel, and the Metropolitan Police station in the Cabildo.
Though Republican governor Kellogg returned to full power
less than a week later (supported by federal forces), the battle

signalled the end of an era and the beginning of a period of insistent racial polarization.

Culturally, to transform the ternary system of racial classification into a binary one, three steps were necessary: the mulattoes or *métis* had to be downgraded in personal worth and social value; mulattoes had to be denied social and legal status as a separate *race;* and absolute purity of white blood had to be demanded of all those in the white category. Three excerpts from *Le Carillon* itself illustrate the white Creole's awareness of these problems and their attempted solutions.

A July 20, 1873, article in *Le Carillon* entitled "Mélange des Races" deplored the consequences of miscegenation. The mixture of races, it said, instead of producing human beings who were superior in both physiognomy and morality, produced people who were unpredictable.

[L]e métis, ainsi le veulent les lois physiologiques, est un être changeant et fugitif; différent de ses ascendants, il transmet la vie à des descendants qui ne sont point semblables à lui. De génération en génération le cours du sang remonte vers l'une des deux sources, pour reprendre son identité. . . . Si les trois ou quatre millions d'individus d'origine africaine, que l'on compte au Sud, étaient répartis sur toute la surface des Etats-Unis, ils ne tarderaient pas à être absorbés dans l'océan de la race blanche; mais agglomérés sur une portion du sol, où, à l'heure présente, ils sont en nombre à peu près égal aux blancs, si la miscégénation se poursuivait entre eux et ces derniers, notre Sud offrirait bientôt le spectacle de ce chaos humain qui fait l'irrémédiable misère de l'Amérique espagnole.

Alors, qu'adviendrait-il de ces populations mixtes et affaîblies, tristes successeurs des vaillants soldats de la Confédération? Il n'est pas difficile de le prévoir. Le flot toujours grossissant de l'immigration blanche du Nord, soigneuse de son identité qui fait sa force, chasserait devant lui les eaux troubles du mongrélisme africano-caucasien, et les restes méconnaissables de la population louisianaise iraient se perdre dans l'exil, sous le ciel des Antilles, du Mexique et des *républiquettes* anarchiques de l'Amérique Méridionale.[5]

More negative feelings toward the *métis* resound in the following unsigned poem written in a Louisiana Negro dialect. In the poem, the author's objective is not simply to denigrate the *métis* but also to deny them categorial status as a separate race.

"Françoése et les Races"

Antouène, mo plus *smart* que toi;
Couté moin bien, et ta oi;
To di que préjugé mouri,
Que l'égalité remplacé li!
—Faut to bien bête pour croi ca!

Ça qui blanc pas lé jamais noir;
Ça qui noir pas lé jamais blanc;
Ça qui jaune, et qui cré yé blanc,
Va jamais cré que yé noir.
—Faut to bête pour pas connin ça!

Jour qu'ein seul milate va croi
Que nous, nègues, cé yé l'égal,
Jour là, to va tournin choal,
Et moin, ma vini blanc, mo croi.
—Faut to bête pour pas comprane çà!

Contre nous, préjugé des milates,
Le va jamais gagnin ein terme.
Yé méprisé nous; aussi, resté ferme,
Car milates—sra nous Ponce-Pilates.
—To pas trop bête pour comprane-çà!

L'égalité, l'*unification*
Va fait ein drôle la race, mo croir,
Puisque l'enfant de cette union
Sra ni blanc, ni jaune, ni noir.
—To pas trop bête pour comprane çà!

Antouène, si nous pas bien veillé,
Milates va metté nous en dedans;
Pour nous yé di ya pé préché,
Mais . . . mo préféré gagnin zaffair avec blancs.
—Lait pur vaut mieux que ça qui mélangé!

Blancs,—cé ein vrai la race;
Nègues,—cé ein vrai la race;
Choal,—cé ein vrai la race;
Boeuf,—cé ein vrai la race;
Cigare l'Havane,—cé ein vrai la race;
    Mais, milates!—cé pas plus ein la race
Que milet cé ein vrai la race,
Ou que cigare mélé cé ein vrai la race [6]
(*Le Carillon*, July 13, 1873, p. 4).

In "Un mulatre audacieux," published in *Le Carillon*, August 9, 1874, the requirement of absolute purity of blood is clear:

Jeudi dernier, après s'être occupé d'affaires usuelles, le club de la *Ligue Blanche* du 5me Ward ferma ses portes et entra en séance secrète ou exécutive. Au moment òu allait commencer la lecture d'une communication des plus importantes, émanée du *Conseil Suprême de la Ligue*—lecture qui ne peut etre entendue que par des *purs*—on aperçut, fort á l'aise assis au milieu des ligueurs, un petit *Monsieur* n'appartenant pas au Club et poussant l'audace au point de vouloir surprendre la teneur des *causeries positives* de l'assemblée, dans le but d'en faire part, évidemment, à nos ennemis—car c'était un mulâtre *pur sang,* s'il y a des mulâtres pur sang, bien entendu.

L'intrus fut expulsé; et bien lui prit de filer sans murmurer, car la moindre insolence de sa part eut donné du travail, le lendemain, à un entrepreneur de pompes funèbres! [7]

In this case, the mulatto in question was presumably recognizable as such; hence the requirement of absolute purity of blood was easily upheld. The problem in Louisiana, however, was that many of those who were phenotypically white might not meet this requirement of purity of white ancestry. Many members of the white elite community became rather sensitive to the problem of purity of blood. A reader of *Le Carillon,* for instance, objected to an article in the paper that called "les Arabes bel et bien mulâtres et quelque peu nègres." [8] The reader exclaimed,

Que doivent penser de cette assertion nos concitoyens Espagnols qui descendent en grande partie des Arabes?

Les Arabes sont blancs, essentiellement blancs, quoique brunis par la lumière et le soleil, comme les blancs de tous les pays chauds qui vivent en plein air. C'est un peuple pur, sans mélanges, d'un type très accentué, qui s'est conservé sans altération à travers la série des siècles. Ils sont comme les Juifs et les Phéniciens, de race Sémïtique, et se disent en ligne droite, descendants de Sem, l'un des fils de Noë (*Le Carillon,* August 3, 1873, p. 1).[9]

Realistically speaking, white Creoles who were descended from Arabs or from Spaniards had little to fear, since traceability to the time of the Arab conquest of Spain and farther back to North Africa was virtually impossible. On the other hand, the threat of exclusion was to become quite real among Louisianians with even a single "touch of the tarbrush."

In the context of increasing racial polarization, maintenance of a racially undifferentiated social category became deeply problematic. Suspicions multiplied about the Creoles' racial ancestry. Genteel, perhaps aristocratic, but totally impoverished white Creoles saw themselves on the brink of losing what little social status they had managed to salvage just before, during, and after the Civil War. Northern newcomers to the city and other non-Creoles began to insinuate rather openly and insistently that all Creoles had at least "a touch of the tarbrush." After all, many of the well-known politicians of the era of Reconstruction called themselves Creole but were also colored. Although white Creoles did not exactly *look* colored, rumors spread that they had skeletons in their closets. Why, otherwise, would they continue to identify themselves as members of the same social group or category as thousands of colored people?

Unable to retaliate successfully or to hold their own economically or politically, white Creoles finally surrendered to the dichotomizing movement. Books, speeches, and articles began the redefining process. Suddenly, most written or public references to Creoles by members of the white Creole community contained explicit definitions of Creole. Very few if any, by contrast, had preceded the Civil War; certainly the proselytized definition insisted upon by white Creoles in the latter part of the nineteenth century and carried through most of the twentieth was new. It was not totally unconnected to the semantic history of the term, but it had more the quality of myth than of history.

There was a veritable explosion of defenses of Creole ancestry. The more novelist George Washington Cable engaged his characters in family feuds over inheritance, embroiled them in sexual unions with blacks and mulattoes, and made them seem particularly defensive about their presumably pure Caucasian ancestry, the more vociferously the white Creoles responded, insisting on purity of white ancestry as a requirement for identification of individuals as Creole. Cable's novels and short stories explicitly defined the Creole as a white Louisianian of French and/or Spanish ancestry, but they strongly insinuated that Louisiana Creoles were de facto far different from the image they sought to convey (Cable 1879; 1880; 1881; 1884a; 1884b; 1959). Moreover, Cable dabbled in Louisiana history to the dismay of many descendants of colonial families (1884a), and consumed much of his time collecting and publishing Louisiana Negro folklore. The mixture of themes in his writings lent support to the white Creoles' worst suspicions about the man and his intentions.

An anonymous pamphlet now generally attributed to poet-priest Adrien Rouquette appeared in 1880 (Rouquette 1880; Le Breton 1947: 319ff; Turner 1966). Furious over the treatment of Creoles in *The Grandissimes* (1880), its author described Cable as a man prompted by a "disguised puritanism assuming the fanatical mission of radical reform and universal enlightenment." He accused Cable of slandering and ridiculing Creole ancestry in order to profit from sale of his works in "the prejudiced and inimical North." He dismissed Cable in the end as an "unnatural Southern growth, a bastard sprout." Cable's treatment of the Creoles had been sufficiently offensive to break up the more than casual acquaintance between Cable and Rouquette and the friendship between Rouquette and Cable supporter Lafcadio Hearn (Le Breton 1947).

A near-obsession with metasemantics ruled much of the 1880s and 1890s. Even the English-speaking *Daily Picayune* contributed its bit in the December 22, 1884, issue. It explained that, "Creole is not used by Americans unless referring to people of Spanish or French descent. The Americans in Louisiana outnumber those of French descent and the native Americans of this state never called themselves Creoles." For their part, Charles Gayarré, the Honorable F. P. Poché, and Alcée Fortier, probably the three most prominent Creole intellectuals of the nineteenth century, led the outspoken though desperate defense of the Creole. As bright as these men clearly were, they still became engulfed in the reclassification process intent on salvaging white Creole status. Their speeches consequently read more like sympathetic eulogies than historical analyses.

In 1885, for example, Gayarré lectured several times on the theme of the Louisiana Creoles, sometimes in French and at least on one well-known occasion in English at Tulane University (1885 ms.; vertical files at Tulane's Howard-Tilton Memorial Library, undated clipping). The papers described the theme of his presentation, "The Creoles of History and the Creoles of Romance," as a "subject of peculiar attractiveness at this time, in view of the discussions aroused by Mr. Cable's novels." In just slightly over an hour, Gayarré made thirty explicit references to "the pure white ancestry of the Louisiana Creoles." The speech was organized in a historical fashion, but the frequent asides and reminders of "true" Creole identity gave it quite a different flavor. For one thing, Gayarré never examined the meanings of *Creole* in use in earlier periods of Louisiana history and instead assumed that the white ancestors of those belonging to white Creole society in the 1880s were likewise identified as Creole in their days. For another, he never even suggested as a possible explanation of Northern or Southern non-Creole white "confusion" over the meaning of Creole the existence of a noticeable group of colored people in southern Louisiana who identified themselves as Creole and were so identified for over a century. Instead, he was insistent and emotional. He began, for example, with a clear indication of intent: "In every nation the human language has modified itself in the course of time. The spelling and pronunciation of words have changed. Their original meaning has frequently become obscured and misapplied. But few have met the striking transformation of the word *Criollo* in Spanish and Creole in French—at least in the United States—if not in any other part of the world, for it conveys to the immense majority of the Americans of Anglo-Saxon origin a meaning that is the very reverse of its primitive signification." Denials of miscegenation are frequent: "From the very beginning to the late war of secession the strongest line of demarkation, I may say an impassible one, was kept up between what may be called these two halves of the population, and not the slightest cause or pretext was ever given for confounding the one with the other." Irked and emotional, he later added:

It is impossible to comprehend how so many intelligent people should have so completely reversed the meaning of the word Creole when every one of the numerous dictionaries within easy reach could have given them correct information on the subject. What could have led to such a delusion in the public mind? Whence the source of so strange an error? The labor necessary to gratify curiosity on that point might be profitless and the fullest investigation might not, after all, solve the problem. But it is important to correct the error itself, whatever may be the difficulty, or even impossibility of finding out its cause. It has become high time to establish that the Creoles of Louisiana, whose number today may be approximately estimated at 250,000 souls, have not, because of the name they bear, a particle of African blood in their veins, and this is what I believe to have successfully done.

F. P. Poché generally concurred, though he was less vehement in his criticism of "the widespread mistake." Speaking to a large crowd on Creole Day at the 1886 American Exposition in New Orleans, he argued that

> those of her children who first saw the light of day in the infant colony, and who were born of the pioneers who brought the light of civilization from France, Canada, Spain and Germany, to the wild shores of the Gulf of Mexico, were called "Creoles," and their descendants have, with becoming pride, been tenacious of that title.
>
> But simple as this origin appears it is passing strange, but equally true, that it is not generally understood, and *that one of the humiliations of the Creoles is to have been at all times misrepresented as to their origin, their character, their morals and their customs* (*New Orleans Daily Picayune,* February 8, 1886; emphasis added).

Six years later Alcée Fortier still found the same topic meaningful and disturbing. He told the members of the Louisiana Educational Association who made up his audience that "we [the Creoles] have been maligned and misrepresented" (1892: 1), "described so fantastically that Northern men coming to New Orleans look for [Creole women] as they would for wild beasts in a menagerie" (1892: 8), and made to look like "insignificant dolls or more superstitious idiots" (1892: 7). Fortier complained about the total picture that Cable painted of the Louisiana Creole, not just the racial question. Cable accused them of "want of energy," of descent from "casket girls, or worse still, says a certain writer," of fear of voodoo, and of speaking a kind of pidgin or Creole English. Fortier countered with mentions of well-known successful Louisianians who "cleared the land by cutting down the primeval forests," "who managed those plantations larger in area than some German principalities" (1892: 6), who were "descended from the best nobility of France" or "trace their lineage to that excellent middle class, called *la bourgeoisie"* (1892: 7). Of Creole women he reverently wrote, "rich and poor, they are enlightened and refined. They know nothing about the voudous, and their hearts are as brave as their souls are pure" (ibid.).

A variety of essays, articles and journalistic notes on the Creoles flourished at the end of the nineteenth century. P. F. de Gournay wrote a piece for the *Magazine of American History* entitled "Creole Peculiarities" (1886). The *Creole Monthly* appeared in 1896; the *Creole Magazine* in 1899 as a sequel to the *Monthly;* and *Creole Fireside* in 1896. All three were published in English and devoted specifically to poetry and short stories, but they were founded and run by white Louisiana Creoles and perpetuated the new tradition of definitional concerns. In 1890, Jules Dayot wrote a couple of pieces for New Orleans newspapers on "the characteristics, home lives, mansions, etc." of Louisiana Creoles (*Daily City Item,* September 10, 1890, p. 3; *Daily Picayune,* September 14, 1890, p. 16). He argued that "their present condition [was] not unworthy of their brilliant past." In 1891, the *Daily Picayune* again printed a piece on the Creoles: "Creoles of New Orleans are pretty little dark-eyed women of Spanish and French descent" (March 28, 1891, p. 10; cf. also Harris 1897).

A new tradition was thus born. Nurtured by the bitterness of Reconstruction days and kept alive by the passing of Jim Crow laws at the turn of the century (Desdunes 1911; Fischer 1968; Labbé 1971; Reed 1965), a divisive new meaning was given to the term *Creole.* For white Creoles, insistence on the exclusively Caucasian composition of the category became a matter of legal survival as well as social tranquility. The Louisiana General Assembly had passed a statute in 1890 requiring separate railroad accommodations for whites and Negroes. By 1900, segregation had become mandatory in train stations, and segregated schools were required rather than prohibited (as the Radical constitution of 1868 had done). After 1900, segregation statutes increased in number. Segregation was instituted in saloons,

neighborhoods, and mental institutions. It even became official
Catholic church policy in Louisiana between 1909 and 1918
(New Orleans Archdiocesan Archives; Labbé 1971). Insinuations of partial African ancestry could have disenfranchised
white Creoles. Little did it seem to matter to them that many of
their fellow, but partly colored, Creoles were severely affected by
racial polarization and legal segregation. The new interpretation took care of that by pronouncing colored Creoles to be
colored and denying that they were Creole.

A number of white Creole organizations emerged to protect
the status of the "true" Creole, to promote the use of French
language in Louisiana, and to preserve French Creole culture.
Among these were l'Union française, founded in 1872; l'Athénée louisianais, formally organized in 1876; the Creole Organization, chartered in 1886; le Cercle lyrique, founded in 1911;
les Causeries du Lundi, organized in 1912; la Renaissance française, created in 1929; and le Reveil français, dating back to
1930. The Creole Organization of Louisiana was particularly
explicit about its raison d'être. Its June 24, 1886, charter proclaimed the need "to disseminate knowledge concerning the
true origin and real character, and to promote advancement of
the creole race in Louisiana." One hundred and four persons
signed the charter and elected F. P. Poché president. Le Cercle
lyrique sought to preserve and advance good music, meaning
continental music, in New Orleans; les Causeries du Lundi, "to
unite the 'elite' of New Orleans Society interested and loving
France, given [sic] them the occasion to exchange their ideas and
to discuss on all subjects relating to France" (Argüedas 1936;
New Orleans Courier, April 17, 1936). The others generally
stressed French language and French culture (cf. vertical files,
Tulane Special Collections).

Reiterations of the new interpretation periodically appeared
in print throughout the early and middle part of the twentieth
century, with Anglo-American friends of the white Creoles
adopting this new interpretation as well. Grace King adhered to

it in her famous *Creole Families of New Orleans* (1921). Paul Villeré implied it in a reading he gave April 29, 1921, at a meeting of the Athénée louisianais, "Le Créole—réflexions l'après-guerre" (1921: 65–85). Flo Field assumed it in her popular play "A la Creole!"—thus winning over large numbers of white Creoles predisposed to criticism (1927). And so did Adele Drouet, writing on Creole lullabies (1927); Lyle Saxon on old Louisiana (1928, 1929); Annette Duchain on how "Creole duelists of 1832 would be amazed to see women descendants fence" (1932); Roger Baudier on the Catholic church in Louisiana (1939) and on family life around the turn of the twentieth century (1943–1951); Harnett Kane on customs of the past (1944, 1958); an author using the pen name of André Cajun on why Louisiana has parishes, police jurymen, Redbones, Creoles, and Cajuns (1947); M. H. Herrin on the so-called Creole aristocracy (1952); Charles "Pie" Dufour on aspects of the history of southern Louisiana (1967); and James Bezou on French influences in the state (1967–1979). In fact, colored Creoles, white priests, and social workers who have worked with the colored Creole population assert today that economically and socially powerful white families of French/Spanish descent or allegiance actively fought the publication of any book or article that referred to, or even implied, that there were people of color in Louisiana who called themselves Creole. They did not always succeed, or have access. Harper & Brothers did publish Rohrer and Edmonson's *The Eighth Generation* in 1960, whose second chapter, "New Orleans Negro Society" freely referred to the coexistence of white Creoles and colored Creoles at various points in the city's history. And a number of graduate students obtained degrees—most at the master's level—upon completion of research projects specifically on colored Creole communities (cf. Jenkins 1965; Jones 1950; Mott n.d.; Palazzolo 1955; Rousseau 1955; Wingfield 1961). The doubt reemerges, however, when we note that none of these theses was published in Louisiana in any form.

Chapter 6

ANATOMY OF THE CREOLE CONTROVERSY

In *State ex rel. Cousin v. Louisiana State Board of Health* (138 So. 2d 829; see Chapter 4), then, the court was embroiled in a conflict whose roots were both cognitive and social. As the court reluctantly acknowledged, public opinion was divided over the racial identity of Louisiana Creoles. And as the court simultaneously implied, too much is at stake in racially stratified societies for advocates of one view or another blithely to accept the existence of contradictory definitions.

Two types of Louisianians consequently identify themselves today as Creole. One is socially and legally white; the other, socially and legally colored. The white side by definition cannot accept the existence of colored Creoles; the colored side, by definition, cannot accept the white conception of *Creole*. The problem is encapsulated in the use of the terms *Cajun Creole* and *Creole Cajun*. These expressions make no sense at all to white Creoles. A Creole in their estimation is a purely white descendant of French or Spanish settlers in colonial Louisiana; a Cajun is a purely white descendant of Acadian colonial settlers in southern Louisiana. The two categories are mutually exclusive subcategories of a strictly white superclass. Like Italian, Irish, or Jewish, they are subdivisions of contemporary white Louisiana society. In the contemporary North American scene, they would fit the white stereotype of a white *ethnic*. (See Figure 6.1.) The expressions *Cajun Creole* or *Creole Cajun* make sense only in an alternative interpretation, wherein *Cajun* signifies colonial Acadian ancestry and *Creole* signifies "racially" mixed ancestry. In this view Cajuns are not necessarily all-white, nor are Creoles

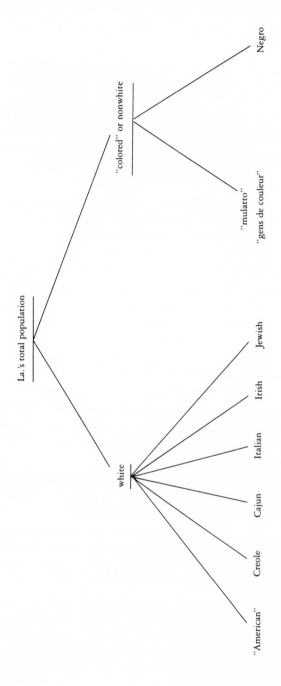

Figure 6.1 The Contemporary White Creole Conception of Louisiana's Social Categories

necessarily the descendants of French or Spanish settlers. Indeed, *Creole* here implies mixed white and Negro ancestry. A Cajun Creole is therefore a "colored" person who has at least one Acadian ancestor; a Creole Cajun is a descendant of Acadian settlers in Louisiana who has partial Negro ancestry. The referents of these two compound lexemes are usually identical, though their specific senses suggest differential weighing of one of the two kinds of ancestries signified by the terms. These uses of *Creole* do not allow for the possibility of there being white Creoles.

There are, in fact, colored Creoles who are virtually ignorant of the existence of whites in Louisiana who call themselves Creole. Often young and only superficially in touch with whites in New Orleans, they find the phrase *white Creole* to be a contradiction in terms. When someone identifies himself as Creole, they assume he means he is racially mixed, although he may look stereotypically Caucasian. Teenagers and young adults often stared at me with surprise and disbelief when I spoke of whites identifying themselves as Creole.

In a less extremist version, *Creole* designates a racially undifferentiated category of all those Louisianians with at least some French or Spanish ancestry. Whites may be Creoles, as may nonwhites. Figure 6.2 illustrates the structural difference between the two alternative conceptions. We see here that for there to be a Cajun Creole or Creole Cajun in variant B, a subclass of the class of Creoles or Cajuns has to be stressed, and only the encompassing class of the other general category invoked. *Creole* is not a racial classification in variant B. Creole and non-Creole, white and colored, are two independent ways to divide Louisianian society.

THE CONCEPTION OF PURITY

The conflict takes the form of an argument over the interpretation of ancestry. Central to the view that has dominated

Figure 6.2 Alternative Nonwhite Views
of the Creole Social Category

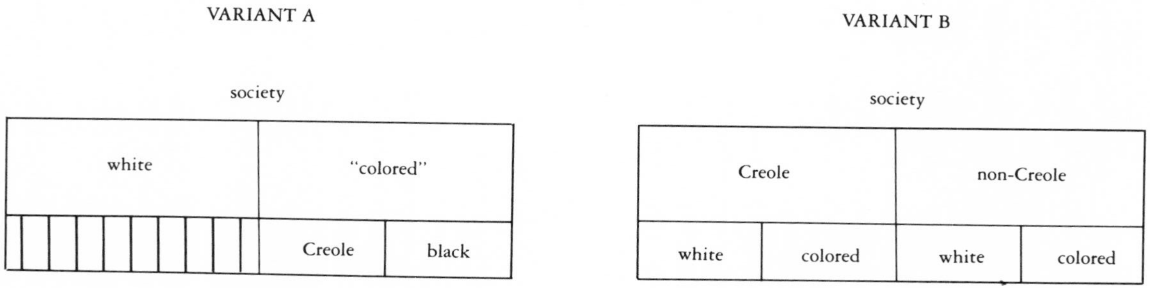

VARIANT A

VARIANT B

white Creole circles in the twentieth century is the concept of purity of blood. Throughout mainland Latin America and the Caribbean, "purity of blood"—although no longer a legal concept—still demarcates elite status (cf. Brito Figueroa 1966; Haring 1963; King 1951; Rama 1970), "blood" indexes ancestry, and "purity" signifies freedom from certain ethnic, religious, or racial ancestries. Physical, psychological, and emotional characteristics are presumably passed on physically from one generation to another in the blood. A person's blood thus embodies his entire ancestry, and mixtures of blood of different social "quality" tarnishes the "superior" of the two while it upgrades the "inferior." From the point of view of those whose blood is said to be superior, mixture of that blood with blood of inferior quality produces impurity. As purity is equated with elite status, incurring impurity lowers social standing. Underlying the distinction between pure and impure blood then is a hierarchical placement of social categories.

The dominant white Creole concept is strikingly similar. It is apparent in a number of expressions commonly heard in white Creole circles. These include the phrases *sang pur* (pure blood), *malblanchi* (literally, poorly cleansed), *touch of the tarbrush, café au lait* (literally, coffee in the milk), and *quatorze carats* (fourteen carats, where twenty-four is pure gold). Metaphors of impurity overlap in these examples. *Sang pur* literally translates as "pure blood" and implies an untarnished ancestry. *Malblanchi* and touch of the tarbrush play upon the notion of dirt. *Café au lait* and *c'est un quatorze carats* suggest measures of impurity.

The sense of tarnishing is very vivid. There is a strong association of tarnished ancestry with polluted blood and of polluted blood with physical dirt. People "touched by the tarbrush" are simply presumed less clean than "pure whites." Polite references to questionable ancestry, for example, include nonverbal signs, such as pressing with one's fingertip on the skin below the eye and pulling down just enough to expose the bottom part of the eye and the inside color of the eyelid. The implication is that the "touch of the tarbrush" would be physically visible.

It is the same expectation that surfaces in white rationalizations of the need for physical distance from the colored. Physical separation between the white and the colored is thought to ensure cleanliness. Many whites continue to oppose integration at least partially on these grounds: integrated schools are assumed to be dirtier than all-white schools. Whites feel uncomfortable sitting next to blacks in buses, streetcars, and restaurants. When Huey P. Long proposed founding nursing programs for colored women (cf. Williams 1969), he did not advocate equal opportunity as much as the idea that white women should not have to soil themselves taking care of colored people.

In white Creole homes, where domestics are almost always colored, there is frequent contact between whites and at least some blacks, and often even visible affection between them. Yet to ensure their own cleanliness, whites insist on functional separation between themselves and their colored servants. Blacks do not sit in living rooms, dining rooms, or bedrooms, unless they are asked to do so on very special occasions. They are for the most part restricted to the kitchen, pantry, back porches, or if they stay overnight, their own bedrooms.

There are some necessary concessions. Blacks continue to be used as caretakers for white children (although they do so now less frequently than they used to). They spend a fair amount of time in children's bedrooms, and there they are allowed to sit, relax, and play with white children. When a white adult enters the room, however, the black "mammie" is expected to show deference to her superior by rising from her chair. Black servants are equated with children in more than one way: they are inferior in status, and are said to be unpredictable, even unruly in public, and untrained in the fastidious manners of "civilized society."

Concessions may also be made when there is serious illness in the household. "Rules" may be relaxed to allow black nurses or servants to offer round-the-clock supervision, but even there separation is prescribed where possible. Colored or black practical nurses are allowed to sleep in patients' rooms, but the women remain fully dressed and sleep, only when their services are not needed, on unopened couches or armchairs. In one household that I observed in detail, the nurse assumed a more traditional black role in the morning by making breakfast for the patient and his family. This was never, of course, her official job; in fact, it was strongly discouraged by the nursing agency that sent her, which feared that it would lower the status of nurses in general.

A direct connection between blood pollution and dirt was clearly implied in this same household in 1976 when two nurses of markedly different color took turns watching over my sick informant. One, the informant's wife often remarked to me, was "black as coal"; the other was so light-skinned that "you'd almost never know she was colored!" My white informants were openly and admittedly fond of both of these women, but they clearly discriminated between them. They thought the latter was "so nice-looking that you might not even mind her sleeping on our own white linen." Of the former, no such statement was ever forthcoming. Near-whiteness of blood was being equated with degree of body cleanliness.

The idea that polluted blood contaminates matter itself is, however, nowhere more evident than in burial practices. Impurities of blood are thought to pollute the entire human body even after death. Thus, the ashes of the "pure" should be kept separate from those of the "impure." Separation is ensured when individual interment is practiced, but it is not always so in New Orleans. The earliest burials in New Orleans were made entirely below the ground (Huber 1974: 4), but most burials since then have been above ground. Most of New Orleans rests on low swampy ground, and water can be found just a few feet below the surface. The first New Orleans cemetery—where people were buried underground following the customs of the regions they had left in Europe—had to be surrounded by ditches (ibid.). When the new cemetery, the St. Louis I, was planned in

1789, builders resorted to the old Spanish custom of group burials in vaults and society tombs above the ground. Most private tombs today consist of two vaults, one above the other, and a pit (*caveau*) or receptacle below (ibid.: 10). The dead are placed in coffins, and these are placed in whichever vault is available in the family tomb. If both vaults are filled when a family member dies, one of the two coffins—usually the oldest of the two burials—is removed to make room for the most recent dead, and the remains found inside the coffin are placed in a bag. The bag is then consigned to the caveau below, where the ashes mix. Family tombs of this type allow numerous generations of relatives to be buried in the same place in the ground. They are a means of keeping the family together even after death. The problem is that ashes mix, and only certain ashes are allowed to mix.

It is obvious from surveying more than a hundred family tombs that spouses of family members are not automatically excluded from a family tomb; it is common to find sons- and daughters-in-law buried in a family tomb. It is not unusual also to find a foster relative or even a white nurse or domestic servant buried in a family tomb. Neither consanguinity nor equality of status is necessary. The one mixture not knowingly allowed is the burial of the "racially impure" with the ashes of the "racially pure." White and colored branches of a family may have adjacent family tombs if the two sides acknowledge their consanguineal relationship. Several informants volunteered examples of this practice in their own families but asked to remain anonymous to protect the families involved. In one typical modern white Creole family, family members remained discrete when they discovered that one of their own had married a woman "of questionable racial ancestry." "This is not *public* knowledge," my informant explained, "but it is public enough that when she died, she was not buried in the tomb along with the rest of the family but was instead buried in a separate tomb next to the family's private enclosure." There are now two separate tombs, one next to the other in the St. Louis cemetery—the descendants of the woman of questionable racial ancestry being carefully buried adjacent to but not in the tomb of "the pure members of the family."

In most cases, nonetheless, white and colored relatives are buried in tombs not so closely situated, thereby publicly denying even the possibility that there might be a distant consanguineal relationship between them. In this sense, burial is the ultimate expression of the boundaries of social categories and of the special importance accorded to the purity or impurity of one's blood.

In the colored Creole uses of the term *Creole,* there is a fundamental rebuttal of the exclusionary principle invoked by white Creoles. Objections are of two sorts. A deep-rooted one is explicit skepticism about the "purity" of anyone's pedigree, any mention of which infuriates many white Creoles. The second objection is to the dichotomization of Louisiana society that white Creoles envision. Colored Creoles believe that dichotomization distorts the facts of Louisiana society by ignoring the continuum of racial types and the history of miscegenation, and that it "unjustifiably" makes other criteria of differentiation insignificant, such as language, wealth, partial French ancestry, education, and religion.

Capturing the flavor of the first objection is the impassioned statement of a middle-aged colored Creole woman in a taped interview in 1962.

> Among the Creoles—and you know the Creoles were not only our color. They were black and all different colors. That's why we call us the Creoles. Now you want to know who the Creoles were? What is a Creole? A Creole is a French and Spanish. That's what I am. To be a *pure* Creole you have to be a descendant of French and Spaniard. Now they say today that a Creole is a mixture, which it is. Creole is a mixture. I talked with a lady in the Vieux Carre when we started the Fiesta. She had *her* version of who was a Creole, and so she would tell the people in the Spring

Fiesta what she thought was a Creole. So when she got with me, she says, well now, I was telling them it was a mixture, Mrs. ————. *I* thought it was a mixture. I says, it *is* a mixture. If you mix two people together it *is* a mixture. If you mix four or five or so on, it *is* a mixture. So [she laughed] she didn't know what to say. So I told her it *is* a mixture. And I say, really and truly, most everybody in New Orleans is a mixture, because there's Italian, there's German, there's Spanish, French and all— you hardly can find *one* pure breed of any nationality here in New Orleans. Isn't that so?

I told this professor that came from Tulane, that came from Tulane here about four, five years ago. . . . He came with some students here, and asked me questions. I told him, I said, you can find me one pure breed of any nationality here. I says, I'll give you my Fiesta which I dearly love. He said, "No, Mrs., I don't think I can." I said, now I don't mean colored, I mean white—like you. I mean *one* pure breed, and I'll give [you] my Fiesta. He says, I won't even try. So, that's what everybody is in all places, not only the South. They *are* a mixture. That's why Hitler had such a troubled time to get [make] his race all one. Now I hate to say that. I shouldn't bring that up, maybe. But we're talking about pure . . . you're talking about breed, aren't you? Who we are and all that. Well, we're a mixture, and you'll find . . . [us] . . . very badly mixed. As far as I know, we're a mixture, we're mixed. I've even had people tell me—call me— that, I'm mixed. But there's nothing I could do to defend myself because my family is very badly mixed. And our people, our grandparents and all call us Creole, and so that's all I know. And I'm Creole (tape stored at the New Orleans Jazz Archives).

The informant eloquently plays upon a double sense of mixture. She argues that "purity" of Creole ancestry is imaginary: who can find a "pure breed" today? But she also clearly recognizes the implications of the white principle of purity when she explains, "now, I don't mean colored, I mean white—like you." She acknowledges the mixed ancestries of her family and friends but minimizes the importance whites might place on her Negro

ancestry by invoking a very general and literal definition of mixture—"if you mix two people together, it *is* a mixture. . . ."

Privately, many of these Creoles delight in stories that question the "purity" of members of the white Creole community,
whether or not there is hard evidence to support the imputation.
The men sneak smiles; the women giggle; children listen attentively. Someone may rub his forearm as if to clean off the dirt.
Names are used sparingly. Suspicion is part of everyday life in
Louisiana. Whites often grow up afraid to know their own genealogies. Many admit that as children they often stared at the
skin below their fingernails and through a mirror at the white of
their eyes to see if there was any "touch of the tarbrush." Not
finding written records of birth, baptism, marriage, or death for
any one ancestor exacerbates suspicions of foul play. Such a discovery brings glee to a political enemy or economic rival and
may traumatize the individual concerned.

Reactions vary. Several families have left Louisiana for California, Chicago, or New England shortly after rumors spread
about their questionable ancestry. Others, as in the well-known
case of boxer Ralph Dupas (102 So. 2d 77; 125 So. 2d 375),
have stayed to fight it out in court. Still others persevere in
efforts to locate those elusive written documents. One classic
case of the latter is that of an older, well-known, and well-liked
white Creole whose genealogical records go back more than six
generations along several lines. Some respected old Louisiana
French Creole names appear on that genealogy—Livaudais,
Fazende, Saunhac du Fossat (a variant of Soniat du Fossat) and
Dreux. But the nagging problem of her mother's mother's
mother's marital status overshadows the otherwise illustrious ancestry. My informant is upset because she cannot find any reference to her MMMH (mother's mother's mother's husband). She
showed me several documents that described the MMM as
a widow; one reference specifically names her as "widow of
Joseph." In my informant's mind, however, the absence of a
marriage certificate is deeply problematic, as it may indicate

that her mother's mother was illegitimate, and this in turn could imply that she was not purely Caucasian. Conflicting hearsay evidence urges this particular informant to continue in her now seemingly interminable search. For one, it seems that her mother's mother's mother lived with her mother and maiden sister in the same house most of her life. My informant's argument is that she would not have been allowed to remain in the fold had she led a disreputable life. Then, there is the mother's mother's mother's claim, which my informant remembers although she was very young when she first heard it, that she and her husband were cousins. This would explain why the mother's mother had the same surname as her own mother. Yet this is all unsubstantiated hearsay evidence. There is no marriage certificate, and there are no birth or baptismal certificates for the children of the MMM.

Suspicion is irreverent. A popular joke in white Creole circles envisions the King of Carnival one year discovering that he had that untouchable "touch." It has Rex not feeling well and seeking professional advice from the best physicians at the world-famous Ocshner Clinic in New Orleans. Complete tests are done. Samples of blood, urine, stool are taken. EKG's and EEG's are done. Still Rex feels weak and nervous about heading New Orleans's traditional Mardi Gras finale. The day the results are in he visits the clinic's chief attending physician, an old-time friend and classmate. Upon arrival, Rex finds the doctor morose and irritable. He has asked to be left alone with this already elected King of Carnival, who now senses that he is seriously ill.

"Well, tell me, Doctor. What is the matter? Do I have terminal cancer?"

"No."

"Tuberculosis?"

"No."

"Some terminal heart ailment?"

"No."

"Some rare incurable disease?"

"No."

"Well, then, tell me for heaven's sake. What is wrong with me?"

"You have sickle-cell anemia. I didn't know how to tell you, but there's absolutely no doubt about it. I'm really sorry."

The association of sickle-cell anemia with the black population makes the racial allusion obvious.

The colored Creole population, however, is torn by the reality imposed upon it by racial dichotomization. If the white Creole community is not all "pure" in the white sense of the word, it is because some of the "impure," that is, the other Creoles, managed to pass. Dichotomization forces those who try to pass to maintain absolutely no contact with the family and the friends they leave behind. Any such contact could arouse suspicion, and with suspicion comes demotion and a return to "colored" status.

The successful *passablanc* breeds both jealousy and pride in the community he leaves behind. It is a situation to which many have reluctantly resigned themselves. They fault not the individuals who pass but the dichotomous system of classification that forces them to pass. Hence, many colored Creoles protect others who are trying to pass, to the point of feigning ignorance of certain branches of their families. Elicited genealogies often seem strangely skewed. In the case of one very good informant, a year passed before he confided in me that his own mother's sister and her children had passed into the white community. With tears in his eyes, he described the painful experience of learning about his aunt's death on the obituary page of the *New Orleans Times-Picayune*. His cousins failed to inform the abandoned side of the family of the death, for fear that they might show up at the wake or the funeral and thereby destroy the image of whiteness. Total separation was necessary for secrecy.

Colored Creole uses of the term *pure* also outrage or puzzle white Creoles. For emphasis one may, for instance, describe a person as "pure Creole" and make no reference at all to the "racial" characteristics of his ancestors. "Pure Creole" could be one who speaks French fluently, is particularly concerned with manners, frequently sprinkles his conversation with old Creole sayings, and associates only with individuals like himself. He is "pure" because he embodies a stereotype of the lifestyle of the Louisiana Creole, a stereotype the white Creoles find incomplete. Mary Belle M'Kellar, a white reporter for the Natchitoches daily newspaper, reported on May 15, 1926, that the Cane River people of Isle Brevelle had what she. called a "naïve" concept of purity. She wrote, "The passing of Sister Marie Therese in Shreveport has caused a soft echo of sorrowing prayers in a little community on Cane River known as Isle Brevelle, a strange community of mulattoes and quadroons descended, some of them from the purest blood of ancient France, who have, as one of them naively told me, 'kept the strain pure' throughout the succeeding years."

But the naivete was hers as well as theirs. Colored Creoles strive for *whitening*, which amounts to a kind of *process* of purification. Like other Caribbean and Afro-American groups (see Alexander 1977; Birmingham 1975; Degler 1971; Domínguez 1973; Frazier 1957; Harris 197; Harris and Kottak 1963; Samuels 1974; Sanjek 1971), these Creoles impose a value hierarchy on the continuum of physical appearance; the whiter a person is, the better his status, and the blacker he is, the lower his ascribed status. Not uncommon is the case of a child sent to the country to be raised by a grandmother or an aunt away from home, because he is too dark for the family. The family's distress arises not from blackness as evidence of "impurity" but from blackness itself as a kind of regression. Similar occurrences in the white Creole community wreak havoc; the birth of a child with apparently Negroid features leads to the inference that the ancestral line itself is tainted, racially impure.

The terms used by colored Creoles to describe physical appearance are often revealing. A "nice-looking" man is invariably a light-skinned man with Caucasian-like features. He is likely to have "good" (straight) rather than "bad" (kinky) hair, and "keen" (sharp, elongated) features. At worst he is brown, certainly not black; at best he is "real fair" or perhaps "high yellow." "Black means evil; that's why we're not black," said one informant. "My soul isn't black. I'm not black. I'm colored but not black. They say that black is beautiful. *Black* is *beautiful?* Yes, when black acts beautifully."

Traditionally, these Creoles have rejected the labels *black* and *Negro* in descriptions of themselves. Seemingly untouched by the civil rights movement of the 1960s, many still prefer to be called colored rather than black. They strongly assert it is a biological fact that they are not black. To be colored is to have some color, to carry some amount of Negro blood in their bodies; to be black or Negro is to have *only* Negro blood, in the words of one older informant, "to come straight out of the jungles of Africa." An old member of the Jeunes Amis (a fraternal benevolence association) put it succinctly when, in 1976, a white southern archivist asked the association's last president for contributions that would allow him to expand his collection of primary sources on black history in Louisiana. The old Jeunes Amis member was vehement: "Jeunes Amis was not a *black* organization! Thommy Lafon [the founder] was not *black.* I am not black. Thommy Lafon would rise up from his grave in sheer anger if he ever knew that you had called us *black!* You will *have* to look elsewhere to find *black* history."

In an autobiographical account on deposit at the Special Collections division of Northwestern State University's memorial library in Natchitoches, Louisiana, Frances Metoyer tells a story of fear and surprise that illustrates colored Creoles' desire not to be associated with persons they considered black. "A few days after we left Little River," she writes, "and come stayed with my mother's mother we went trip cane and cut them down for the meal. That was my grandfather's cane and the sype [syrup] was ready. Late that night they sent a man to bring us a pitcher of hot sype and the man was named Lewis Metoyer, and he was real dark and my sister saw the man before we came to the door and she had never seen a dark man before in her life and she started screaming and from that day she has never eaten sype yet."

There are many such stories. Part of the lore tells of "paper bag" dances and "comb tests." The color of a brown paper bag is said to have served as a test for admission. People darker than the color of the paper bag would automatically be excluded. The "comb test" likewise kept unwelcome visitors from entering a Creole party. Anyone who could not pass a comb through his hair without getting it stuck would be excluded. I am uncertain about the prevalence of either of these two customs in the recent past. Roland Wingfield reported in a 1961 master's thesis on a sector of the colored Creole population in New Orleans that one informant swore "people say that Creoles still do this in the country. In C———, for instance, there is a blind man who sits outside the dance hall with a big black comb in his hand. He also claims that he can tell the color of a person by touching his skin" (Wingfield 1961: 84). It is true that I personally was unable to find a single informant who would vouch that such practices continued either in New Orleans or in the country. And during nearly a year and a half of participant observation, including attendance at innumerable balls, feasts, picnics, and parties, I never witnessed even the semblance of such a test being put into practice. But undoubtedly, lore serves to preserve color consciousness.

In the same vein, marriages between light-skinned Creoles, usually women, and dark-skinned non-Creole blacks, usually men, are often described as *mixed* marriages. Parental objections are common though often veiled. References may be made to differences in religion, level of education, or occupational background. After all, most blacks are Protestant and most Creoles are, at least nominally, Catholic. But in private, and after a few drinks, the color question frequently surfaces. "I know he's not good enough for ———," said one informant of her daughter's boyfriend. "He can't help it he's so dark. Everyone tells me she can do *much* better, but you think ——— will listen to me, her mother? She already tells me I'm old-fashioned." In another case, a university-educated black man from a Protestant family in uptown New Orleans was never fully accepted by his wife's staunchly Creole family despite his education, position, and manner. They were thought to have a mixed marriage and only half-Creole children.

One impassioned defense of a nondichotomized system of racial classification is worth transcribing here. Four prominent black and colored politicians and educators called a meeting in the heart of the most colored-Creole New Orleans neighborhood to discuss problems of race, class, and power in New Orleans. Fourteen people attended. About halfway through the group discussion, a woman in her thirties turned excitedly to the people sitting near her and explained, "All of these things they're talking about boil down to the *great divide*. The fact is that this country is divided into two separate sectors, white and black, and all the other divisions come second. White/black is the great divide." At this point, having commanded the attention of the rest of the group, she repeated the point. The moderator of the meeting then suggested, "the question is how to bridge that difference." She replied, "The country is splitting farther and farther apart. Everything is seen in black/white terms. Now the blacks are becoming blacker. There is black food, black ideas. Why is Arthur Ashe playing a *white* sport? Tennis is a *white* sport! And why, what happens when you have an argument with someone who is black, and they tell you you don't agree with them because you don't *think black!* The country is splitting apart. Integration? Integration means the black kids go to a white school and the school becomes black. That's what integration means."

A lawyer: "The thing is that there is more horizontal integration than vertical integration. Black lawyers get together with white lawyers much more often than black lawyers get together with white laborers."

A skilled laborer:

"That's right. There's really an element of class involved. A man who's walking around barefoot with ragged clothes, whether he's white *or* black, won't be admitted into the house of a Rockefeller!"

An academic: "As E——— said, there are other divisions in our society besides the white-black one. Class is very important—as the people who grew up here in the Seventh Ward know very well. We know that better than anyone else perhaps in the whole country!" Everyone chuckled. The Seventh Ward (see Figure 6.3) is known for its heavy concentration of colored Creoles. Although many of these Creoles are poor and unskilled, they regard themselves, and are generally regarded in the New Orleans black community at large, as pretentious and elitist.

Original speaker: "That's right, but the primary division in this country is still white and black!"

Moderator: "Well, what can we *do* about it? How can we change it?"

Original speaker (frustrated and fishing for an answer): "Well, I suppose, we could educate people but I don't know how long it would take to change that, and I don't think it's going to happen anyway."

MANIPULATIVE SOLUTIONS

Three types of reactions show rejection of the coexistence of contradictory senses of Creole identity. I shall call the older white Creole reaction the struggle for monosemy, the younger colored Creole reaction the consolidation of a racial dichotomy, and the younger white Creole reaction the escape to ethnicity.

The Struggle for Monosemy

Typical of the staunch white Creole's adherence to a racially exclusive interpretation of Creole is his ability to ignore even carefully worded remarks that acknowledge multiplicity of meaning. A 1976 article in a medium-brow monthly magazine epitomizes diplomacy, subtlety, and sensitivity. It begins with

Figure 6.3 New Orleans Ward Boundaries

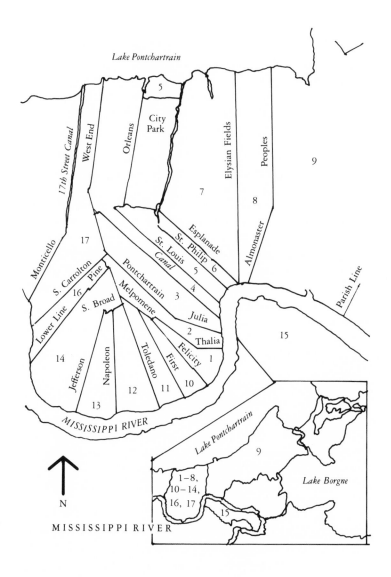

brief though colorful descriptions of three contemporary scenes and the three characteristic reactions to the word *Creole* (Wonk 1976: 47–57). The first takes place in a cottage off St. Bernard Avenue. The hostess, described by Wonk as having "soft black hair and olive skin," picked up a set of family pictures.

"Would you call that child a Negro?" asks the woman. . . . Look at that man, would you say he was black?" Snap. "Does that woman look like a Negro?"

"It used to be," says the lady, "there were three letters you could mark when you applied for things: W or N or C.

"There was White or Negro or . . . what I marked was C . . . which stood for Caucasian."

"Stood for what?" shouts the son incredulously.

"Some people said it stood for Caucasian," says his mother, "some said it stood for Creole."

Her son starts laughing uncontrollably. "Yeah, mama," he says, "and some say it stood for Colored."

The second scene pictures an "attractive young woman (milky white skin, jet-black hair)" in an antique-filled house off St. Charles Avenue. When Wonk mentions he is doing a story on Creoles of color, she reacts immediately.

"Theah are no such things as Creoles of colah," she says.

"Well," I begin, "the people I've been talking to describe themselves as. . . ."

Her face flushes with very convincing Latin anger.

"Theah are no such things," she repeats, "as Creoles of colah."

In the third scene, "a dark-skinned Negro with no pretensions to Latin background *or* Caucasian features" sits at a Rampart Street bar with Wonk. He reacts with annoyance when Wonk indicates that he is doing a story on the Creoles of color.

"Oh . . . I had a boyhood friend who was light-skinned. He married one of those London Avenue *passablanc*. When I went to

visit him, the old mother-in-law said to me: 'Do you know you're
the first black man who's been in my home in a long, long time.'"

Continuing to proceed with extreme caution, Wonk explains
clearly that he knows there are those who disagree and "who
maintain that the word 'Creole' may only be applied to those
who are born in a colony or former colony (in this case Louisiana), whose immediate ancestors are of European origin" (1976:
49). But he adds, "the word is also used to describe anyone with
a colonial French or Spanish heritage, regardless of race. And,
very commonly in New Orleans but even more so outside the
United States, Creole means someone of French background
with Negro blood—the Creole of color" (1976: 49–50). Despite Wonk's careful wording, at least one white Creole felt com-
pelled to respond in print.

The defense of Creole whiteness here rested on amateur linguistic analysis. *Creole*, the writer claimed, is correctly used as
an *adjective* to describe *certain* blacks, but never as a noun. I
quote here from a letter to the editor of the *New Orleans Magazine*
(July 1976: 10):

> It is also impossible not to quarrel with the same writer [Dalt
> Wonk] on his article, "The Creoles of Color." I suggest that he
> speak with someone of authority on the matter, such as Pie
> Dufour.
>
> "Creole" is both a noun and an adjective. As a noun it de-
> scribes the American born child or descendent [*sic*] of aristicratic
> [*sic*] European parentage, usually French and Spanish. As an
> adjective it means "of the New World," such as a "Creole" Negro
> as opposed to an "African" Negro, or a "Creole" tomato, a variety
> grown in the United States.
>
> It is true that many persons of partial Negro ancestry did call
> themselves "Creoles," but this was a corruption of good English.
> The proper term was "Creole Negro," or "mulatto."
>
> R. J. Caire
>
> Pass Christian

It is not an uncommon position. White Creole informants often explain that use of the term *Creole* as adjective is by loose extension from the true meaning of *Creole;* thus, for them, *Creole* modifies Negro the same way it modifies tomato (that is, means "born, raised, or grown in the U.S."). In this analysis the categories Creole and Creole Negro are totally discrete but may become confused if the *Negro* in *Creole Negro* is deleted. This may not be good linguistics, but it is the way some people explain the use of *Creole* to refer to persons of color.

Similar defenses of Creole Caucasian purity are common occurrence. Some take place in predictable settings; others do not. Some, of course, are intra-Creole settings. At a well-attended conference on the French in Louisiana at the University of New Orleans in the spring of 1977, for example, Professor George Reinecke, who comes from an old and respected (though not particularly well-to-do) white Creole family, explained that *Creole* is used in a variety of ways by different groups of Louisianians and hence should be accepted as having a host of meanings. During the question-and-answer period, a conservatively dressed man in his late fifties or early sixties openly criticized Reinecke: "Just because some blacks choose to use our term Creole to call themselves by doesn't mean it's correct." (The word *blacks* was strained, perhaps because in private most middle-aged and elderly whites still call blacks "Negroes" or "niggers.") Reinecke was attacked for being out of line.

A typical setting for the defense of Creole whiteness is the encounter with outsiders. When I asked an archivist if I could have access to some of his church records, for example, he remarked adamantly: "You know, so many people are confused. Creoles are not the descendants of mixed racial couples; they are the descendants of the French and Spanish settlers of long ago."

A third common setting is a conversation in the presence of an audience of non-Creole whites. The defense of whiteness can be sudden and unpredictable. My first white Creole contact, for example, then a third-year law student, quizzed me immediately upon hearing that I was in New Orleans to study the Creoles. "I presume you know," he began, "that Creoles are not black. You won't get very far in this town if you think differently." I had not even known he was Creole, nor was this an interview situation. Yet surrounded by fellow law students, most of whom were not native Louisianians, this mild-mannered informant rose in unprodded defense of Creole Caucasian purity.

So emotionally charged is the controversy that several Tulane academics, natives and nonnatives alike, asserted in no uncertain terms that I would not be able to study both the white and the colored Creole communities. One was simply skeptical of anyone's ability to penetrate both social networks; another was vehemently opposed to "a nice young woman getting involved in such a sensitive, even dangerous, issue."

The apparent exaggeration has some basis in fact. From time to time emotion stirs up threats of violence. In 1968, members of the board of directors of the Creole Fiesta Association, a colored Creole social organization, received a series of threatening letters from angry whites who wanted the association to drop the term *Creole* from its official name or terminate its activities altogether. Founded in 1952, this association does little more than hold two or three dances a year, a few picnics, a small number of generally old-fashioned social events, and an annual parade. Its purpose, as explained in 1962 by its founder, Mrs. A. C. Synigal, "is to give scholarship and for culture and for charity for our race" (Jazz Archives 1962). The association does not proselytize, is fundamentally a social club, and has almost never functioned as a political interest group. At its peak it had no more than 200 members. Only the use of *Creole* in the name of the organization evoked emotion, but the emotion was great enough to provoke threats of physical violence. Several letters made explicit threats. At least one threatened to kill members of the Fiesta board when they reached the corner of Esplanade and Claiborne avenues on their annual parade. Duly frightened, the board approached the FBI. Round-the-clock protection for participants allowed the Fiesta to hold its scheduled parade, but the incident made them schedule only daytime parades in later years. The FBI concluded that a group of angry whites from St. Bernard Parish and not the Ku Klux Klan had precipitated the entire incident.

The Consolidation of a Racial Dichotomy

The civil rights movement of the past twenty years has taken its toll in the colored community. Candid remarks made in private at the beginning of my fieldwork there stressed how sensitive the word has become. "Creole?" asked a twenty-two-year-old. "It's no longer something people talk about, you know, after the sixties. It's no longer cool." More extensive discussions shed further light on the problem. One twenty-four-year-old schoolteacher, for example, told me she does not like to use the term because she doesn't believe any such separate group ever existed. "It was just a way in which society divided blacks against blacks. It is an artificial distinction," she argued insistently. But to put such remarks in perspective, one should note the kind of pressure that colored Creoles have experienced since the start of the black power movement. This woman's family staunchly considers itself Creole. The woman herself, like most members of her immediate family, is light-skinned, though too non-Caucasian to pass for white. While in school she was often ridiculed, often criticized, by non-Creole blacks for being Creole. And she claims she is still taunted at the school where she teaches because of her Creole heritage. People call her German because her last name is German. "It's quite a subject," she repeated several times. Then as we stood on the sidewalk, the teacher, a white male friend of hers from the North, and I noticed a young man in his twenties enter the house across the street. Her friend turned to her and remarked that this fellow was an example of what he had often noticed in New Orleans, really white, fair skinned but with kinky hair. My informant concurred and added, "Yeah, he lets it grow long so it will look more Afro."

Afros have "saved" many of the young light-skinned colored Creoles who choose now to identify themselves as black and disavow any connection with colored Creole society. The Afro has become symbol of their social and political affiliation. So keen was the criticism of Creoles by non-Creole blacks, especially in the early 1970s, that light-skinned teenage boys whose hair was straight began to put vinegar on their hair to make it kinky. A couple of young informants swear that several of their friends are beginning to grow bald, and they attribute this loss of hair to their frequent shampooing with vinegar. Afros may be the current hairstyle among black Americans, but among young male colored Creoles they are political symbols, too. It is no accident that seventy-eight of the eighty-five thirteen-, fourteen-, and fifteen-year-old boys who were confirmed at Corpus Christi parish in the heart of the colored Creole community on May 20, 1977, light- and dark-skinned alike, had Afros.

A perceptive and sympathetic northern white man who studied and taught in the Creole community from 1964 to 1968 and again in the mid- and late seventies experienced the changes himself. During his first stay, he lived in the dormitories at Xavier University, a "black" Catholic university traditionally dominated by colored Creoles. Xavier felt more like an extended family than a university. Students could ask dormitory porters to pick up pizzas for them, and for only a small tip, the porters would do it gladly. Faculty and students felt that they lived in a privileged family environment. But that had changed drastically by 1968. The faculty, he reported, experienced "rapid turnovers"; departments became "overly competitive"; and the black power, black-is-beautiful movement invaded the campus. He remembers scuffles between students of different "color." The term *Creole* fell into disuse.

Answers to a parish census taken in 1968 in the heart of the old colored Creole community corroborate the extent of the tension between Creoles and non-Creoles in the black community at the time. One of the questions asked if anyone in the immediate family had ever *felt* discriminated against. Few admitted they had, but of those who openly admitted having felt discriminated against, the overwhelming majority complained of discrimination by non-Creole blacks towards Creoles, rather than discrimination by whites against them. Every single one of these complaints came from middle-aged or elderly colored Creoles.

Observers believe the change has been essentially completed in black or colored high schools and colleges in New Orleans. It is certainly difficult to get teenage sons and daughters of old colored Creole families to identify themselves as Creole. At St. Augustine's, the nationally respected black Catholic high school for boys, it is nearly impossible to find a student who will so identify himself. They consider themselves black; even those who look so Caucasian that they could pass for white consider themselves black. As the school principal, himself light-skinned and a graduate of St. Aug's, said, "the kids all consider themselves black now and with pride. They're not Creole, they're black." "Are you opposing Creole to black?" I asked. He immediately responded, "Oh yes, definitely."

Illustrative of the ongoing movement is a documentary entitled "Proud Free Men" narrated by another graduate of St. Augustine's and shown at the school in the spring of 1976. The term *Creole* is rarely used in the film, and then only as an adjective in the phrase *Creole Negroes*. Preferred appellations are *gens de couleur*, free men of color, and "the upper class of the Negro community." Oscar Dunn is described as the first *black* lieutenant governor of Louisiana, even though he was light-skinned. Thommy Lafon, well-known colored philanthropist and founder of the very Creole Jeunes Amis fraternal association, is described as having had "olive skin with straight steel-like hair but *never having tried to pass*" (emphasis added).

When in the spring of 1977 I hired a twenty-year-old colored Creole to administer a short questionnaire to people in their teens and twenties, he was initially enthusiastic. The question-naire asked each respondent to list the ten people or families he or she felt had the highest social position in New Orleans, and to give a reason for each choice. It also asked them to list the ten Creoles (or Creole families) they felt held the highest social posi-tions in New Orleans. Teachers at two schools, one heavily white Creole, the other heavily colored Creole, had already cooperated with me. At the white school, the questions were considered troublesome, but the teenagers still responded to them. At the "black" school, only thirteen of nearly two hundred students complied with the request. I then hired the twenty-year-old man to collect the information himself in a more informal and individual manner. We had two training sessions. Both times he listened attentively and did just what I wanted in practice inter-views. I asked him how many sets of responses he thought he could get. He suggested fifty to a hundred. I reminded him as I was leaving his house both times that I only wanted him to approach Creoles, and both time he mumbled apologetically that to be sure in each case he would have to ask the person himself and that that would be a problem. "People don't like to use the term," he insisted. "It has bad vibes these days." Periodi-cally I would call to find out how the interviews were going. Invariably he would respond "slowly, but I'll do more next week." When the time came for my departure, he announced that the folder in which he had placed the answers to my ques-tionnaire had been stolen from his car the night before. He never claimed that the car itself had been stolen, just that valuable invisible folder. Irresponsibility was not the cause.

In private, in closed family situations, or under pressure, many of these children of staunchly Creole colored families will admit that they are Creole, but they do so only to a limited extent, and when they do it stands out. In one such case, a young man in his early twenties mounted the bar at a popular jazz club frequented by Creole and non-Creole blacks as well as by pro-gressive, young, and often nonnative whites. It was three o'clock in the morning, and the bartender estimated that he had been drinking for several hours. Dancing wildly, he suddenly announced to the world about him, "I'm a Creole [kʁeɪɔl], man, Creole . . . yeah, yeah, I'm a nigger." Just minutes before, a much older inebriated black man had called his wife a quadroon, and amid ripples of laughter he had asked his wife if she knew what quadroon meant. "He means a little, light-skinned white man's woman nigger," he had explained. Though everyone had smiled and joked about the old man using the term quadroon, nervous giggles suggested that he had broached a subject that people did not talk about publicly any more. Hence, my informant's spontaneous self-identification as Creole had come under pressure. If one taboo had been broken, the other might as well also be.

More common are partial self-identifications, such as descriptions of parents, grandparents, or ancestors as Creole, or very Creole. Some will go so far as to say they are half Creole, a quarter Creole, or simply part Creole. But few would volunteer full self-identification as Creole the way middle-aged and older colored Creoles do. Certainly few would do so with pride.

The Escape to Ethnicity

A parallel, if distinct, process is taking place in young white Creole circles. Many tease their grandparents for being Creole, but they do not assume that that also makes them Creole. Typically they refer to themselves as French or part French, pointing to the country of origin of their ancestors rather than to the social identity of their more immediate progenitors. The pattern is particularly clear in responses to a brief questionnaire I gave high school students at a heavily Creole white school. The questionnaire consisted of eight sets of questions posed in a specific order so as to minimize questioner bias. These were:

1. Why are you taking French? Pressure from your family? Personal interest? Your own background?

2. Have you ever been to France or any other French-speaking territory?

3. Does anyone in your household speak French to you? Do you have any relatives now living who learned French at home as children? Are there any deceased relatives *you* knew personally who learned French at home as children? What are these people's relation to you?

4. Do you have any French ancestors? Can you name them and give their relation to you?

5. How would you define the term Creole? How would you define Cajun?

6. Would you identify yourself as Creole? Cajun? Or as what?

7. Has anyone else in your family studied French in school? Who? (I.e., brother, sister, father, mother, etc.)

8. Can you name any New Orleans families you think are Creole? or Cajun? or French? [1]

The questionnaire was administered by the head of the Romance language department to all high school students at the school who were then taking French as a foreign language. Of the 111 students who answered the questionnaire, only 14 (12.6 percent) identified themselves as Creole, though 71 (64 percent) admitted having French ancestry and an even higher number belong to families otherwise identified in the community as Creole. A note attached to the students' responses reflected the teacher's own dismay. She, too, was a white Creole. "What a shame," she wrote, "that these girls don't for the most part realize something that is so indigenous to their culture here in New Orleans! But I clearly see that our task as teachers of French, is cut out for us."

Combined answers to several of the questions show the emerging pattern of ethnic classification very clearly. One student, for example, answered question 4, "Do you have any French ancestry?" with "Yes, I'm about 3/4 French." When asked how she would define the terms *Creole* and *Cajun,* she put question marks next to the terms and left the space blank. In answer to question 6 ("Would you identify yourself as Creole? Cajun? or as what?"), she wrote "French," though her family is well-known in uptown Creole circles as Creole. Finally, asked to name Creole, Cajun, and French families in New Orleans with which she was familiar, she listed her own family and three other family names, all of which she identified as French.

In the more advanced classes of sixteen-, seventeen-, and eighteen-year-olds, the responses were more detailed and suggest better knowledge of their ancestry. Yet they, too, denied being Creole and in a number of cases quite openly rejected that label, preferring instead phrases such as "French" or "American with French ancestry."

The following four sets of responses were given by the four students in the most advanced course in French at the school. The pattern noted above is persistent and pervasive.

"Anna"—No one speaks French at home fluently. My grand-fathers speak French some—both are living. My great-grandparents spoke French at home. My grandmother was a Tremoulet and speaks a little French. My grandfather Breiten-moser speaks French some also. *Both sides of the family have a French history.*

Creole is a mixture of French. It is a blend of cultural language and English. It is proper, but acceptable to certain social classes. Cajun is a more common type of French spoken. It is from rural background such as farm areas. *I consider myself as an American with a French and German history of relatives.*

Creole names: *Toussaint l'Ouverture* [black leader of the Haitian Revolution]. Dixie Roto [a magazine] wrote an article on this.
Cajun names:
French names: Boisfontaine, de la Barre, Bordeau (emphasis added above).

"Brenda"—Often I speak to my mother in French. *My great aunt lived in France for seven years and speaks it.* There are no deceased relatives that I knew that spoke French at home.

Yes [I have French ancestors]. Pierre Joseph Favrot, great (?)

grandfather—have French cousins in France but don't know their names, have a marquis who is a relation.

A Creole in my opinion is someone who is a mixture of French and Spanish ancestry, but who speaks French. A Cajun is someone of French and English background but is usually in the lower middle class.

No, I'm not Creole or Cajun. I'm American, with a mixture of French, Irish, and British background.

I can't think of any New Orleans family I think is Creole. I know Edwin Edwards is Cajun but not from New Orleans. Otherwise I can't think of any Cajun family. I read an article about Creole families in the paper recently (*Times Picayune,* Vivant [section]).

French families: Favrot, Livaudais, de la Houssaye [all three usually thought of in New Orleans as white Creole families] (emphasis added above).

"Christine"—No one in my house speaks French. My grandmother was raised speaking French as well as English. My great grandmother, now deceased, spoke French also.

My mother's family was French. My great uncle and their fathers were French but I am not aware of their names. George Howe? Baldwin.

I think of Creole as a long-standing family of French-Spanish background who contribute many of their customs to the southern area. The Cajuns are French people who settled around the mouth of the Mississippi and derived their own type of French language.

I am neither Creole nor Cajun. I am of a mixed German and French background.

I cannot think of a Creole family name. My great aunt, Mrs. Clifford Baldwin, is a Cajun but I don't know her maiden name. Edwin Edwards is also a Cajun.

The Favrots and the Magne's are two families that I know are French (emphasis added above).

"Delores"—[I take French in school] *because my family is predominantly French* and because I have traveled in France.

Yes [I have ancestors] on my father's side, but I don't know all their names.

Creoles: The customs and language of a section of French
people which has been changed by the influences of environment
and time.
Cajuns:
I consider myself an American with strong French-bound feelings.
Also with a background of German, Irish, and Swiss.
Fontaine, Gendron, these are two Cajun names.
Some French families are: Boisfontaine, Favrot, Magne. [No
families are labeled Creole.] (Emphasis added above.)

The past and the present have influenced these youths' responses. While students generally refused to identify themselves as Creoles, they perpetuated the interpretation of *Creole*
proffered by white Creoles in the twentieth century. To the question of definition of *Creole,* nearly all responded that it meant a
descendant of the early French and Spanish settlers of Louisiana.
Only three of the students associated *Creole* with the black population, and all three of these described themselves as having
French ancestry but not as Creole. Two denied being Creole
themselves; the third defined *Creole* as "a native southern Louisianian (mostly black)," and was uncertain of her own ancestry.
She responded, "I am Creole?" The only black student in the
pool claimed she did not know how to define either *Creole* or
Cajun; yet she identified herself as "Afro-American with a little
Creole background (mother's side)."

A perceptive fifty-five-year-old informant was himself quite
surprised when a younger Creole neighbor of his identified himself and his lifestyle as Creole. The fellow had made some remark about a woman who lived down the street who, in his
terms, did not know how to enjoy the delicacies of life. She did
not like shrimp or crab or oysters, and he found this rather hard
to believe. Suddenly his eyes lit up, confident that he had determined the reason for such unusual taste buds. "Well," he argued, "she's not a Creole, that's probably why!" My informant
shook his head in amazement, not because he thought the young
fellow had said something outrageous but because he did not

imagine that someone that young today would still be so overtly conscious of a Creole identity and culture.

Whereas young colored Creoles today live under black pressure to be black, young white Creoles live under pressure of "misrepresentation." The commitment of earlier generations to withstand the pressures put upon them by others has waned, to a large extent because the pressures have become internalized. Younger white Creoles see less sense or purpose in denying the existence of colored Creoles and prefer instead to yield the name rather than fight fear of "misrepresentation." Young colored Creoles, for their part, reacting to the binary classification of race in the United States, try to enhance pride in their African ancestry, however small it might be. With the removal of legal sanctions for discrimination, the gradual development of equal rights with whites, and the expansion of the black middle class, young colored Creoles find less reason to keep apart and more sense in a common black identity.

Part III

MANIPULATING THE PRACTICE AND THE PRACTICE OF MANIPULATING

Chapter 7

THE CRITERION OF ANCESTRY

What form, then, does the individual manipulation of identity take? So far I have traced the outline of a legal framework of racial classification that both set the limits of possibility of identity within the law and created, by its example of frequent manipulation of those limits, the condition of possibility of manipulation itself. Individual action has regularly tested and challenged those limits, but it has also usually found the institutional framework resistant to the pressure of individual choice.

The power of collective action has been evident in the semantic transformations of Creole identity that I have tried to explore in Part II of this volume. Crucial broad-based semantic change occurred at moments critical to the power and status of a sector of the population that was subjected to a near-siege mentality. Individual figures pioneered in the campaign to redefine the identity, but they are remembered as heroes rather than quacks because their goals had the backing of influential, if not always sizeable, sectors of the population. And yet throughout I have identified individuals who did not fit, who took the same facts and drew different conclusions, whose behavior smacks of deliberate manipulation of the legal and semantic system in their time and place for explicit individual ends.

Is there a contradiction here? The rooting of manipulation in the regional political economy and its encoding in the law suggest a model of category formation in which individuals manipulate identities only when they engage in concerted aggregate action. Challenges to the structure of classification, however, indicate a clear lack of closure in the processes of classification. Popular lore dismisses them as deviant or exceptional cases; Barth would rely on them to push for a transactional model of persisting group differentiation. The problem is how to integrate evidence of the exercise of individual choice with evidence of institutional and sectoral structuring of social categories. Wherein and to what extent is there successful exercise of choice of self-identification? And what makes those choices *possible?*

All propositions about Creole identity assume it to *follow* from ancestry. Neither social achievements nor individual exercise of choice play any role in any of these propositions. And yet here, as in the societies Barth examined, there is substantial flow of personnel across the boundaries of both white and colored Creole categories.

To begin with, the genealogies of Creole families provide evidence of numerous ancestors who were neither French nor Spanish or who did not arrive in Louisiana before the Louisiana Purchase. Irishmen and Englishmen, New England Yankees and German settlers, Italian noblemen as well as Italian peasants, all appear in the extensive recorded genealogies of white Creole families. Even some of those said to be quintessentially Creole exhibit substantial non-French and non-Spanish ancestry (cf., e.g., Beckwith 1893; Deiler 1909). The de la Vergne family tree, for example, includes the Anglo-Saxon Clair Gibbons, the late-nineteenth-century Frenchman Count Charles de Bony de la Vergne, the Swede Gustavus Schmidt, the Anglo-Saxon Hincks, the Alsatian Jean George Troxler, the Germans Jean Adam Haidel and Jacob Shaf, the eighteenth-century Swedes Charles Frederic D'Arensbourg and Marguerite de Wurtenberg, to name but a few. Among the ancestors of James Amédée Stouse are German Oehmichens and Wiltz, Anglo-Saxon Wolfs, Talbots, and Stouses, and Italian de Reggios. George William

Nott, his daughter Isabel McKay, and her children descend from the Irish Macartys and the New England Yankee William Nott. Claiborne Perrilliatt and Clarisse Grima are direct descendants of Governor William Claiborne, whose second and third marriages were to Creole women. The Bezous have Italian ancestors through the Bouligny line. The Urquharts' Scottish ancestry enables historian Kenneth Urquhart to head a worldwide Scottish clan. The extensive Fortier family (cf. Cochran 1963) descends from Alexis Ferry, Gustave Bouligny, John Zweig (whose descendants gallicized the name into *Labranche*), and Jean Baptiste Grevenberg from Flanders. The Westfeldts are Creole, the Nolans are Creole, the Baldwins are Creole, and the Miltenbergers are Creole. Even the very proud and very Creole Villerés have Swedish, German, and Acadian ancestry. And the wealthy and powerful Bernard de Marigny of the late eighteenth and early nineteenth centuries married the daughter of a well-to-do Pennsylvanian by the name of Evan Jones, who was American consul in New Orleans during the early territorial years (Family papers; oral genealogies; C. P. Dimitry 1892 in Arthur and Kernion 1931; King 1921).

The point is that Creoles were never fully endogamous. Marriages with nonnatives, non-French, non-Spanish, and individuals not descended from French or Spanish colonial settlers took place throughout the nearly three centuries of Louisiana history. Creoles intermarried even when they outnumbered other social groups, and they have continued to marry outside the group during the past century.

Family patterns varied somewhat. Some remained largely endogamous during the period of intense opposition between Creoles and Americans from about the time of the Louisiana Purchase to the Civil War. Some became even more endogamous during the era of relative impoverishment late in the nineteenth century. These Creoles chose to marry cousins rather than risk the already tenuous status of the family by marrying "classless" *nouveau riches*. But others quite openly married out. The de la

Chaise, Villeré, Perret, Cruzat, DuVerjé, and Sarrat families, to name a few, maintained a generally endogamous pattern. But others, such as the children of Gustave Bouligny and Octavie Fortier, chose exogamy instead. Of the eight children of Gustave and Octavie, only two married Creoles by any definition. The oldest, Felicite Bouligny, married a man named John Fox with no known prior connection to Creole families. Alice married Robert F. Spangenburg; Gustave, Ellen Davenport; Arthemise, Albert Baldwin from Watertown, Massachusetts; Nathalie, Dr. Andrew Smyth from Ireland, and Octavie, a certain John S. Wood. Likewise, their children and descendants have tended to marry Anglo-Saxons: Felicite Fox married George Clark; Henry Fay Baldwin II married Cora Lillian Holman; Amelia Baldwin married William Thompkins West; Robert Bruce Baldwin married Madeline Mayer, and so forth, as indicated in Figure 7.1. Since those who did marry out kept themselves at least partly within Creole society, the ranks of the white Creoles became increasingly heterogeneous.

Colored Creole genealogies reveal similar patterns of mixed ancestries. Surnames alone suggest the extent of intermarriage among the ancestors of contemporary colored Creoles. There are Colemans, Johnsons, Millers, Halls, McDonalds, Sheiks, and Williamses, as well as a host of French and Spanish surnames. There are Caucasians and Negroes, Amerindians as well as East Indians, Jews as well as Arabs in the genealogical charts of colored Creole families. Kara Rousseau discovered that the majority of the people she interviewed "traced back only two or three generations to their white ancestry" (Rousseau 1955: 109–110).

Colored Creoles may acknowledge the mixtures to a greater extent than white Creoles. But the reality of mixed ancestry has the same implications for both: self-identification as Creole entails an element of choice of group membership and is not the simple corollary of ancestry. One chooses to stress a particular ancestral connection over the other possible ones.

The interplay between possibility and choice shapes the

actual composition of both Creole communities. Both self-identified "groups" underrepresent the class of descendants of French and/or Spanish colonial settlers in Louisiana. Not everyone with French and/or Spanish colonial ancestry identifies himself or herself as Creole or is so identified by others.

Poché (1886) and Gayarré (1886) estimated in the late nineteenth century that there were 250,000 Creoles in the white community of southern Louisiana, and there are nowhere near that number today. Even if we assumed that both of these scholars overestimated the size of the white Creole community for social or political reasons or simply defined the term *Creole* loosely, we would still be able to note remarkable reduction in the size of the white Creole community over the past century. The 1970 United States Census showed 1,468,440 speakers of French in all of Louisiana, but the vast majority of these were Cajuns who spoke Cajun French rather than the continental French associated with the Creoles (cf. CODOFIL estimates on Table 7.1: U.S. Census I, part 20). Of these alleged speakers of French, 1,371,235 lived outside New Orleans proper; only 97,205 resided in the New Orleans metropolitan area itself. Some years ago we would not have been justified in differentiating Creoles from Cajuns in terms of residence, but today the Creole community restricts itself mainly to New Orleans and assumes that all families without at least one residence in New Orleans are Cajun rather than Creole. Thus, we may eliminate French speakers from outside New Orleans and are left with less than a hundred thousand. Still, not all of these are socially identified as Creole. Of them, 1,056 are foreign-born French-speakers, and an unspecified number are Cajun speakers who migrated to the city. The New Orleans telephone directory contains numerous stereotypically Cajun surnames such as Boudreaux, Guillot, Hebert, Landry, Le Blanc, and Thibodaux. Of the French or Spanish names appearing in the 1977 New Orleans phone book, a particularly well-connected white Creole remarked in writing, "The Cajun names are the most prolific!" One informant identified 378 names in the New Orleans phone

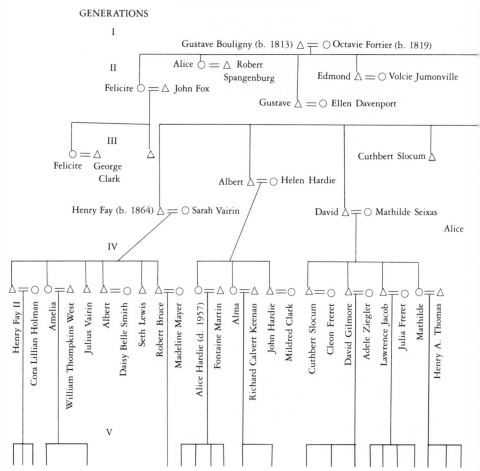

Figure 7.1 The Descendants of Gustave Bouligny and Octavie Fortier, Showing the Extent of Exogamy in Post–Civil War Generations

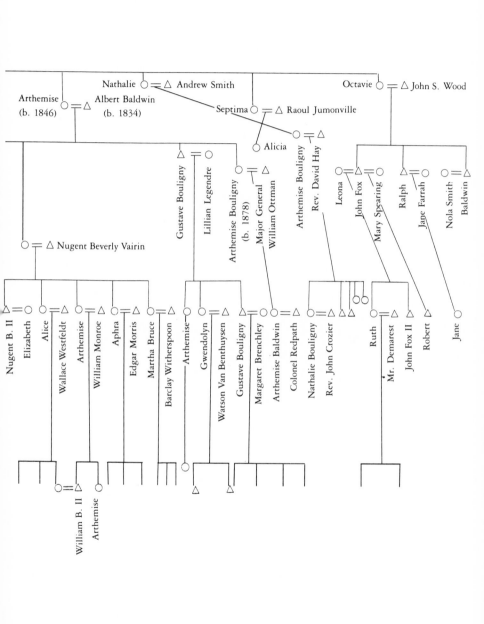

Table 7.1

French-speaking Population of the Southern Parishes
of Louisiana in 1970

The parishes included in this list are those stretching from the Texas border in the east, as far as Avoyelles in the northeast, and to the mouth of the Mississippi in the southeast.

Parish	Population	French-speaking	Percentage of French-speaking population
Acadia	52,109	27,845	53.4
Allen	20,794	4,949	23.8
Ascension	37,086	7,001	18.9
Assumption	19,654	8,876	45.2
Avoyelles	37,751	19,898	52.7
Calcasieu	145,415	34,607	23.8
Cameron	8,194	3,478	42.4
Evangeline	31,932	24,222	75.9
Iberia	57,397	25,216	43.9
Jefferson	337,568	45,769	13.6
Jefferson Davis	29,554	14,049	47.5
Lafayette	109,716	57,138	52.1
Lafourche	68,941	43,101	62.5
Plaquemine	25,225	4,736	18.8
Pointe Coupee	22,002	4,468	20.3
St. Charles	29,550	6,700	22.7
St. James	19,733	5,686	28.8
St. John the Baptist	23,813	5,265	22.1
St. Landry	80,364	38,550	48.0
St. Martin	32,453	25,655	79.1
St. Mary	60,752	13,279	21.9
Terrebonne	76,049	29,953	39.4
Vermilion	43,071	29,843	69.3

The French-speaking population in all of Louisiana was estimated at 1,468,440. These parishes of south Louisiana have the highest percentages of French-speaking population, but the other forty-one parishes, including Orleans, have a French-speaking population of nearly 700,000.

Source: U.S. Bureau of Census, census of 1970.

book as either Creole or Cajun. Boudreaux, Hebert, Landry, and Le Blanc—which had the most entries in the phone book—were immediately described as Cajun names.

In addition, the 1970 count of French speakers in New Orleans includes whites as well as blacks and all the shades in between. The census did not differentiate between white and colored Creoles or between Creoles and Cajuns. The actual number of French-speaking white Creoles in Louisiana today is very small. Dr. Jedah Johnson of the University of New Orleans has estimated that it may be as small as 5,000 (symposium at UNO, March 24, 1976).

Since many Creoles today do not consider French their native tongue, other indicators of Creole identity have become important. Many older white Creoles in New Orleans say that the Creole is "a forgotten man." Creoles also see themselves as belonging to an essentially closed community of limited size. One elderly man remarked, "If someone is worth knowing, we probably know them already, and if we don't know them already, they're probably not worth getting to know." Other white Creole informants voiced the same feeling. Were all the descendants of French and Spanish colonial ancestors included in the group, its size would never permit such a sense of exclusivity to persist in the community.

Many individuals who could by definition call themselves Creole call themselves something else instead. Some never stressed their Creole ancestry, out of either choice or ignorance; others have crossed social boundaries and "become" Cajuns, Italians, Irish, Americans, or a host of other social identities. Intermarriage over time plays a crucial role in this process of becoming. I pressed one particularly staunch white Creole several times on the question of eligibility to Creole identity:

Q: If only one of your parents is Creole, can you be Creole?
A: Yes, of course, there are many people around like that.
Q: What if only one of your grandparents is Creole? Can you still be Creole?

A: Yes, I think so. Again there are a lot of people here that are Creoles like that.

Q: What if only one of your great-grandparents is Creole? Can you also then be Creole?

A: Well, there I think you'd have to say that it depended on how they identified themselves, if they spoke French, married French, that kind of thing.

Intermarriage gives descendants the possibility of changing their social identity. Intermarriage also solidifies one's social ties with a particular community. It is said that a Creole does not stop being a Creole simply because he *acts* like *un qui a faim* (a starving man), *un Créole poi rouge* (a red-beans-and-rice type), *un chacalata* (term for white trash), or *un déclassé d'une basse classe* (a member of a lower class). But it is said also that he is well on his way to becoming something else when he marries a non-Creole, especially if he marries beneath the group.

A four-generation cycle is implicit in many white Creoles' comments. A family's identity, they suggest, is little affected by the actions of a single generation. When two successive generations persist in marrying and socializing outside Creole society, doubts may arise both in the family and among Creoles in general. When the third generation continues the pattern set by the previous two, the transformation accelerates its pace. The fourth generation is thought to be the clincher. It may affirm the leanings of the previous three or reclaim Creole status. If it chooses the first, the process of becoming is thought complete; if it reclaims Creole status, it would move back into the Creole community, although the memory of the three previous generations would keep it more at the peripheries of the Creole community than at its core. It would then be up to the fifth generation to bring the family back into the community's core.

The vast majority of rural Creole families became Cajun over the past century. They continue, of course, to descend from the same French or Spanish colonial settlers they claimed before they became Cajun, but they now choose to stress Acadian over

Creole ancestry and to associate with other descendants of Acadians more than with Creoles. Only in St. Martinville in southwest Louisiana are there still Creole families, at least in the opinion of white New Orleans Creoles. They have maintained close social contacts with New Orleans Creoles throughout the history of Louisiana and are said not to have married into Cajun families. Five St. Martinville families are generally identified as Creole: the De Blanc de Neuveville, Peltier de la Houssaye, Olivier de Vezin, Pellerin de Vezin, Pellerin de Chatillon, and De Clouet de Piedre. Two others, D'Emeville and Montault de Monbereau, are now extinct. A professional Creole genealogist added at the bottom of the list of Creole families of St. Martinville that he compiled for me: "These were the TopMost Families who first came to St. Martinville. Not to be confused with the Acadians." It is also worth noting that he entitled the list "Noble Families Settling in St. Martinville called 'Le Petit Paris,'" knowing full well that I had asked only for the names of St. Martinville Creoles.

This same genealogist also put together a list of names of New Orleans Creole families (see Table 7.2) and noted on the side, "Some branches of these respective families still retain their standings while others have not." He was referring not only to the alleged noble status of these thirty-five families and their descendants but also to their status as Creoles, since the two identities, in his view, imply each other.

"Underrepresentation" is equally evident in the black and colored community of southern Louisiana. We have seen that colored Creoles proclaim themselves descendants of French and/or Spanish settlers in Louisiana as well as of Africans and children of Africans born in the state, and that they consider themselves racially mixed, descended for the most part from the large antebellum population of free people of color. A comparison of estimates of the number of likely descendants of such nineteenth-century Louisianians with estimates of the size of the colored Creole community today in New Orleans is revealing. As I showed in Chapter 2, manumission laws and social customs had

Table 7.2
New Orleans Family Residents (Spanish and French), May 25, 1977
(According to a Well-Known White Creole Genealogist)

1. De Leaumont
2. Le Gardeur de Tilly
3. Trudeau
4. Carriere de Malozé
5. Enoul de Livaudais
6. Jumonville de Villiers
7. Marin d'Argoté (Spanish)
8. Dubreuil de Villars
9. De Verges
10. La Bedoyere Huchet de Kernion
11. D'Aunoy
12. D'Aquin
13. D'Oriocourt
14. Roy de Villeré
15. Arnoult
16. Bouligny (Spanish)
17. De Fazende
18. Forstall
19. De Lavilleboeuvre
20. Soniat du Fossat
21. Seré de Villede (Spanish)
22. Hardy de Boisblanc
23. Lebreton D'Orgenoy
24. De Brierre
25. Dusau De Lacroix
26. Lacestiere De Labarre
27. Verloin De Gruy
28. Pitot De Beaujardiere
29. De La Vergne
30. De Reggio
31. D'Arcantel
32. Daspit De Saint-Amand
33. Bauchet De Saint Martin
34. De Montreuil
35. Levert (formerly De Vert)

so favored the racially mixed child over the "pure Negro" since the earliest days of the colony that most of the free-colored throughout the antebellum period of Louisiana history were racially mixed. Two sets of figures suffice here to stress the point. By 1778, 248 of 353 (70.2 percent) free people of color in New Orleans were "mulattoes" or "quadroons." By 1850, the proportion had gone up to 8,058 out of 9,961 (80.9 percent).[1]

We can, therefore, confidently assume that at the very least most descendants of the free population of color of Louisiana during the first decade of the nineteenth century could qualify as Creoles today following the old definition. The 1805 census of the city of New Orleans enumerated 1,566 free people of color. If I add to these the 1,977 free persons of color who took refuge in southern Louisiana between 1805 and 1810 following the revolution in St. Domingue, the total comes to 3,543 at the end of the first decade of the nineteenth century (U.S. Census 1805; *Biographical and Historical Memoirs of Louisiana* 1892). Using the standard equation for determining natural population growth,

$$P_t \; = \; P_o \; x \; e^{rt}$$

where t is the number of years elapsed between the two years in question, r is the rate of growth of the population, P_o and P_t are the sizes of the populations at the beginning (1810) and at the end (1980) of the period in question, and estimating r at a conservative 2 percent, we arrive at an estimate of about a hundred thousand individuals today with French and/or Spanish plus Negroid Louisianian colonial ancestry.

The 2 percent rate of growth I use in that calculation is in keeping with the annual rate of growth (2.3 percent) of the total colored/black population of New Orleans, calculated from the census figures for 1860 and 1960 (see Table 4.2). But it may, in fact, be too low a rate. Except for the period from 1791 to 1803, the rate of growth of the free-colored population of New Orleans did not drop below 2.3 percent until the fifth decade of the nineteenth century.

For the early years, of course, there are a number of valid explanations for these exceptionally high rates of growth. The early populations were so small that it was possible to double or triple the size of the population with relatively small increments to the settled population. Moreover, during the first one and a half centuries of Louisiana history, miscegenation persistently added new individuals to the sector of the free-colored. Accretions to the racially mixed population came through sexual unions between whites and black or Negro women, not only by natural growth of the population of colored marrying each other. Even the 1805 New Orleans household census suggests the numerical importance of miscegenation as source of racially mixed children. Of the 1,391 households listed therein, 8.6 percent consisted of a white man and an adult colored woman. Many of these households also included one or more colored children. An additional 11.5 percent of the households had at least one adult white man and an adult woman of color. While we can assume that the woman was employed as domestic servant or nurse in some of these households, it would be unrealistic to make that assumption in all cases. In addition, 19.8 percent of New Orleans households at the time were strictly colored, meaning that fully one-fourth of the households in New Orleans that were white, or contained whites, also had free adult women of color in them, and 10 percent of the households that included whites consisted of a single adult white man and a single adult woman of color. These 10 percent seemed clearly miscegenetic (1805 census).

Though miscegenation was to continue for many years past 1810, clearly the rate of growth of the racially mixed population did not remain as high as in the eighteenth century. Had it remained, for example, at 5 percent from 1810 to 1977, there would have been almost 15 million descendants of French and/ or Spanish colored residents of Louisiana either in the state or throughout the country by now. Today there are far fewer people in Louisiana even when we take whites, coloreds, blacks, and others all into account: the entire population of Louisiana was 3,641,306 in 1970. This means that while 5 percent may be unrealistically high, 2 percent must be considered conservative, and with it the estimate of one hundred thousand derived above.[2] This estimate takes into account only natural rates of reproduction, not accretion from miscegenetic unions whose importance was signalled above.

With all the foregoing caveats, we are still confronted with a significant gap between the estimated number of people eligible to call themselves Creole by colored Creole definition of Creole today and the number of people who do so. Wingfield estimated in 1961 that there were between twenty and thirty thousand Creoles of color in the New Orleans area: sixteen thousand parishioners at Corpus Christi (ten thousand of whom had French names and/or mixed ancestry), six thousand parishioners at Epiphany, and roughly six thousand more from other Catholic parishes of the city—in other words, about a third of the Negro Catholic population of New Orleans (1961: 20). One could question his figures and argue that his scope was too narrow, that not all Creoles registered themselves with a Catholic parish even if they were Catholic, and that there were Creoles outside New Orleans proper. But the members of many racially mixed communities elsewhere in Louisiana call themselves by names other than Creole and do not participate in the same social network as the New Orleans colored Creoles. Although Sister Frances Jerome Woods (1972) uses the term *Creoles of color* to describe the members of an old and established semirural racially mixed community, few members of the community identify themselves as Creole. Mostly they use their well-known surname as social identifier. In traditionally Cajun areas of southwest Louisiana, racially mixed descendants of French and/or Spanish colonial settlers tend to identify themselves as Cajun rather than Creole, although there are a few exceptions. In the parts of southeastern Louisiana closest to New Orleans, one finds greater use of the term in black/colored communities

(Jenkins 1965; oral information). But usually these outlying groups of self-identified Creoles of color are connected to the New Orleans community through commerce, friendship, marriage, or kinship. Even if one were to double or triple Wingfield's estimate to take into account those who might not belong to the typically Creole Catholic parishes, the product would still not quite equal the conservative estimate derived above of those. eligible to call themselves Creole.

"Underrepresentation" is the product of three processes. The first has become particularly evident since the height of the civil rights movement, which was intent at least in Louisiana in turning Creoles into blacks. Despite the popularity of this change in identity in recent years, it is not an altogether new process. Collateral branches of contemporary colored Creole families long ago passed into the non-Creole black community, mostly outside New Orleans. Ruth Samuels, whose most recent fieldwork was on male/female relations in a non-Creole black neighborhood of uptown New Orleans (1974), discovered some French or Spanish ancestors even in the shallow genealogies of her informants. Generally dark-skinned and non-Catholic, her informants would comment upon their non-African ancestry but would not necessarily assume that knowledge of the fact changed their social identity.

Another common way of changing one's identity is passing into the white community. It is not easy to compute the frequency of passing. The social, economic, and political consequences of this change of social identity are so great for the individuals involved that people are unwilling to divulge information to strangers about those who have passed or who are currently in the process of passing for white. But it is possible to draw up reliable estimates, nonetheless. As late as 1941, Blanchet claimed that the most successful colored Creole businessmen were those who passed for white, at least in their public lives (1941). She went so far as to name several families and businesses known in the Creole community to be passing for white. Inconsiderate and unethical though it might seem to do that, it is doubtful that it affected the lives of those mentioned by name for two reasons: first, because it was never published, and second, because those mentioned in this master's thesis are generally known, in the colored Creole community, to be passing for white. Their names came up in several private conversations I had with informants long before I discovered the dusty, forgotten thesis.

Quantitative estimates might be drawn from informants' accounts of the past and present behavior of families living on several blocks within walking distance of Corpus Christi Church, the heart of the colored Creole community from around the turn of the century. Of the eight colored families on one of these blocks, one had a son who passed completely into the white community. Other members of his family itself often passed as well, although they did so only in certain public contexts such as buses and schools and not in others. Another family on this block was described as passable. They generally accepted their racially mixed ancestry but in some situations passed for white. One of the daughters, now in her late thirties, told of getting a job at a large respectable and expensive department store where she was assumed to be white. But her nerves did her in. She was terrified they would discover that she was colored, and soon resigned. Yet another of these families permanently passed and moved recently to California where they live as white.

Of the fourteen households on another block, two have totally passed, although informants smilingly explained to me that "they go strictly for white but we know." A nephew of another local resident "looks so fair he too goes for white; his mother who kind of passes put him in a white school and he's passed since." Close relatives of the owners of five other houses on this block have passed. In one case, the owner is an older lady whose children have all passed and moved into different neighborhoods of the city to avoid association with the colored Creoles. In another, it is one of the man's sisters who currently passes. In a third case, the owners have never passed themselves permanently, though informants frequently asserted that they, too, could pass "because of the way they look." Instead, one brother and one sister became white and moved to California to avoid suspicions.

On a third neighboring street, three of the six families either currently pass or have already completely passed into the white community. One refuses to admit any colored ancestry even in the privacy of colored Creole neighbors' homes. Another one of these is an elderly couple who refuse to join Corpus Christi parish because it is commony regarded as a colored Catholic parish. They used to belong to Sacred Heart parish just down the street when that church was integrated, but were incommoded by the founding of Corpus Christi Church in 1917. When Sacred Heart Church closed down and its records were deposited at Corpus Christi, this elderly couple vehemently protested. They claimed after all to be white, so why should their records be on deposit at a colored church? Recently the elderly lady became ill and unable to attend Sunday mass at her primarily white parish. Since Corpus Christi was around the corner from where she lived and her regular parish church much farther away, she called Corpus Christi rectory to ask to have Holy Communion brought to her at home. So long as she did not have to be seen with the colored people who attend mass at Corpus Christi, she would have no complaints. But she became furious and ill-at-ease when the priest showed up. They had sent the *one* black priest then serving this Josephite Mission parish. The third case of passing on this block is that of a middle-aged couple in which the husband is in the process of becoming white. The wife either cannot or will not join him in the process, so for the time being he restricts his white identity to his job and his public activities outside the immediate neighborhood in which he is known to have colored ancestry. A fourth family on this block does not pass, though one of the daughters moved away to California where she lives as white. The adjacent side street consists of only

three houses, but even here one of the three resident families
passes for white.

Though a quantitative estimate here is necessarily only an
approximation of the pervasiveness of this complex and delicate
reality, it is still worth noting that eleven of the thirty-one families surveyed— more than a third of the families on these four
blocks—have members who pass for white at least part of the
time. The constant flow of colored Creoles into the white community is a major source of underrepresentation in the colored
Creole community. Moreover, on the whole, they do not attempt to socialize much with white Creoles because the latters'
obsession with purity of blood and genealogical research makes
such passage difficult. They prefer instead to move to "neutral"
neighborhoods not associated with any one particular social
group, often to the more modern sectors of the city or the
quickly expanding suburbs to the east and west of Orleans parish. Here they are often surrounded by recent migrants from the
North and the West who do not know, or do not care about, the
details of social classification in New Orleans. Passage into this
white community is much easier. When asked about their family backgrounds, they mention only those ancestors who were
white or looked white, then claim ignorance of other branches of
their families. Often the ones who initiate the social transformation ensure acceptance of their children and grandchildren by
the white community at large by keeping the unhappy details of
their ancestry even from their children. Passage out of the colored Creole community generally means passage out of the Louisiana Creole communities altogether.

The third main reason for underrepresentation within the
colored Creole community is passage of individuals with French
or Spanish colonial ancestry into other social groups outside of
New Orleans. Like the white Creoles in the countryside in
southwestern Louisiana who married into Cajun families, so did
many colored Creoles, even those related to members of the
colored Creole community of New Orleans. In the midst of

speakers of Cajun French and exposed to customs associated with the Cajuns, former colored Creole families became Cajuns—some white, some colored, and some with unclear racial identities.

Like the rest of the American South, the Louisiana countryside is dotted with special groups that Edgar Thompson has called "little races" (1972). They usually call themselves Indians and deny any African ancestry. A number of former colored Creoles have moved into the various groups of this sort present in Louisiana. Many of the so-called Houma Indians have colored Creole ancestors in various generations (Parks 1974). The same is true for many of the so-called Redbones and the various "Indian" family networks of the Red River area of central and northwestern Louisiana (NSU archives at Natchitoches). The descendants of these colored Creoles who married into allegedly Indian families could, by the criterion of ancestry most often invoked in New Orleans today, qualify as Creole in the colored community. But by choice, they are "Indians" rather than Creoles.

Here is a prime example of the interplay between possibility and choice. The legal, political, economic, and epistemological conditions do not exist that would enable these colored Creoles, as a group, to claim white status. But the conditions *have* allowed them to proclaim for themselves an alternative, conceivable, and realizable identity—that of American Indians. The phenomenon, in its general form, is evident among both white and colored Creoles. Macroprocesses determine the arena of possibilities, but the arena always allows for the exercise of choice within its boundaries.

Chapter 8

THE LOGIC
OF DEDUCTION

What then of the possibility of "overrepresentation"—the existence of Creoles who do not conform to any contemporary definition of the term in the social circles in which they operate? We have argued that "underrepresentation" results from the exercise of choice by those *eligible* to claim Creole identity. The interplay between structural and epistemological possibility, on one hand, and individual choice, on the other, is clearly evident in that process. But, at least on the surface, the existence of Creoles who do not exhibit the defining attributes of *Creole* is more problematic. It would be easy, for example, to take it as evidence of the relative irrelevance of official or social definitions in actual processes of identification. But at what price? One obvious price of buying the view that definitions can be so easily circumvented would be sheer disbelief that so much of Louisiana history has been embroiled in an incessant haggling over apparently inconsequential definitions of identity.

The fact is that criteria other than ancestry are frequently used to identify individuals as Creoles. The question is how and why those alternative criteria have come to be so freely employed in instances of labeling, and to what extent they can be viewed as the product of individual manipulation of the system of social classification. I concentrate here on the five main *indexical* markers of Creole identity: physical appearance, speech, propriety, religious preference, and elite status.

LOOKS

Physical appearance is a heavily weighed factor in the identification of Creoles, especially in the black community. Specific ancestries are thought to produce specific discernible physical traits. Hence those who bear such physical characteristics are suspected of being Creole and are even at times introduced as Creoles.

The stereotypic white Creole has milky white skin or a light olive complexion, pitch black hair, dark eyes, medium to short stature, and a slow, deliberate gait. (S)he is pictured in many of the romanticized defenses of the Creole that flooded the market from the mid-nineteenth to the mid-twentieth centuries. The prototypical Creole beauty had mysterious deep-set eyes that evoked images of passion. Creole families could be distinguished from American families by their darker eye and hair color and the olive tint of their complexions. Today many Creoles are blond, red-headed, or brunette, tall, medium in height, or short. Some are heavy; many, quite slender; most look quite average in weight. There are brown eyes and blue eyes as well as green eyes. A room full of white Creoles suggests no single European national stereotype, but rather evidence of the various European streams of immigrants to populate North America. Family portraits likewise suggest the rarity of stereotypic Creole looks in southern Louisiana today. Typically, white Creole households have four or five portraits of ancestors hanging on the walls. And though the standard tour of a white Creole house includes showing off the family portraits, most are identified by name and relationship but not by reference to physical appearance. Only the one or two per household thought to epitomize Creole identity almost always evoke reference to physical appearance. "He was really Creole, wasn't he?" is a standard accompanying phrase. The Creole-looking Creole is generally singled out.

Still, for a person who fits the stereotype, looks facilitate the process of becoming Creole. Creoles make comments about those members of the Creole community who in their opinion look very Creole, and wonder if someone they know in the community could confirm their suspicions that a certain person they saw at the drugstore, the market, the boutique, or a restaurant was Creole "because he looked just so Creole!" For the researcher with dark hair, dark eyes, and Mediterranean complexion, Creole associations of ancestry with physical appearance were a godsend. *Looking Creole* facilitated entrance into Creole social circles; no one ever questioned my presence at social events.

Looks play a crucial role in the colored Creole community. A Creole is expected to be light-skinned, if not nearly Caucasian in appearance, have dark but nonkinky hair, medium height, and a look of self-confidence. Since Creole identity is partly derived from racial mixture, any evidence of racial mixture in a person's physical appearance, such as dark skin and straight hair or a wide nose, fair skin, and very curly hair, is taken as signal of Creole ancestry.

In everyday situations in the colored Creole community of New Orleans and in the black community at large (cf. Samuels 1974), *Creole* is often taken to mean simply racially mixed. Indicative of this perceived relationship between Creole identity and a specific phenotype are the comments made by ten adult members of the colored Creole community when shown photographs of twenty widely varying physical types. These black-and-white photographs of ten male and ten female college freshmen depict a range of physical appearance approximating a continuum from the Nordic blond, fair, blue-eyed type to the Negroid dark-eyed, dark-and-kinky-haired type. All the men wore coat and tie; all the women had respectable necklines and neatly combed hair. Shot against the same white background and with the same amount of light, the photographs were as standardized as possible. The pictures were shuffled so they would appear in random order. The informants were asked if they had any comments to make about the pictures. Every colored Creole divided the lot into whites, Creoles, and blacks, although they differed on the kind of personalities, socioeconomic position, sensuality, and degree of beauty they assigned to the photographed individuals. The responses appear even more significant when compared to comments made by ten adult white Creoles who saw the photographs under similar circumstances. Not a single white Creole suggested that a person looked Creole, though there were several individuals in the photographs who would seem to fit their image of the Creole. Instead, each white Creole informant divided the lot into whites and blacks. Certain individuals were difficult to classify, they admitted. They said they just *couldn't tell* whether the individuals were white or black.

Colored Creole emphasis on physical appearance as an index of social identity is so great that they frequently make comments about people's identities quite spontaneously, when looking at photographs, attending wakes, watching television or gossiping at weddings. Typical of such customary behavior were the reactions of five middle-aged women to pictures of the founders and staff members of the People's Life Insurance Company of Louisiana in a booklet that commemorated the company's fiftieth anniversary. The pictures were taken in 1972 when the company was still dominated by New Orleans Creoles. The five observers lamented the sale of the company to a larger black insurance company based in Atlanta, arguing that "they were going to break up this family affair." Examining the group photograph of the home office personnel, these women immediately picked out the darkest, most Negroid girls, and pointed out that they were not Creole, not connected by family ties to others on the staff or the board of directors, and not Corpus Christi types—all three things thought to imply each other. In addition, my informants wondered how these eight girls had ever gotten their jobs, since the other thirteen at the home office had obviously gotten theirs because of their family ties and social connections.

In fact, they made no mention of the physical characteristics of the three men in the picture—one of whom was as dark as the eight girls singled out above—or of two of the women they identified as Creole who were significantly more Negroid than the rest. These others were Creole, part of "the family," for reasons other than physical appearance, so my informants selectively blinded themselves to the reality of their phenotypes in order to continue with the preferred illusion that Creoles and blacks could be distinguished from each other on the basis of physical appearance.

Bullied by the interviewer, informants acknowledged that there are Creoles who are very black, but they would qualify their statements, adding that Creole identity consisted of more than just physical appearance. In one such conversation, a woman in her mid-thirties described her high school and the students in it. She had attended Xavier Preparatory School, which, although located uptown, attracted primarily Creole students from the Corpus Christi parish neighborhood. There were a number of "uptown people" there at the time, but this informant claimed that she did not know many of them well, and that her friends were almost all "seventh warders." Then she added, "and it's not really that they were dark only; we've always had black Creoles but there were . . . well, they looked so dark, and while we'd always had some dark ones at C. C. well, we'd known them for so long, they didn't look so dark. The other ones looked much darker, but I guess it's because we didn't know them."

In another conversation with a very dark Creole, the logical problem posed by black Creoles surfaced. His mother's maiden name was French, and the family Catholic. Fishing for information, teasingly, I asked if his family was Creole. "Yeah, I guess we count as Creole! People tease me about that at school. You little Creole! Most people think of Creoles as high yellow, you know, very light, but when you look deeper into it, Creole has more to do with background, traditions, and family." He pointed to his own face as he made the statement.

SPEECH AND THE IMAGE OF SPEECH

Ability to speak French well, preferably as a first language, has for years been diagnostic of Creoles. As fewer and fewer people speak the language of their forefathers, however, the logic is applied cautiously. Not knowing the language fails to become a criterion for exclusion, and usually not even a reason for suspicion. But as a corollary, those who do speak French fluently have that to their advantage when they begin to associate themselves with the Creole community.

Contrary to non-Creole belief, the language that both white and colored Creoles associate with their own communities is Continental French, not the language known as Louisiana Negro Creole. Alcée Fortier wrote extensively about Louisiana Negro Creole at the turn of the twentieth century and transcribed, inter alia, folk tales and proverbs. Morphologically and lexically, this Louisiana Negro Creole resembles Haitian Creole and is usually thought to have been derived from the language spoken by the slaves of the refugees from St. Domingue who came to Louisiana at the beginning of the nineteenth century. For years it was predominantly a language of rural blacks in southern Louisiana. It was neither the language of the white Creoles (as is substantiated by volumes of letters and writings of these people in the eighteenth, nineteenth, and twentieth centuries) nor the language of the New Orleans colored Creoles (also confirmed by letters, poems, publications, and records of clubs and benevolent associations throughout the nineteenth and twentieth centuries). The various archives consulted in this research yield ample proof of actual Creole linguistic use in family papers of white Creoles, in the records of the Jeunes Amis and Francs Amis benevolent associations of colored Creoles at the turn of the twentieth century, and in the writings of the poet Lanusse (1845) and the self-styled historian Rodolfe Desdunes (1911).

To complicate matters, both white and colored Creoles, like

most residents of southern Louisiana at the time, knew a fair amount of Louisiana Negro Creole. In both communities today elderly men and women still remember sayings and proverbs in Louisiana Negro Creole. To both, it was a source of amusement, garbled French, though to colored Creoles it was also a source of embarrassment. Most strove publicly always to speak "perfect French" so as not to be confused with the rural, uneducated blacks who spoke Creole. Still, they could recite certain jingles, songs, and proverbs in Creole and smiled when I showed them some that white Creoles Fortier and G. W. Nott had collected up to the 1920s and 1930s (cf. Nott 1926).

The name given to the Haitian-like language spoken in rural Louisiana creates confusion in certain ranks of New Orleans society. Many non-Creole blacks believe those who speak or spoke Creole were Creole. One such lady from a small town just west of New Orleans very proudly asserted that her mother was Creole because she spoke Creole. By no other standards did she qualify as Creole, at least not by any of the New Orleans Creole standards. Her sole claim to Creole identity was her knowledge of Louisiana Negro Creole. When I confronted New Orleans Creole informants with this woman's assertions, they shook their heads, obviously irked by the pretensions of someone they thought so clearly ineligible. Of course, they argued, she wasn't Creole. Indeed, her speaking Creole proved that she wasn't Creole.

Speakers of Continental French, who were born in France or are children of Frenchmen who moved to Louisiana in the past hundred years, complicate the picture. A number of these incorporated themselves socially into Creole society and are frequently thought to be Creole. Older Creole informants may argue about one of these Louisianians' social identity, some supporting, some denying the person's claims to be Creole. In these cases, the person's popularity, respectability, and reputation usually play the determining role. If he is well accepted socially and brings honor to the community, few are those who challenge his claims. If, on the other hand, he is a source of embarrassment and dishonor, few will be those who do not challenge his claims as a Creole.

RESPECT AND PROPRIETY

In customary behavior, we find similar deductive processes. Though few practices today truly distinguish either group of Creoles from non-Creoles in southern Louisiana, a host of idiosyncrasies, medical beliefs, courtship patterns, and above all rules of propriety were associated with both Creole communities in the past and survive in public opinion as characteristic of Creoles. Roger Baudier incorporated many of these associations in a series of newspaper articles, "Historic Old New Orleans," published from 1943 to 1951. I refer to them here because one informant thought they were so descriptive of everyday life in the Creole community of his youth that he regularly cut them out of the paper and stored them in boxes for more than thirty years.

Propriety and family prestige occupy a central role in the image of the Creole. Even when Creoles engaged in gossip, which Baudier and elderly Creoles today all describe as frequent, lively, and typical of the Creoles, they remembered the honor of the family. One of Baudier's sketches is particularly apt.

In the family, Cousine Odaline—or Dada as most folks knew her—was notorious for her descriptive expressions and pithy comments, although in social circles Dada was very much *à cheval* [dignified and proper]. . . . Nonc Justin had to invite her to the various functions, but he did not relish her presence, nor did his wife, Tante Armantine. Dada smiled affably and chatted with groups and individuals, but they knew that she had *des idées baroques,* and they were always fearful she would shock somebody with some blunt comment—*un coup d'hache,* as Armantine put it, if somebody stroked her the wrong way in her pet peeves (Baudier 1951, July 26).

Dressing properly was paramount for years. Even today, though styles afford greater comfort and flexibility, propriety and elegance in dress remain a hallmark of white Creoles. Older Creoles lament the passing of certain dress habits. They would like to see younger women wear white gloves and hats when they go out, the way some older Creole ladies still do, and they would prefer to see Creole men always in jacket and tie. "When Ananas went out on the street," Baudier wrote, "no matter how short a distance, she was dressed up 'en grande toilette, corsetée, ficelée, poudrée, gantée, voilée'. . . . In the summertime, when the family sat on the front gallery, or on the marble front-steps, taking the air, there she was, 'tout attifaillée, comme pour grande cérémonie,' Urbain always remarked" (Baudier 1949, February 17). Today this type of behavior is rare, but its rarity ironically strengthens the association with Creole identity, for it is assumed that only those who are true Creoles would bother to dress like that and be so concerned with propriety.

Already in 1949, Baudier had noticed how these inferential patterns might lead one to consider a person more or less Creole. On August 11, he wrote of Tante Elise,

> She was a Creole lady in every sense of the word. The unwritten code of propriety was at the tips of her fingers. . . . She was always annoyed when Hortense came on visits—boisterous in talk and laughter, careless about her subjects of conversation and inclined to gesticulate. When she was gone, Elise would say gently, 'Elle n'est pas très Créole'. . . . Creole ladies certainly had no business to visit a barber shop, even if a boy had to get his haircut. That was a man's task to accompany him.

Contemporary examples abound. One wealthy Creole characterized a certain well-known Creole woman as Creole by accident of ancestry alone, therefore not very Creole.

> "PAUL": That woman! She is really rock bottom. I've never understood how a nice man like him would marry her.
> INTERVIEWER: What exactly do you mean?

"PAUL": Oh, it's everything. Especially the things she says. She really says things that no one with any sense of propriety would ever say. Really gross.

INTERVIEWER: But she's a ————, isn't she? [I gave him her family name, evidence of a long line of Creole forebearers.]

"PAUL": Bah! Yes, she is, but *that* doesn't mean anything. This is what I meant by so many of the *ge-ge* Creoles being fallen people. And why should ———— [her husband, whom "Paul" likes and respects] stoop so low?

It is worth noting that this informant is fairly closely related to both the man and his wife and that this enters little into his estimation of her. But the process works in the other direction as well. By their discretion, their manner, their dress, and their social interests, the spouses and friends of old-time Creoles conform so much to the highest traditional standards of Creole propriety that for all practical purposes they acquire Creole identity.

In the colored Creole community, we note parallel processes. An older colored Creole lady might not wear gloves and a hat when she walks down the street, but she is always carefully dressed in dress or pantsuit. Decency of dress matters more than styles the white Creoles consider elegant.

More focal, however, is mode of address and pattern of social interaction. Older Creoles complain that many children and teenagers today do not adhere to the rules of basic propriety. They claim these kids walk past homes of people they know without so much as greeting the acquaintance sitting on the porch, walking out of his house, or working on the lawn. This, they claim, would never have happened before the mid-sixties. Yet from this observer's vantage point, what stands out is how often these youths follow the "rules," rather than how often they fail to do so.

Fourteen- and fifteen-year-old boys in wild Afros and patched blue jeans may blurt out a greeting so quickly and inarticulately that it is barely comprehensible, but they still do so. Older people are still addressed as Mr. and Mz., as are others thought to have higher social or economic status. Informants interpret such greetings as signs of respect and decry what they believe is the tendency of non-Creole blacks to use only first names in personal greetings. Thus, formal greetings are thought to differentiate the Creoles from the non-Creoles, and from their use or lack of use inferences are drawn about a person's social identity.

To a Creole there are no strict rules for forms of address, but there are fundamental notions of propriety that help individuals choose a given form for any one individual. The choices are calling a person by his or her first name or nickname; using the title Mr. or Mz. (shortened informal version of Mrs.), followed by the person's first name or nickname; calling him or her by last name alone; or addressing the person by title, Mr. or Mz., followed by the person's last name.

First names and nicknames are the most informal and most familiar. Generally they are not used when a person wishes to index respect. Children and adolescents, close family members, good friends close in age, and those who ask to be called by their first names to avoid feeling old are addressed by first names or nicknames. First names preceded by titles index familiarity and affection coupled with respect. This form is frequently used by children to address close friends of their parents or a long-time neighbor. Informants often found it difficult to explain why they use these forms of address since they convey mixed messages. On one hand, they indicate respect but on the other, "a sort of closeness." One Creole friend had difficulty explaining to me why she called a woman Mz. Mary. The woman was in her late fifties or early sixties, a generation or so older than my informant, had lived around the corner for years, had been a good friend of my informant's mother but was now also a close friend of hers. At times Helen would attribute it to their "sort of closeness," at times to her desire to be respectful. "Well, about Mz. Mary," she would say, "I don't know why I call her that, but about the rest I *think* I can explain it. No real reason for Mz. Mary—that's all I know. But it has to do with showing respect, or at least not too much familiarity."

So important is the balance struck between familiarity and respect in such relationships that friends often address each other this way in the presence of their children so as to teach the children the appropriate form of address. Though Helen, for example, had difficulty explaining specific instances of this pattern of address, she readily saw the overall pattern. "Like Mz. Barros, she works at the Credit Union. I call her that because she calls me Miss Helen and that's because she has two fourteen-, fifteen-year-old girls and she wants them to show me respect. She doesn't want them calling me Helen, so she calls me Miss Helen to get them to call me Miss Helen. But you see if my mother were still around Mz. Barros would have her daughter call her Mz. Canterre."

Using a person's surname in address increases the expression of respect and the lack of familiarity. Surnames alone are not all that frequently used. They are thought to be flatly impersonal and therefore usually inappropriate within the community. They are perhaps most frequently used in semipublic address between schoolteachers, and they are thought awkward in most other contexts within the community. When it does happen, Creoles either get annoyed or become downright curious about the motives for such impersonality. Joy is a perfect example. For several years she interpreted this other woman's habit of calling her by her surname alone as a sign of covert hostility. Then she began to wonder. She is now convinced that the woman simply did not know her first name at first, and that she learned her last name from business files at their mutual place of work. Out of habit, Joy thinks this woman continues to call her by her last name alone though Joy assumes she must know her first name as well by now.

Utmost respect is indexed by use of title and last name combined. Creoles often refer to other Creoles as Mr. or Mz. So-and-So when speaking with strangers outside the community, even if in person they prefer a more informal form of address. They believe it inspires greater respect from strangers.

Manipulation is not only possible; it is also common. For amusement as much as for emphasis, individuals can upgrade or lower the degree of implied respect by choosing forms of address that are not quite appropriate. For laughs, for example, "you might call a good friend Mr. or Mz. So-and-So. . . . Hello, Mz. Gladys, how are you? Or like when you'd walk into the office and I'd say well, hello, Mz. Virginia, how are you today?" People are called different things by different people in accordance with the kind of relationship they have with each other. But all Creoles are expected to pay careful attention to forms of address, to indicate both community spirit and propriety. Middle-aged and older people in particular are noticeably sensitive on this point. According to one informant,

> My mother had a really close friend, Mz. DuRochelle; but at home we always heard my mother talk about Christine this and Christine that. So one day Christine called my mother. My brother picked up the phone and *he* didn't know what to say, so he called my mother and said, "Mom, it's for you. It's . . . Christine." And Mz. DuRochelle heard it, I guess, on the phone, 'cause when my mother picked it up Mz. DuRochelle said, "I didn't know I went to school with him!"

Concern with respect and propriety is pervasive. It is a frequent topic of conversation for mothers of all ages, because of their conscious attempt to ensure that their children bear a proper sense of respect. This maternal concern embodies the dual nature of Creole notions of respect and propriety. It is true that proper, respectful behavior is honestly valued and preferred, but at the same time that it is appreciated in the abstract, it serves as a symbol of Creole identity. To perpetuate the tradition of propriety is to ensure the maintenance of the group itself.

The point is patently evident in derisive remarks about non-Creole blacks—that they don't know how to behave at social gatherings; that they don't know that it is bad form to pay someone a visit at mealtimes unless one has been invited to the meal;

that they don't know how to eat at a public restaurant or how to walk properly; and that they *certainly* don't know how to speak proper English. Not surprisingly, the stereotype is that the colored Creole speaks softly in public places especially outside Creole surroundings. The non-Creole black community tends to interpret that as pretense and arrogance, while the white community sees it as "amazingly good manners."

The Creole is generally conscious of that image and seeks to perpetuate it. I see it in Mardi Gras balls, which like white balls double as forums for presentation of debutantes, as well as in concern with correct usage of English. At the start of each Mardi Gras ball, the young women come out onto the dance floor one by one and are escorted on their walkabout by a member of the club that sponsors the ball. High status white and colored balls are very similar in this regard. The one noticeable difference between them is that colored debutantes tend to be much more formal in the way they walk and the way they curtsy than their white counterparts. The former take short, interrupted steps in line with the slow beat of the music; the latter walk slower than usual but without the cadence expected on formal occasions of the sort. Older former debutantes are on hand always before and during these balls to help the younger women. Still, the white Creoles are more relaxed, less concerned with absolute formality than the colored Creole debutantes.

The deliberateness of the colored Creole balls parallels their concern with correct usage of English. Black English, which they call "speaking flat," draws little esteem in the colored Creole community. Most can imitate it, some do so for political reasons—either to get black votes or to avoid hostility from non-Creole blacks on the job—but most also make a point of avoiding flatness in most contexts within the Creole community and in racially mixed situations outside. Teachers spend a great deal of time correcting speech and demanding clear enunciation. Parents chide their children for using double negatives, the negative *ain't,* or the phone "d" instead of "th." It is said that certain people speak very slowly to avoid falling into flat speech. Others are embarrassed by discussions of correct speech if they feel that their own is not quite up to par. Many are also embarrassed when whites adopt one or another element thought to make speech flat. Innocently, for example, nearly a year after beginning fieldwork, I used the word *ain't* in a conversation with a Creole friend. Before I could say anything else, she turned to me in shock and said, "Now don't you go picking up the worst of our habits." Fascinated by her reaction, I began to experiment with a host of other informants, all of whom soon commented on my new form of speech. Some of the younger ones were amused; some of the older ones became suspicious of my intentions and disapproving of my "carelessly sliding speech"; several seemed embarrassed, wondering if they indeed spoke that "flat" often enough for me to pick it up. I sounded too familiar for comfort.

Creole businesses, churches, and service centers in general exhibit the same concern with language. Receptionists and telephone operators in particular must speak standard English. Many blacks are turned away at job interviews at least in part because "they do not speak clearly enough." Thus speech patterns, too, are indices of group membership. A very dark Creole, for example, would maximize his knowledge of standard English in a job interview of this type, and he would be spoken of, not as a black or nigger, but as a dark-skinned or brown Creole. Likewise, a non-Creole black fluent in standard English has a good chance of obtaining the job otherwise restricted to Creoles. As a result, he becomes at least partly accepted by the Creole community.

RELIGION

Religious identification holds a similar place in the logic. Much of the known lore of Creole culture—the devotion to the

Virgin Mary (*la Sainte Vierge*), picnics at New Orleans cemeteries on All Saints' Day (November 1) every year (*les Tous Saints*), the celebration of Mardi Gras itself just before Lent, and devotions to St. Jude (the patron saint of impossible cases), St. Anthony (who helps locate lost articles), St. Peter (who will open the way), and a host of other saints thought useful in particular circumstances—derives in part from Catholicism. There is the liturgical calendar, the concept of sainthood, the theological posture of the church on the place of the Virgin Mary in God's universe. In fact, French and Spanish cultures are so strongly associated with Roman Catholicism that Louisianians assume all persons with French and/or Spanish ancestry are Catholic and that most Catholics in the state are people of French and/or Spanish ancestry.

Of course, not all of those who celebrate wildly during Mardi Gras plan to fast during the Lenten season, nor do all participants at All Saints' Day picnics believe in life after death. Certainly not all of those who get married in Catholic churches are religious, nor are all those who attend Catholic schools. The question is, what do Louisianians consciously or unconsciously do with their expectation that ancestry implies religious affiliation and religious affiliation, ancestry?

Older white Creoles frequently speak of the anticlericalism of their forefathers and the unbending faith of their foremothers, a pattern not uncommon in Mediterranean societies.[1] The combination of male anticlericalism and female devotion frequently resulted in large enrollments in Catholic schools and weak male attendance at Sunday masses. The Ursuline Order and the Order of the Sacre Coeur educated girls, while Jesuits and diocesans attempted to educate boys. St. Augustine's Church and St. Ann's Church downtown and the New Orleans Cathedral in the heart of the French Quarter were for years magnets of Creole society. But even here women predominated, with men generally standing in the back of the church or outside discussing business, politics, or each other.

It is not insignificant that the non-Creole, non-Catholic ancestors of persons unequivocally accepted as Creole by today's
Creole community generally yielded in matters of religion to
their Catholic spouses. It is remarkable that there are so few
Protestants and no known Jews in the white Creole community
given the relative frequency of intermarriage in the eight or ten
generations of life in southern Louisiana. Many are nonpractic-
ing Catholics, many agnostics, many atheists, but few profess a
non-Catholic faith.

Jeanne Argüedas, writer and novelist, caught much of the
essence of this symbolism in her account of a visit to Popo and
Mémé D'Abadie on 1717 Kerlerec Street within the last fifteen
to twenty years (Argüedas n.d.: 7). Seventy-five-year-old Mémé
reminisced about *les temps passés* as she looked out onto her
backyard.

> Carree used to come an sketch here, dat an de shrine an my
> house too. Oh what a fine artist she is'. She used to come early in
> de morning an sit on her leetel camp stool painting. I asked her:
> "Carree, chere, so early? You don been to Mass, it is Saint Joseph's
> feast day, you know?"
> "Oh, no! I don go to Mass, I am Protestant."
> Ma Chere when she say dat, I feel a blow in my heart, Protes-
> tant! You an all de family such good Catholics. Ah non, pas
> possibl. Ah! Jesus, Marie, Joseph, St. Pierre, Ste. Barbe, Ste.
> Anne. We must pray for her, me every day I light a leel canel at
> de alter for her. It is very sad, because you know only Catholics
> go to Heaven!

Mrs. Aphra Vairan Morris also stressed the significance of
religion for group identity though she herself is not a practicing
Catholic. In a long taped interview taken September 10, 1975,
she frequently mentioned religious beliefs and religious identity. The night her father's mother died she remembers sitting at
dinner very quietly until her father said, "Of course, she *did*
believe in God." Mrs. Morris added, "my mother and father

didn't go to church scarcely at all which was unusual I guess in that circle. The Bernards, for instance, our neighbors were very religious." And later in the interview:

> There again you see I always seem to be bringing up religious differences but religious differences did affect the way we were brought up. Let me say this: my grandfather and my grand-mother, one was a Catholic; the other was an Episcopalian or something. My grandfather and grandmother had thirteen chil-dren of whom only six or seven lived. My grandmother was permitted to raise the girls as Catholic; my grandfather would raise them [here I presume she meant the boys] as Episcopalian or whatever. He had the prerogative. My mother was really nothing as far as religious affiliation went (Friends of the Cabildo tape).

She was never much of a practicing Catholic, but she never be-came anything else. One could easily begin to pass out of the community by becoming Protestant, Jewish, or Moslem. To pass into the Creole community, it was crucial but not definitive to become Catholic.

The influx of Irishmen, Italians, and German Catholics in the middle of the nineteenth century and of Central and South Americans in more recent years complicated the task of social identification in New Orleans. These newer immigrants, too, were traditionally Catholic. The distinction between Catholics and Protestants was no longer quite equivalent to the distinc-tion between Creoles and non-Creoles, at least in a narrow sense of the term *Creole*. One could not infer that a person was Creole from the mere fact that he was Catholic, though it would be difficult for him to become Creole without somehow affiliating himself with the Catholic church. Chances were greater if the person was French Catholic, spoke French, and attended a French-speaking Catholic church. Through cultural and social affiliations, he and his descendants would have strong claims to Creole identity. It is precisely through language, customs, and

religion that the descendants of many of the Frenchmen who
arrived in Louisiana after the colonial period claim today that
they and their ancestors have always been Creole.

Catholicism is strongly associated with the colored Creoles.
Records of St. Louis Cathedral and St. Augustine's Church
throughout the nineteenth century show the continued participation of persons of color in the Catholic church (cf. Notre
Dame Archives; Augustine 1893; Baudier 1939). In 1826,
Henriette Delille, a light-skinned educated free woman of
color, organized a group of women of color for the purposes of
carrying out charitable, educational, and social activities in the
colored community. In 1842 they formally became the religious
order of the Sisters of the Holy Family. A school was organized
by them informally in 1850. It opened officially in 1867. Some
three hundred women belong to the order today, though not all
are colored Creoles. Their school, now well over a century old,
continues to provide high-quality religious education to hundreds of black or colored Catholic girls.[2]

With the beginnings of segregation in the Catholic church of
Louisiana in 1895 (Labbé 1971), certain churches became associated with the colored Creole community. The Josephites and
the Sisters of the Blessed Sacrament, two primarily white
orders, took on missionary work in Louisiana's black and colored
community. Late in 1916, Corpus Christi Church opened its
doors on St. Bernard Avenue in the Seventh Ward, within walking distance of an increasing number of colored Creole families.
In 1919, Corpus Christi parish was split in two, with the area on
the edge of the French Quarter going to the newly formed parish
of the Holy Redeemer. On April 7, 1920, the Josephites bought
St. Ann's Church on St. Philip Street slightly west of Corpus
Christi and turned it from a white into a colored parish. It was
renamed St. Peter Claver. Epiphany was founded northeast of
Corpus Christi Church in 1948. Accompanying each church
from the beginning was a parish school run by the Blessed Sacrament Sisters. Though Josephites founded additional churches

during this period in New Orleans, Corpus Christi, Holy Redeemer, St. Peter Claver, and Epiphany became nearly synonymous with Creole in the black community. By implication, membership in these churches was thought to signal Creole identity.

Parish membership is of far greater significance here than one might otherwise assume. References to third parties frequently include mention of the person's parish membership if he is Catholic, or of his nonmembership in the speaker's own parish if he is not. References to specific parishes carry with them images of the person's social identity, from the chances that he might own his own house to the likelihood of his being Creole. Blessed Sacrament, for example, is located far west of Corpus Christi or the French Quarter in the heart of a black neighborhood thought to be almost completely non-Creole. Yet it is a Catholic church, and those associated with it have at least that on their side if and when they seek to establish a Creole identity. Somewhere along the line, it is often assumed, there must be French and/or Spanish ancestry.

St. David's and St. Philip's are two intermediate cases. The former, founded in 1937, was created out of part of the territory of Holy Redeemer, across the channel to the southeast of the French Quarter. Though some Creoles do live in the area and associate with Seventh Ward Creoles, many non-Creoles also reside there. A member of St. David's parish may or may not be Creole. St. Philip's, founded in the late 1940s, caters primarily to residents of the Desire housing project, which is strongly disclaimed by Creoles. Yet it was started as a mission outpost of St. Raymond's, which is much more closely associated with colored Creoles. Some connection between these parishes and the Creoles is often invoked.

Then there are more recent parishes founded to keep up with New Orleans' expansion to the east. St. Paul's is thought to be an outgrowth of Corpus Christi, an image reinforced by the presence of Josephite priests who founded it. St. Raphael's, though not segregated nor initially associated with Creoles, is currently full of colored Creoles who moved out of the Corpus Christi parish area towards Gentilly Woods in the 1950s and 1960s. The same is true of St. Gabriel's, which serves the communities of Gentilly Woods and Pontchartrain Park. Creoles do not generally infer from a person's membership in one of these two parishes alone that he is Creole, but certainly that he might be so.

Catholics remain in the minority in the New Orleans black community. Hence information about a person's Catholic heritage or Catholic upbringing is weighed heavily and favorably by the Creoles. They recognize to some extent the popularity of the Catholic church among blacks today (cf. Frazier 1957; *Josephite Harvest* records; discussion with Josephite priests), and the possibility of converting to Catholicism. But few are keenly aware of the role of religious conversions in establishing or reconfirming claims to Creole identity. Unlike physical appearance and ancestry, which are ascribed, religious affiliation can be changed at will, as can the social and cultural connotations of the new religious identity acquired with it. In the thirty years between 1925 and 1954, when Corpus Christi parish had the largest number of members in its history, an average of twenty-four adults converted to Catholicism each year. A total of 712 converts received the sacrament of baptism during this thirty-year period. Well over a thousand have converted from the founding of the parish in 1916 to the present (Corpus Christi Church records; cf. also Palazzolo 1955). This is not an insignificant number. During the early and mid-fifties, the church estimated a total of between fifteen and twenty thousand parishioners, but this included children as well as adults. Since then the number of registered parishioners has steadily declined as younger and middle-aged Creoles began to move out to Gentilly, Pontchartrain Park, and New Orleans East. From sixteen thousand in 1954, it slid to an estimated seven thousand in 1975 and 1976. And, of course, as the parish diminishes in size, so does the number of conversions. From 1969 to 1975 there were only eighty-eight official conversions, at an average of twelve to thirteen a year; yet the ratio of conversion rate to parish size remained nearly identical during both periods. A steady influx of non-Creole blacks is discernible throughout the sixty years of Corpus Christi history.

Another way to look at the rate of influx is to compare the number of children baptized with the number of adult conversions. The former is a measure of the natural growth of the Creole population; the latter, a step at least in the process of crossing boundaries. From 1925 to 1954, 11,149 children received the sacrament of baptism, and 712 adults converted. Conversions amounted to 6 percent of the total number of new parishioners. From 1969 to 1975, 1,357 children were baptized and 88 adults converted. The number of convert baptisms remained remarkably similar—6.1 percent of the total number of baptisms at Corpus Christi.

The desirability of Catholic identity, especially Corpus Christi Catholic identity, is evident as well in the number of people who participate in various activities of Corpus Christi parish life. Large crowds assemble nearly every Sunday morning for mass at 11:00 A.M. and 12:15 P.M. Around a hundred altar boys, between fifteen and twenty-five of them ages sixteen, seventeen, and eighteen, alternate assisting at mass. Parishioners claim the size of the crowds has diminished little in the last twenty years, a remarkable observation given the substantial reduction in the number of registered parishioners over this period. In fact, many of those who attend Sunday mass at Corpus Christi are not registered parishioners and all are not baptized Catholics. For the latter, the social activities of the parish—and Sunday mass is certainly an important social function here— serve as mechanisms of incorporation into the Creole community. For the former, Sunday mass is a ritual of community participation and reaffirmation of identity. Many of these are younger or middle-aged Creoles who moved out of the parish in recent years but spend time with parents and grandparents in the area every Sunday. Corroborating this observation are the church's own records showing the aging of its parishioners. The population dropped from sixteen thousand to seven thousand between 1954 and 1975; proportionally baptism and weddings decreased even more—baptisms from 396 to 146, and weddings from 98 to 36. Deaths, in contrast, increased from 94 to 109. Had the age distribution not changed over this twenty-one-year period, we might have expected there to be 173 baptisms, 43 weddings, and only 41 deaths. (See Table 8.1.)

ELITE CONNOTATIONS

Implied in the way in which looks, speech, manners, and religion index Creole identity is a strong Creole claim to elite status. It is explicit in attitudes to work, hierarchy, accomplishment, and self-reliance. It is particularly manifest in opposition to the identification of *certain* families as Creole.

Work

A white Creole, for example, is expected to shun all manual labor for pay outside the privacy of his or her home. In standard Mediterranean fashion, white Creoles associate manual labor with working-class or lower-class status, and freedom from manual labor with the status of the social elite. So ingrained is the avoidance of manual labor for pay that white Creole women impoverished by the Civil War refused even to sew for others, unless it was in the privacy of their own homes where they would not be seen by others. Forced to supplement the family's income by their own work, these women sought employment "in nice, classy stores" as salesladies, schoolteachers, and clerks. They would accept employment even in domains thought to be characteristically middle-class. They would shuffle papers, sit behind a desk, or stand behind sales counters "in nice stores," but

Year	Weddings	Baptisms	Funerals
1917	68		
1918	74		
1919	88		
1920	61		
1921	55		
1922	50		
1923	66		
1924	52		
1925	41	283	
1926	84	266	
1927	66	326	
1928	66	349	
1929	60	327	
1930	81	354	
1931	71	373	
1932	58	330	
1933	60	335	
1934	95	356	
1935	62	346	
1936	90	369	
1937	80	353	
1938	69	380	
1939	95	373	
1940	149	371	
1941	101	395	
1942	146	461	
1943	148	432	
1944	93	413	
1945	125	386	
1946	200	545	

Table 8.1 (*continued*)

Year	Weddings	Baptisms	Funerals
1947	158	581	
1948	119	557	
1949	85	491	62
1950	98	468	77
1951	89	434	77
1952	90	425	80
1953	94	395	94
1954	98	396	94
1955	78	372	70
1956	103	408	73
1957	86	355	84
1958	82	358	91
1959	83	376	81
1960	102	345	108
1961	104	300	91
1962	119	309	87
1963	122	370	101
1964	84	367	128
1965	100	382	125
1966	105	262	129
1967	93	311	90
1968	95	280	139
1969	95	239	108
1970	61	221	112
1971	69	248	85
1972	73	184	118
1973	42	153	111
1974	41	152	110
1975	36	146	109
1976[a]	32–33	134–140	98–102

[a] Estimates extrapolated from data through June 19.

they would starve, it is said, before accepting any job that required public subservience to anyone below them in status. The genealogies of white Creole families today contain numerous examples of Creole women in need who sought ways to earn money without losing face.

One middle-aged informant, for example, reported that two of his four great-grandmothers were widowed rather young. His father's mother's mother managed to remarry within five years and gain support for herself and her children, but his mother's mother's mother did not and found herself in need of outside income. In a family history he kindly prepared for me in 1976, he wrote of the latter:

> Laure Bordelois was a blue-stocking who when her husband died after the Civil War, to look after five young children undertook to teach in other people's schools, then to found her own elementary school, to do fine sewing after hours, and to make numerous attempts at publication of essays and verse in French, without great success. She won a medal in some provincial French competition, and published an "Histoire de la Louisiane racontée aux enfants" of which I have a copy. She may be responsible for strong anti-clerical tradition in her branch of the Andry family.

A somewhat older Creole speaks of a female relative of the postbellum period who found herself in need of work. Great-grandfather Meunier's father's mother's father lost substantial amounts of money during the Civil War, leaving himself nearly destitute and with ten children to feed. Henri's father's mother's sister, Tante Julie, married but was widowed early in life. Finding herself alone and concerned about the fate of her two unmarried sisters, Tante Julie opened a small school on the other side of their house on Ursulines Street and lived off the income it generated. Henri's mother's mother also taught school during the Civil War and in the period immediately following. It was, in his words, "a way to support the family in trying times."

The many small white private schools that sprung up after

the Civil War offered employment opportunities to a host of white Creole women. Among these, l'Institut Guillot, l'Institut de Mlle. Picard, Pardet's, the Pinac Institute, and Mme. Vatinel's were probably the best known, but many were simply run on a very small scale by single or widowed women and lasted only as long as the supplementary income was needed. Older informants mentioned attending schools of this sort at "Mrs. Bouligny's," "Mrs. Gregory's," "the Bourgés'," and "the Urquharts'." At the Bouligny school near the turn of the twentieth century, for example, Mrs. Amelia Baldwin West remembers that there were three teachers. "I went to my cousin's school," she said, "on Esplanade Avenue, the Misses Bouligny, Miss Marie Schmidt and Miss Lizette Bouligny." "My cousin," she continued, "Miss Madeleine Arnaud, taught me my ABC's and everything we had was in French. We had lunch there. We brought our own cups and saucers. It was a regular Creole lunch" (Friends of the Cabildo tape, September 3, 1975). Schools were family affairs for both teachers and pupils. They afforded teachers respectability in the midst of penury.

Charles Patton Dimitry's journalistic and genealogical series on Louisiana families (1892/93) confirms these patterns of female employment. Though he covers forty-four families (or branches of families) and well over a thousand names for the period from 1718 to 1893, he mentions only seventeen women with careers, jobs, or professions of any kind, and only two or these antedated the Civil War. The remaining fifteen included five nuns, three general educators, two writers, one music professor and singer, and four women described as composers, musicians, or artists who do not seem to have made a living from their work in the arts. Not a single woman is mentioned in any form of manual or menial labor, or for that matter, not even in sales or clerical work. Though in reality a number of impoverished Creole families did begin to see their women work for money, it is clear that only artistic or pedagogic work was considered truly respectable in the late 1800s. Most of the families who are described in detail in Dimitry's series did have working women at the time, but he chose not to mention all those jobs that did not accord with the elite image of the "old Louisiana family."

Manual labor was also not considered respectable for men. People snickered disapprovingly at one informant's uncle who, "unlike the ideal of the Creole gentleman was very fond of working with his hands, even owned a half-interest in a bicycle shop for a while." While manual work was just a hobby for him, it was still a source of friction at home and in the Creole community.

Dimitry's family histories reflect this much as well. Not a single man mentioned in the series is described as a skilled or unskilled laborer. Though more than a thousand people are mentioned in the series, the occupations of only 260 men appear in Dimitry's 44 columns. Taking only the history of each family since arrival in Louisiana and focusing on the occupation requiring the most training or achievement of each individual mentioned (important since many dabbled in other matters, such as planters in government or doctors in business and military officers in agriculture), we arrive at a telling distribution of income-generating activities among white Creoles in the eighteenth and nineteenth centuries. (See Table 8.2.)

Of these, military commissions tended to be more frequent in the eighteenth century during colonial times and official legal training much more common after 1803. Businesses that attracted many of the Creoles included the cotton and sugar exchanges, the importation of wines, shipping and transportation, and insurance. Smaller businesses not directly tied to the booming sugar and cotton economies of the Gulf Coast of Louisiana are conspicuous by their absence from the list. There are no construction companies, no cloth importers or clothing factories, no retail stores, no crafts, and no food service establishments. Late in his life a Dr. Ducatel did go into the dry goods business, which was not altogether respectable, but being a physician he could compensate for his gall with his status.

It has always been very déclassé to be in "the food business"

Table 8.2
Primary Occupations of Males (1718–1893) in the White Creole
Community, According to Charles Patton Dimitry (1892/1893)

Primary occupation	Number	Percent
Planters	56	21.5
Lawyer/notary public (judges included)	48	18.5
Military officers	34	13.1
Owners of business and top executives (non-planters)	28	10.8
Middle-level government officials	26	10.0
Physicians	25	9.6
Sales, clerks	16	6.2
Journalists/writers	11	4.2
Priests/clergymen	4	1.6
Educators/scholars	3	1.1
Engineers/surveyors	3	1.1
Bankers	2	0.8
Chemists	2	0.8
Architects	1	0.4
Stockbrokers	1	0.4

Source: Series on "Louisiana Families," *Times-Democrat,* January 10, 1892–
January 29, 1893.

itself. A middle-aged Creole swears his grandfather "would
never have dreamed of inviting or having a well-known figure in
the food industry over at his house." He explained:

It was respectable to be in the dry goods business but not in the
food—grocery—business. My grandmother's grandfather was
in the grocery business, I'm fairly sure, but the family has always
referred to him as being "in business."

When ———, my mother's first cousin, found himself destitute during the 1930s Depression, he decided to open up a grocery store. That way he'd be able to have food readily available for his own family and make a little money as well. Well, ———'s first cousins on the other side were outraged, particularly the two or three unmarried girls who told him that they could no longer look up at anyone. They were so ashamed that a member of their family had become a grocer.

Stigma against the food industry has visible effects on the composition of the white Creole community. Several Louisiana families with French and Spanish colonial ancestry are usually taken not to be Creole by the more discerning white Creoles largely, if not exclusively, because of their business interests in supermarkets, groceries, or restaurants. When I asked a very sensible, intelligent, well-traveled older informant what he thought about the social identity of two such families, he immediately injected, "But wait, you're now getting out of the family!" The remark is particularly significant since my informant is indeed rather closely related to both of these families.

Stigma is also attached to occupations thought to be generally dominated by social groups they deem socially inferior to them, especially occupations associated over the years with the Creoles of color, whom they see as "colored" or "black." There is more than a general indictment of manual labor; there is a taboo against occupations associated with light-skinned blacks. White Creoles are afraid that they will *become* colored Creoles in the minds of the white population if they acquire external characteristics of the colored Creoles. One informant perceptively called this "tainting by association." Another gave me an example of the power of such inferences out of his own past. He fondly remembers a friendship he had with a serious, intellectually inclined boy who for years was warmly welcomed at his house because he was quiet and enjoyed discussing books. My informant also not so fondly remembers how when he was sixteen one of his aunts spoiled the friendship by suggesting that the boy might not be quite white. She offered no genealogical information to support her contention, but appealed instead to the power of inference. As my informant put it, "You know, this boy isn't pure white. His father may be a pharmacist, but his uncles, they are stonemasons and you know what that means."

The pharmaceutical profession was above suspicion, but stone-masonry was not. Pharmacists were professionals, and professionals were considered respectable. Very few professionals in Louisiana were colored, so it would be safe to assume that if the man was a pharmacist and looked essentially Caucasian he was probably white; and that if the family had a French name, French ancestors with familiar Creole names and identified itself as Creole, it was probably also Creole. But the uncles' occupations associated them with manual labor in general, and the colored community in particular, in both cases associations that conflicted with the preferred image of the white Creole. Although the boy's family claimed to be white and Creole, the woman's inferences sowed the seeds of suspicion. Within weeks, the boy's visits were discouraged and finally terminated. Within months, his family saw most of its social ties to the white Creole community weakened and eventually severed. In the end, the boy lost his social identity as a white Creole. Only in the privacy of his own house could he claim to be white Creole without someone frowning, smiling, or snickering. And without the support of the social group, claims to Creole identity lost first their significance, and second their reality. Whatever the boy's family's prior social identity, it is clear that occupation had played a major part in establishing its claims to white Creole status and that it was occupation as well that was now undermining these same claims.

It is significant that only one of more than three hundred people identified as Creole by a group of white Creoles today is a blue-collar worker; this young man is in a special category since he is physically disabled. Moreover, he has a college degree and works as a handyman only for Creole families, whom he believes understand and respect his position, and only because he is too handicapped to find more suitable employment. All these conditions make the young man a very acceptable exception.

The rest present a picture of essentially middle-class respectability, a far cry from the picture painted by Dimitry at the turn of the twentieth century, but still one that does not conflict with the white Creole's image of himself as elite. The 190 individuals aged thirty and over whose occupations (before retirement) were something other than housewife appear in Table 8.3.

Education is the primary source of employment now, just as plantation agriculture was in the nineteenth century. Archival, genealogical, preservation, and real estate work also hold a special attraction for white Creoles today, as might be expected from a group whose past is deemed more glorious than the present. Among those in business for themselves, only a handful really own large companies or real estate holdings. Most have small shops, agencies, or small family businesses. Practically all of those over thirty own the house they live in, or share ownership of some old family house with other members of their immediate family. On paper, therefore, most appear to be rather wealthy, but many are short on cash. Many frequently complain about shortage of liquid cash with which to cover annual property taxes on their houses, houses that in many cases they have inherited or bought with money acquired from the sale of ancestral real estate. They are in many ways the epitome of an impoverished aristocracy.

Hierarchy in Debauchery

Juggling the reality of relative impoverishment with persistent claims to elite status takes ingenuity and poise. Where wealth is lacking and power questionable, white Creoles invoke ancestry as a source of prestige. To operationalize these claims in social life, they create clubs that restrict membership to Louisianians like them, or found chapters of national genealogical societies in New Orleans to support their claims to membership in a hereditary aristocracy. Societies for which genealogical proof of

Table 8.3

Primary Occupations of White Creoles in Sample (1975 – 1977)

	Number	*Percent*
Educators	46	24.2
Owners of businesses	29	15.3
Physicians	15	7.9
Middle-level functionaries	14	7.4
Clerks	14	7.4
Lawyers	10	5.3
Secretaries	8	4.2
Real estate agents	7	3.7
Librarians/archivists	6	3.2
Insurance salesmen	5	2.6
Genealogists	5	2.6
Engineers	3	1.6
Tour guides	3	1.6
Journalists	3	1.6
Architects	3	1.6
Priests	3	1.6
Artists	3	1.6
Medical technicians	2	1.0
Pharmacists	2	1.0
Stockbrokers	2	1.0
Travel agents	2	1.0
Receptionists	1	1.0
Gardeners	1	1.0
Salesladies	1	1.0
Accountants	1	1.0
Bookkeepers	1	1.0
	190	99.9

descent from early settlers is a requirement for membership are predictably popular among the Creoles. They are thought to screen out the masses of non-Creoles.

Founders of New Orleans and Louisiana Colonials require of their members proof of descent from colonial settlers in Louisiana and are therefore the most Creole of the genealogical societies, at least by the criterion of ancestry. The New Orleans Chapter of the National Society of Colonial Dames of America, the National Society of U.S. Daughters of the American Revolution, and the Sons of the American Revolution also require genealogical proof of descent from early settlers. These, too, allow the willing Creole a sense of exclusivity that counterbalances the loss of economic and political power. But non-Creoles as well as Creoles belong to these chapters of national societies, since they only require descent from colonial settlers somewhere in the United States and do not restrict membership to descendants of colonial settlers in Louisiana. The inference that a person is Creole is stronger if he is a member of Founders or of Louisiana Colonials than if he is just a member of the New Orleans chapters of these national societies.

Beyond the lure of the genealogical societies is Mardi Gras itself. There is the public Mardi Gras that most tourists see and the private Mardi Gras through which much of New Orleans social structure can be seen. While the parades entertain the tourists, formal balls occupy the social life of thousands of New Orleanians. Anyone can watch the parades, but only those with special invitations can attend New Orleans Mardi Gras balls. The principle of exclusivity appeals to the Creole community.

Each ball is given by an incorporated group called a *krewe,* which sets policies for the admission of members and approves or rejects individuals as guests. Though the primary purpose of each krewe is to plan, design, and coordinate activities connected with the annual ball, the krewes serve broader social functions. As social clubs, they provide members with a sense of belonging and in many, if not most, cases with a sense of personal worth or status. Members frequently identify themselves with the krewe or krewes to which they belong. Regular meetings throughout the year provide continued social contact between members, creating or reinforcing many-stranded relationships among them. By excluding others and tightening social ties, the Mardi Gras krewe gives at least the illusion of being an elite institution—hence its great appeal in the Creole community.

Although the Creoles did not found the first official Mardi Gras krewe, many of the earliest krewes founded in the postbellum period were heavily Creole, and most were at least partly Creole. The strain of Reconstruction, loss of political power, and relative impoverishment created a favorable environment for the formation of exclusive clubs. Twelfth Night, Rex, Momus, and Proteus—founded in 1870, 1872, 1872/73, and 1882 respectively—attracted white Creoles and non-Creoles alike. The next seven krewes founded in New Orleans were mostly Creole: Atlanteans, Elves of Oberon, Nereus, High Priests of Mithras, Olympians, Athenians, and Mystery. The sudden interest of white Creoles in Mardi Gras krewes coincides in time with the great defenses of the white Creole by men such as Charles Gayarré and Alcée Fortier, and with the founding of social clubs aimed at perpetuating the French language and French culture in Louisiana. Indeed, these movements are probably not unrelated. As political power waned and socioeconomic status grew increasingly questionable, the Creoles sought club membership to legitimize their elite status. Mardi Gras krewes offered an exemplary opportunity. They were then quite limited in number and were strongly associated with the social and economic elite of their day. Founding Mardi Gras krewes was a way to earn status by association.

Unfortunately for the Creoles, other social groups have since followed their example. By the 1930s, non-elite non-Creole krewes had made their appearance. Following World War II, the field greatly expanded, reaching its peak perhaps in the last decade. From twelve at the start of World War II, the number of white Mardi Gras krewes soared to sixty-three by 1970. And these included only those mentioned by the press. In fact, more than a hundred Mardi Gras balls are now given every year in the New Orleans metropolitan area. Two or three have been added each year since 1970 from the fast-growing New Orleans suburbs; at least eighteen institutionalized and named balls are given each year in the colored/black community, according to colored Creoles; and there are always hundreds of more informal balls and parties thrown throughout the metropolitan area during the Mardi Gras season.

The multiplication of Mardi Gras krewes robbed the Creoles of the mechanism of elite recognition that they had ingeniously adopted at the close of the nineteenth century. Membership in a krewe alone could no longer signify elite status. There were too many krewes, too many members of krewes, and too many participants at Mardi Gras balls. Though membership in a krewe, any krewe, could enhance the prestige of an individual from a nonelite sector of the population, it could not invest him with elite status. The institution of the Mardi Gras krewe had been democratized.

For white Creoles, as for elite non-Creoles, the current solution to the problem is the constant hierarchization of Mardi Gras krewes. First, there is a clear differentiation between acceptable and non-acceptable krewes. Of the hundred or so, only nineteen or twenty are thought acceptable. In the words of one concerned informant: "The majority of Carnival krewes are 'not social'; they are 'worthless,' 'way down.' Some of them, of course, are all right. I don't mean that they're not otherwise respectable, but you see, like the Moslems or the Alhambra, anyone who's a member of one of those organizations is eligible to be a member of the krewe; there are no selection procedures, like there are in the clubs that *are* social!" Although social worth and respectability are concepts Creoles have trouble delineating, they use the terms freely. Essentially the elite monopolize social worth and respectability. A man is respectable "if he is generally accepted in his occupation, the clubs, his community, if there is no scandal afflicting his family and his lifestyle is honorable." In a nutshell, he is respectable if he is an accepted member of the elite. Social worth and respectability come full circle. They are the properties of the members of the group and of no others.

Creole claims to elite status today require a clear dichotomization of "social" and "nonsocial" krewes, or "worthwhile" and "worthless" krewes. Within each broad category actual ranking is difficult, if not at times impossible, but such ranking matters little to today's Creole. What does matter is the inclusion in the category of the "worthwhile" of all those krewes currently or formerly associated with the white Creoles.

On separate occasions I asked ten white Creoles to rank the many Mardi Gras krewes of the 1970s. Invariably, the five oldest Krewes received the highest grades, and the next seven oldest were rated anywhere from acceptable to very good. The remaining seven or eight acceptable ones were drawn from krewes formed in the period between the wars: Osiris, Pierrettes, Iris, Mystic, Harlequins, Prophets of Persia, Marionnettes, Apollo, Bards of Bohemia, and Caliphs of Cairo. Of these, the Pierrettes, Harlequins, Marionnettes and Apollo are high school and college-age krewes whose respectability derives from the social positions of the members' parents. They are not always counted among the acceptable krewes, because they are considered derivative of already established organizations. Iris suffered a significant change in membership in the late thirties and forties, after it resumed its activities following a nine-year lapse. The new Iris is rarely included in the list of acceptable or social krewes today, though the old one frequently is. Caliphs of Cairo was mentioned by one family as acceptable, but it is worth noting here that members of this family have been deeply involved in this krewe in the past. The only truly acceptable krewe that postdates the 1920s is Achaeans, but this krewe consists of young men of elite families well-connected to the old Mardi Gras organizations. There is a strong correspondence between age of the krewe and its "acceptability." (See Table 8.4.)

This association strengthens Creole claims to elite status. Traditional Creole krewes were among the oldest. Though pass-

Table 8.4
Mardi Gras Krewes with All-White (or Mostly White) Membership
(through 1970)

Year Founded	Krewe
1857	Comus
1870	Twelfth Night
1872	Rex
1872–73	Momus
1882	Proteus
1891	Atlanteans
1895	Elves of Oberon
1896	Nereus
1897	High Priests of Mithras
1903	Olympians
1910	Athenians
1912	Mystery
1916	Osiris
1921	Pierrettes
1922–29	Iris (a new Iris founded in 1938)
1923	Mystic
1925	Harlequins
1927	Prophets of Persia
1928	Marionnettes
1929	Apollo
1933	Bards of Bohemia
1937	Caliphs of Cairo
1937	Noblads
1940–42	Adonis
1948	Alpheus
1949	Naiads
1949	Achaeans
1949	Hera
1949	Janus
1949	Mokana
1950	Okeanos

Table 8.4 (continued)

Year Founded	Krewe
Postdating 1950	Alhambra
(none considered	Alla
by white Creoles	Ancient Scribes
to be socially	Anubis
acceptable)	Babylon
	Bacchus
	Bal Masque
	Bards of Bohemia
	Carrolton
	Choctaw
	Diana
	Dorians
	Elenians
	Endymion
	Eros
	Freret
	Hebians
	Helios
	Jason
	Juno
	Jupiter
	Mecca
	Moslems
	Niobeans
	Omardz
	Pandora
	Pegasus
	Prometheus
	Sparta
	Thoth
	Ulysses
	Venus
	Zeus

ing years have increased the number of non-Creoles in these traditional krewes, white Creoles on the whole continue to speak of most of them as Creole krewes and Creole balls. Informants may disagree when they attempt to identify the specific krewes they consider Creole, but all of the krewes they suggest as Creole fall within the category of the acceptable. The responses of ten well-connected white Creoles to my request for identification of specific Creole krewes are illustrative. (See Table 8.5.) They varied from a low of two to a high of five. No two informants mentioned exactly the same set of krewes. Altogether ten krewes were mentioned. Obviously there is greater consensus on some than on others, as with Mystery and Olympians over the rest of the krewes. But for all the variance in informants' responses, there remains a clear identification of Creole identity with age, and age in this case with prestige.

Yet another way for impoverished Creoles to support their claims to elite status is to study the genealogies of wealthy, prominent New Orleans families who do not regard themselves as Creole and to try to identify in the genealogical record of such families someone of French and/or Spanish ancestry, cultural affiliation, or political allegiance. Just as people claim famous figures as ancestors, Creoles often claim that certain socially prominent people are Creoles, regardless of how they may identify themselves. A kind of affirmative action takes place. I indicated earlier that large numbers of the population of southern Louisiana could claim Creole identity if the criterion of ancestry alone were used. But I have shown, too, that in Creole identity there is an element of choice. Obviously, to claim that a prominent person who does not identify himself as Creole is a Creole is to deny or challenge this element of personal choice.

The memberships of the five most prestigious Mardi Gras krewes include a number of individuals who identify themselves as Creole, but they also include a large number of people who are identified as Creole by less successful Creoles, although they do not identify themselves as Creoles. Likewise, Creole informants

Table 8.5
Mardi Gras Krewes Considered to be Creole by Ten White Creole
Informants (1975–1977)

A: Atlanteans	F: Mystery
Olympians	Nereus
	Olympians
B: Mystery	
Nereus	G: Mystery
Olympians	Oberon
	Prophets of Persia
C: Atlanteans	Proteus
Momus	
Mystery	H: Atlanteans
Proteus	Olympians
Twelfth Night	Proteus
D: Mithras	I: Mithras
Mystery	Mystery
Nereus	Prophets of Persia
Olympians	
	J: Mithras
E: Atlanteans	Mystery
Nereus	Oberon
Olympians	Twelfth Night
Proteus	
Twelfth Night	

Total votes per krewe:

Mystery	7	Twelfth Night	3
Olympians	6	Mithras	3
Atlanteans	4	Oberon	2
Nereus	4	Prophets of Persia	2
Proteus	4	Momus	1

took great pride in calling twenty-six of the thirty-seven official debutantes of the 1976/77 season Creole.[3] Each year in late August the "Vivant" section of the *New Orleans Times-Picayune* devotes an entire issue to the year's debutantes. Each girl's picture is accompanied by a brief biographical sketch that includes the names of her parents, the high school she attended, her college career to date, employment experience, travels, and hobbies. It does not include even a brief family genealogy. Yet several informants independently and without prodding from me went through the seventeen-page section in an effort to determine who was and who was not Creole. Most of the debutantes said to be Creole, were, as one informant put it, "Creole through the mother's side." Informants then went through educational, behavioral, and residential characteristics of the debs to seek confirmation of their claim that over two-thirds of the girls were Creole. They were particularly pleased to note that eleven of the debs had graduated from the Academy of the Sacred Heart (the Sacre Coeur), and that two had gone to Mercy Academy. The ten from Louise S. McGehee School were also probably mostly Creole. Although that school is secular, its principal at the time was a former Catholic nun, and the school has attracted Creole girls for some time. Of the ten at Metairie Park Country Day, at least a few would also be Creole. As expected, none of the debutantes had attended a public high school. All were in college: twelve at Sophie Newcomb (Tulane), twelve at LSU (Louisiana State University at Baton Rouge), nine in other schools throughout Louisiana and the South, one in France, and, as the paper noted, "three . . . in (heaven forbid) Yankee country" (*Times-Picayune* August 29, 1976, sect. 4, p. 12). The higher educational profile could not prove that they were Creole, but it was certainly in accord with Creole values of the past century. Finally, twenty-six of the thirty-seven debs called Uptown their home. Four more lived in the Garden District between Uptown (strictly speaking) and downtown; four lived in Old Metairie; one in the French Quarter; one on a plantation on the other side of the river from New Orleans, and one in Gretna.

This residential distribution revealed the wealth and prominence of the girls' families. Uptown is the most prestigious part of town. The Garden District has gorgeous old mansions. Old Metairie attracts many of the children and grandchildren of prominent families and is, without a doubt, the most prestigious of New Orleans suburbs. That there was only one debutante from the French Quarter itself is not surprising, nor does it conflict with the inference that most of the debs were Creole. By the 1870s and 1880s newer immigrants of Italian, German, and Irish extraction had moved in significant numbers into the French Quarter (Vieux Carré Property Survey, the Historic New Orleans Collection). Low in status by the standards of the old Creole families and alien in much of their lifestyles to that of the elitist Creoles, the immigrants clashed with their French-speaking neighbors. The Creoles claim that they were driven out of the Quarter towards the end of the nineteenth century by the advance of the immigrant population.

The claim is somewhat ill-founded, because the immigrants would not have been able to move in if the Creoles had not begun vacating their homes in the Quarter. Rents were low enough for immigrant occupation. The houses were often ill-kept, and the Quarter was not as glamorous, spacious, or seigneurial as the growing uptown neighborhood of the Anglo-Americans. In the midst of challenges to their social status, the Creoles sought further dissociation from the working classes who occupied the bottom of the social ladder. The exodus culminated in the second and third decades of the twentieth century. First the Creoles moved to the peripheries of the Quarter, to the section just north of the Quarter called Trémé (associated with the parish of St. Ann mentioned above), and to the immediate vicinity of Esplanade Avenue on the eastern edge of the French Quarter. The ten to twelve blocks on Esplanade closest to the river housed the better-off Creoles, the magnificence of these Esplanade homes contrasting with the functional modesty of many of the houses in Trémé. By the beginning of the second decade of this century, however, the movement uptown had begun. The Ursuline Academy for Girls moved uptown in 1912, the Chalaron family in 1918, the Notts in stages between 1924 and 1928; the Villeres, de la Vergnes, Miltenbergers, and Larues all moved uptown. Along with them went the Academy of the Sacred Heart, which moved from the Quarter to St. Charles Avenue in the heart of uptown New Orleans. Loyola University of the South opened its doors uptown (also on St. Charles Avenue) in 1910.

The places of residence of members of the Athénée Louisianais and l'Union Française over the years document the movements away from the Quarter and uptown. In 1876, roughly two-thirds of the members of Athénée lived below Canal Street, with about half actually living in the Quarter. By 1916, two-thirds still lived below Canal, but only five of the thirty-nine members lived in the French Quarter itself. By 1939, the number below Canal had plummeted to only a third of the total membership, and only four of the ninety-four actually lived in the French Quarter. The membership of l'Union Française was somewhat different, somewhat less well-to-do than the Athénée members, and more tied to France. It had originally been founded as a society of recent French immigrants intent on helping hardship cases in France and supporting each other. The pattern of movement among these people was more to the north of the Quarter near Bayou St. John than actually to uptown New Orleans. But even here the two main patterns of evacuation of the French Quarter and movement uptown are well illustrated. Whereas some two-thirds of the members of l'Union Française lived in the Quarter in 1872, only two of thirty-six (less than 10 percent) still lived in the Quarter by 1938. And whereas only three of forty-one (less than 10 percent) resided uptown in 1872, eleven of thirty (over a third) lived there by 1938.

The apparent split indicated here between members of the Athénée and those of l'Union Française was neither complete nor lasting, but it does index the spread of socioeconomic positions of Creole families and their differential assimilation into the Anglo-American community. It is not surprising that most of the Creole debutantes of 1976/77 lived uptown; debutantes come from well-to-do families who can afford the expenses of a formal debut. Outfits, parties, and dinners connected with the debut easily run into the thousands of dollars. People expect the vast majority of Creoles making formal debuts to come from uptown New Orleans and its outposts, the Garden District and Old Metairie.

Claiming wealthy and prominent individuals as Creole enhances the social status of all Creoles, but it also extends the boundaries of the category. Non-Creole members of Comus and Rex told me that there are no more than ten prominent Creole families in New Orleans today. The names of these families appear often enough in newspapers, Mardi Gras listings, and civic announcements to be recognized generally in New Orleans as prominent and influential. Many of the not-so-prominent Creole informants identified all of these families as Creole, although the discerning few who are themselves prominent and Creole in every possible way question a number of these families' claims to Creole identity. Indeed, several of the families have French or Spanish ancestors, but they do not date back to colonial times. One has a name that first appeared in Louisiana in colonial times, but may not be descended from that colonial ancestor. Several of these families are described as recent *arrivés*, and as newly prominent figures in the community they appear to be sensitive and defensive concerning their background. For members of at least two of these families, it is problematic, even embarrassing, that they never lived on (or near) Esplanade. They may explain their nonconforming residential characteristics by claiming that life was safer and schools better uptown even by the turn of the twentieth century. But their nonconformance with the pattern serves as constant source of suspicion about their "true" social identity. Individuals such as these form part of the Creole community primarily, if not exclusively, because of their current sociopolitical influence or economic power. Without their elite status their claims would be far weaker. And without these politically and economically powerful individuals to claim as Creole, the impoverished community of Creoles would have only tenuous claims to elite status. The symbiosis is functional, but clearly conducive to over-representation.

The Best and the Brightest

Indicative of similar colored Creole claims to elite status is the pride they take in St. Augustine High School in the Seventh Ward. A January 21, 1976, article in the *Figaro* vividly captured the unabashed elitism of St. Aug's in its title, "Are St. Augustine's Blacks New Orleans' Best and Brightest?" For obvious reasons numerous colored Creole informants called my attention to the article. It began with the statement that St. Aug's "may very well provide the best secondary education in town—in any school, black or white," and that its "academic record is truly incredible—especially for a school only twenty-five years old." It mentioned the four Presidential Scholars the school produced in the previous decade (who made up 20 percent of the entire number chosen in the state from all Louisiana schools); it mentioned the five St. Aug's alumni graduating from Harvard that year and noted that Metairie Country Day could boast only two, Isidore Newman only one, and McDonough 35 also only one. It quoted Warren Bell, television station WDSU's weekend anchorman, Presidential Scholar, and Yale graduate, who simply said that "the Josephites were as effete and elite as the Jesuits, and they made us uppity and elite." Then he added that "the other blacks at Yale used to talk about those 'New Orleans Nigros.' Even in New Haven, they knew what St. Aug's was. A lot of times, we came in and took things over." "To black New Orleans," the article insisted, "St. Augustine means quite a lot more. Going to St. Aug's means starting life with an extra shove and a few advantages that other, less fortunate people don't have. Ambitious black families will scrimp mightily to keep a son there. (Tuition is $645 a year.)" So strong is the sense of superiority of everything and everyone surrounding St. Aug's that Alden McDonald, president of the Liberty Bank, "makes a big point of telling everybody that he got where he is even without a St. Aug's background."

Located in the heart of the Seventh Ward, within walking distance of Corpus Christi parish and run by the same order of Josephites that is historically linked to the colored Creole community, St. Augustine is the pride of the Creole community and symbol of its claims to elite status. Not all of its students today would be considered Creole by Creole families of the neighborhood, but all are forever members of a growing community intimately linked to the heart of the colored Creole community.

Elitism and pride derive largely from the privileged legal status of the persons of color whom Creoles tend to claim as ancestors, but much is also educational and occupational in origin. A few years ago, a black radio announcer accused the Creole Fiesta people on the air of being separatists. Active Fiesta people, incensed by the dangerous publicity but privately proud of their avowed separatism, got him to retract the statement "every hour on the air" for a period of three days. Later, two of the heads of the organization went to the Bicentennial Commission to criticize them for not supporting the activities of the Fiesta, which like other culturally oriented groups in the city sought to keep alive traditions of the city's historic past. The Bicentennial Commission offered them money to compensate for the oversight, but they refused to accept any. "Creoles have pride," they told me. "We know they didn't expect us to refuse their money but we told them that all our needs were taken care of."

Economic independence is highly valued in the colored Creole community. Being on welfare is a source of embarrassment, and many of those who succumb to government aid eventually drop out of the community. On the other hand, blacks with steady jobs, respectable professions or financial independence frequently marry into the community and become Creole at least by association.

The Creoles' image of economic independence is rooted in the socioeconomic condition of the free people of color before the Civil War. They were slave owners and land owners; above all, they were skilled laborers. Of the 1,834 free Negro heads of households in New Orleans in 1830, 752 (41 percent) owned at least one slave (Woodson 1924: 9–15; 1925: 31–38). New Orleans' persons of color were far wealthier, more secure or established than blacks elsewhere in Louisiana. Indeed, of the 964 colored slaveowners in Louisiana in 1830, 752 (78 percent) lived in New Orleans, and only 212 came from elsewhere. Conservative estimates of the value of real estate owned by the free people of color of New Orleans from the 1830s to the Civil War start at about $2 million (Puckett 1906: 59, 61–62; De Bow 1857: 217; Everett 1952: 227–228; de Gournay 1894: 513; Reinders 1965: 280–281). Estimates vary as widely as the tax records on which they are based. But whether the figure is a "mere" $2 million or the more substantial $22 million claimed by de Gournay in 1894 for the antebellum period, New Orleans' free Negroes still owned more real estate than free Negroes in other American cities (Jackson 1942: 138; Harris 1936: 7–8; Wright 1921: 185). If $2 million is divided by the 10,689 free people of color listed living in New Orleans in 1860 (U.S. Census 1860), the per capita real estate value of the city's free people of color would appear to have been $187, or slightly more than $1,000 per head of household—not an insubstantial figure for its day. In addition, tax records often greatly underestimated real estate values. Real estate, slaves, stocks, bonds, business property, horses and wagons were generally undervalued. In fact, in the case of slaves, market prices were two to three times greater than assessed value (Reinders 1965: 281). It would not be far-fetched under these conditions to suppose that the average free-colored household in New Orleans in the 1850s owned several thousand dollars worth of real estate.

Education and occupation contributed to the economic independence of the antebellum Creole of color. Although colored Creoles cannot boast an ancestry dominated by professionals (as white Creoles can or at least do), they still take pride in the firm footing of the free people of color in the New Orleans economy in the years before the Civil War. The vast majority of free-colored adult males in New Orleans in 1850 were skilled workers. (See Table 8.6.) Only 179 were classified as laborers; only 70 to 100 more might be considered holding unskilled jobs (cf. also Reinders 1965: 275). Thus between 80 and 85 percent of adult colored males in New Orleans at the time were educated enough and technically trained enough to be skilled workers, clerks, teachers, even medical doctors. In fact, the ratio of skilled to unskilled among free-colored men was considerably higher than among Irish and German immigrants (cf., e.g., Reinders 1965: 274).

Economic security helped counteract the effects of laws of the 1840s and 1850s that increasingly restricted the freedom of the free people of color (Everett 1952; Stahl 1942). Free-colored rights to own property, to buy and sell, and to sue were never challenged.

Throughout the years, the free people of color and many of their descendants carved out their own occupational niche. Printing, baking, sailmaking, glazing, lithography, engraving, and piloting were controlled by whites, who generally excluded blacks and colored from these crafts. By mid-nineteenth century, much of the service sector in hotels, restaurants, and transportation had become essentially German and Irish. By the 1850s the docks had been turned over to Irish immigrants. But the free people of color retained control over a series of crafts now traditionally associated with the colored Creole community, alleged descendants of the free-colored. Carpentry and cabinetmaking, cigar manufacturing, masonry, housepainting, and plastering dominate the economic image of the colored Creole. Less than half of all free-colored New Orleans males over the age of fifteen in 1850 practiced these crafts, but those who did dominated the profession.

The plasterer's union, the bricklayer's union, and the car-

Table 8.6
Occupations of Free-Colored Males over 15 Years of Age,
New Orleans, 1850

Apprentices	4	Jewelers	5
Architects	1	Laborers	179
Bakers	1	Lithographers	1
Barbers	41	Mariners	10
Barkeepers	2	Marketmen	25
Blacksmiths	15	Masons	278
Boardinghouse keepers	18	Mechanics	52
Boatmen	37	Merchants	64
Bookbinders	4	Ministers	1
Brickmakers	2	Musicians	4
Brokers	9	Music teachers	1
Butchers	18	Overseers	11
Cabinetmakers	19	Painters	28
Capitalists	4	Peddlers	9
Car men	39	Pilots	2
Carpenters	355	Planters	2
Cigarmakers	156	Sailmakers	2
Clerks	61	Sextons	1
Coachmen	10	Ship carpenters	6
Cooks	25	Shoemakers	92
Coopers	43	Stevedores	7
Doctors	4	Stewards	9
Engineers	1	Students	7
Gardeners	9	Tailors	82
Gunsmiths	4	Teachers	12
Hostlers	3	Upholsterers	8
Hunters	7		

TOTAL   1,792 (1,463 were labeled mulatto)

Source: Statistical View of the United States, *A Compendium of the Seventh Census* (Washington, D.C., 1854), p. 81.

penter's union—the three crafts most strongly associated with the colored Creoles—were founded around the turn of the century by Creoles of color, and Creoles of color continue to this day to dominate the upper echelons of all three organizations. The locations of these unions' business offices today show their strong Seventh Ward affiliation. The plasterers' union (1419 St. Bernard) is just a few blocks down the street from Corpus Christi Church; the bricklayers' union (414 North Galvez) is in Trémé, the old and decaying Creole neighborhood, just east of Canal Street; and the carpenters' union (315 South Broad), of the three the one to have strayed the most, is but three blocks southwest of Canal Street, just west of the traditional Creole neighborhoods. In a city the size of New Orleans, the location of all these unions' business offices in one small neighborhood is clearly by choice rather than accident.

But as economic opportunities have expanded for blacks, colored Creoles have shifted occupations in accordance with their claims to elite status. The equation of skilled labor with elite status has been called into question. Carpentry, bricklaying, and plastering attract fewer and fewer young men of colored Creole families. Instead, Creoles seek professional training and clerical or bureaucratic occupations, but rarely blue-collar jobs. In the past decade more than 90 percent of St. Augustine High School's graduates have gone to college. Few seek any form of manual labor upon completion of their college courses.

The move is strong to occupations that require more years of schooling and carry high status nationally. Only 5 percent of Charles Palazzolo's 1954/55 sample of heads of households of Corpus Christi parish could be considered professional (Palazzolo 1955: 121) and 31 to 32 percent, at the most, white collar. Yet occupations requiring higher education ranked at the top of a list of occupations that Roland Wingfield asked informants to rate in 1960/61 (Wingfield 1961: 92; see Table 8.7). Earning power may have played a part in the ranking, but it was clearly not the main determinant. Priests were at the top, though nationally in a separate survey they were ranked eighth (Wingfield

*Table 8.*7
Wingfield's 1961 Comparison of Rank and Scores Accorded to
Occupations by Creole Sample Population and Population Surveyed
in the National Opinion Research Center Study

Occupation	Ranking		Score	
	Creole	*National*	*Creole*	*National*
Priest	1	8	97	86
Physician [a]	2	2	96	93
Supreme Court Justice	3	1	96	96
Lawyer	4	7	93	86
College professor	5	3	91	89
Architect [b]	6	5	91	86
Dentist [b]	7	6	91	86
Banker	8	4	86	88
Building contractor [a]	9	9	83	79
Public school teacher [a]	10	10	82	78
Undertaker [a]	11	11	75	72
Carpenter	12	14	68	65
Insurance agent [b]	13	12	68	68
Mail carrier [b]	14	13	67	66
Plumber [b]	15	16	66	63
Barber [b]	16	17	65	59
Singer in a night club	17	20	61	52
Automobile repairman	18	15	61	63
Restaurant cook [b]	19	18	52	54
Truck driver [b]	20	19	51	54
Taxi driver [a]	21	21	50	49
Dock worker [b]	22	23	46	47
Restaurant worker [b]	23	22	44	48
Janitor [a]	24	24	40	44
Shoe shiner [a]	25	25	27	33

Source: Roland Wingfield, "The Creoles of Color," master's thesis, Louisiana
State University, 1961, p. 92.
[a] Same rank for Creole and national sample.
[b] One rank difference between Creole and national sample.

1961: 121); college professors were fifth, before architects, dentists, bankers, and contractors. Traditionally Creole occupations fell in the middle of the ranking, above unskilled service workers but below professionals. Yet, as if to assert traditional Creole claims to elite status, carpenters were ranked higher in this community than they are nationally.

Much of the tension between current and traditional symbols of elite status finds its way into Mardi Gras club memberships. Colored Creoles attend between eighteen and twenty official, named, annual Mardi Gras balls. The balls are not all run by Creoles, though all claim some degree of elitism and exclusivity, which ideologically, at least, links them to the Creole community. Seven balls serve as debutante cotillions. Most require their guests to wear formal dress or specific costumes. The names of several suggest exclusivity and worth: Original Exclusive 20's, the Exclusive 20's, the Plantation Revelers, the Beau Brummels, the Rhinestones, and the BonTemps. The Bunch Ball, the Capetowners, the Vikings, and the Zulus[4] suggest special group identity. Invitations to the balls are free, but members must pay dues during the year. Membership dues range from a low of $50 to a high of $500 a year. The fee is high enough to attract only the better-off as members. Indeed, dues are so high in at least one case that their main function is to exclude "the riff-raff." In the best of the white balls, members pay only $100 to $200 a year in dues; several of the black balls require much more, indicating that financial ability is at times considered more important than looks or ancestry.

The Bunch Ball combines financial ability with occupational status. The members are mostly professionals, doctors, lawyers, and professors. Their reputation is symptomatic. They are respected for their educational achievements and standard of living, but they are disliked for their overt snobbism and get labeled *nouveau riches*. One informant argued bluntly that "they consider themselves a bunch of jackasses; they prance around in capes and drummajor hats."

At the other end of the spectrum is the oldest of the colored

Mardi Gras balls, the Original Illinois Club. Founded in 1894, it has been to many a monument to self-respect and a symbol of colored Creoles' relentless struggle to assert their rights to separate and elite status. Jim Crow laws were sweeping the South; white Creoles saw their social status increasingly challenged by unknowing immigrants and adverse economic conditions. The colored Creoles' response to both was a salvaging operation: the formation of an exclusive club that would maintain the highest standards of propriety among its members and their families, and would serve as a cultural and social oasis for them. The majority of its founding members were skilled workers and craftsmen. They *were* the colored elite. But few were professional or elite by modern standards of the Creole community. Family connection, a tradition of literacy, and a style or manner became trademarks of the club. Then in the spring of 1926 a split occurred within the ranks of the Original Illinois Club. Informants often cloak discussions of the split with an air of secrecy or confidentiality. They say the members disagreed on club policy or were simply incompatible. But the source of alleged incompatibility was tension between two concepts of social worth, the traditional family-oriented, color-dominated standard of distinction and one based on achievement rather than ascription. An older Creole confided that "the Young Men's people were not accepted in the Original's social world, they didn't have the right *blood line!*"

Association with the Original Illinois Club strongly implies Creole identity. Association with the Young Men's initially distanced one from the Creole community. Yet as the years go by and the Young Men's Illinois Club gains prestige with age, the implication that the Young Men are not Creole disappears and is replaced by the expectation that, in fact, they are Creole through social connection, if not necessarily through ancestry.

The Creoles have been quick to adapt strategies that maintain their elite status throughout changing economic conditions. Most significant is the incredible push to acquire higher education. Whereas Palazzolo found in 1954/55 a median of 8.3 years of schooling for members of Corpus Christi parish age fifteen and older (Palazzolo 1955: 107), today's equivalent in a sample of 356 Creoles identified as such by a team of informants is 13.3; 29 did not complete high school, 164 are high school graduates without college education, 48 have some college education, 89 are college graduates, and 26 have graduate or professional training. Among the 191 still living in the Seventh Ward in or near Corpus Christi parish, the median is somewhat lower (see Table 8.8), but not nearly as low as Palazzolo reported in 1954. The difference in educational achievement between the Creole residents of the Seventh Ward and those now residing elsewhere is significant and symptomatic of yet another Creole strategy for maintaining elite status. The educated pursue economic opportunities wherever they may present themselves. Since the mid-1950s, these have often come from out of state. Only 35.7

Table 8.8
Educational Achievements of Adults in the Seventh Ward Compared to Those Living Elsewhere in New Orleans or Out of State
(1975 – 1977)

	Seventh Ward	Percent	Outside	Percent
Some graduate school	4	2.1	22	13.3
College graduates	29	15.2	60	36.4
High school plus at least one semester more	18	9.4	30	18.2
High school graduates	111	58.1	53	32.1
High school dropouts or below	29	15.2	0	0.0
	191	100.0	165	100.0
Median years of schooling	12.2		13.3	

percent of the college-educated in this sample remains in the Seventh Ward. Nineteen live to the northeast of the Corpus Christi area in Gentilly, fourteen in the brand-new suburbs of New Orleans East, sixteen in southern California, six in Texas, two in older suburbs across the river from the Seventh Ward in New Orleans, two in Chicago, one in Europe, and fourteen scattered throughout the United States. Note as well that all twenty-nine Creoles without a full high school education live in the Seventh Ward, and that 62.5 percent of those without a college degree still live in the Seventh Ward.

As education increases, people move out, first to Gentilly, then to Pontchartrain Park, and more recently to New Orleans East. Some leave the state altogether, usually to go to Los Angeles, where the Creole community is now sizeable enough to stage a small Mardi Gras celebration each year, to identify a particular Catholic church with Corpus Christi, and to support several grocery stores, barbers, and travel agents. The residential pattern is so strong that it becomes part of the Creole process of inferring group identity.

When a Creole identifies a person as Creole, (s)he is not necessarily saying that that person has French or Spanish colonial ancestry, or that (s)he is white or colored. (S)he may be making a statement about the person's looks, place of residence, manner of speech, or the socioeconomic characteristics of his or her nineteenth-century ancestors. All the connotations or associations of Creole that exist today, and many of those that have been passed down through the generations, play a part in a Creole's decision to identify himself, herself, or others as Creole.

Analytically it is a classic case of pragmatics in the long run determining semantics (cf. Silverstein 1976; Domínguez 1984). When Creole became the label for an interest group during the nineteenth century, it ceased to designate an aspect of a person's identity that was interesting but politically insignificant and became the name of a social group as well as of a social category. Characteristics of members of the group began to affect the meaning of the term by affecting the connotations of the category. When the people identified as Creole were generally well-educated, land-rich, and politically powerful, *Creole* came to connote these characteristics. When the people identified as Creole were proud, colored but light-skinned, refined, and well-educated, *Creole* came to connote pride, near-Caucasian features, social refinement, and education. Likewise, when Creoles were stereotyped as impoverished aristocrats, the senses of *Creole* came to include the notion of an impoverished elite. Socioeconomic associations in turn became indices of Creole identity. Identification as a member of the category would imply a certain look, a certain type of behavior, a certain economic status, a pattern of residence, a religious affiliation, a pattern of schooling, and memberships in certain social clubs. In turn, a certain look, certain behavior patterns, a particular economic status, and specific residential, religious, educational, and social characteristics might lead to the inference that a person was Creole.

Identities may be institutionalized metasemantically (by defining the labels of identities), but they are shaped in the long run by the pragmatics of labeling. Like other lexemes, identity labels acquire meanings in and from their contexts of usage. A different kind of manipulation goes on here. It is not the visible, public, and political manipulation of definitions of identity by either individuals or groups that alone turns "non-Creoles" into "Creoles." It is what I would call a *logical* manipulation—based on implication and inference rather than the sheer exercise of power, one in which individuals are both the doers and the agents.

Chapter 9

CONCLUSION

I argued at the outset that non-Louisianians either tend to assume that Creoles are people of mixed African and French ancestry, or admit that they are confused about the racial and ethnic identity of Louisiana's Creole population. That non-Louisianians would not know who or what a Creole is should not in itself be all that surprising. The issue here, however, is how and why there is also little consensus today among southern Louisianians about the definition of a Creole and the racial and ethnic characteristics of the state's Creole population. The chapters of this book have examined forms and processes of social classification that impinge on the identification of Louisiana's Creoles and account for the lack of consensus. They have, in the process, also illustrated dimensions of social classification that carry significant analytic and political implications beyond the boundaries of Louisiana. I shall attempt in this final chapter to highlight those implications as I bring together the pieces of the puzzle.

To begin with, the existence of alternative definitions of *Creole* and of alternative criteria by which persons come to be identified as Creoles undermines a number of common assumptions about ethnic identity. At this point the Barthian approach seems useful and applicable.

For one, most individuals have a large number of potential identities by ancestry alone. A person who moves back far enough in the family genealogy is likely to find ancestors of different national origin, social class, and in many cases even racial origin. Thus, identification with a particular national, social, or racial group actually entails selecting out of that large number of ancestors one or several with whom to identify. The person's "ethnic" identity cannot, therefore, be biologically determined, for that would require the person to take into account all of his or her ancestors and not just a selected few. Selection involves an individual act, an act of choice, and a set of conditions—social, economic, epistemological, and political—that make only certain choices possible.

But there is more. The dispute between the two sectors of Louisiana's population that identify themselves as Creole, in addition, hinges on the status connotations of the labels *Creole, white,* and *black.* The long history of African slavery in the United States and of white ownership of African slaves left in Louisiana, as in other parts of the United States, a traditional association of whites with upper status and of blacks with lower status. To white Creoles today the mere suggestion of possible African ancestry invokes a lowering of social and economic status for the people in question. To colored or black Creoles, on the other hand, the claim of at least partial European ancestry accords the group in question a status (or an expectation of status) higher than that accorded to "pure" blacks. Moreover, to colored or black Creoles the association with early European settlers in Louisiana signals a tie to the state's "old families" and, by extension, to higher social status. Thus, to identify someone as Creole is to invoke in the course of a particular conversation historically linked connotations of social and economic status. But this is not to say just that "ethnic" identities have status connotations; it is to say that New Orleanians' perception of status, of how things used to be and how in their opinion they ought to be, is often the major criterion by which individuals are identified as Creole. What many of us normally assume to be likely *connotations* of membership in a particular group are, in the case of southern Louisiana often, if not always, the crucial variables that individual New Orleanians manipulate in making themselves members of a group, or in identifying others as members of a group. Status, then, is frequently more of a determining factor in group membership than genealogical ancestry.

Actually the efforts of many individuals in different sectors of the population in southern Louisiana to define exactly who or what a Creole is testify ironically to how many people in the region could actually qualify as members of the group. Clearly there would be little need to define *Creole* if Creole identity were naturally given or otherwise unambiguously delimited. It is precisely because so many people from different sectors of the population claim to be Creole using one or several *possible* criteria that some of these sectors push to formulate definitions that make Creole identity more precise and, thereby, more exclusive. But, of course, in formulating definitions they guarantee, perhaps unwillingly and unwittingly, that the lines they draw around "Creole identity" are far from "natural."

Further supporting the Barthian argument, individuals clearly jockey for position by taking into account the status association of the labels *Creole, white,* and *black,* considering in the process the range of identities available to them and relying on any of those possible criteria. Most often they will identify with the group or sector (for which they qualify) that is highest in status or with which they wish to identify for social, political, or economic reasons in the context in which they find themselves. Thus, within the course of a lifetime a New Orleanian may identify himself as a member of several groups and, if successful in eliciting recognition of each of those identities from appropriate sectors of the population, may come to be identified by members of different groups as one of their own. Despite the serious attempts by many New Orleanians to delimit the boundaries around the group with which they identify, the common jockeying for position means that there are no fixed boundaries around any groups and that it may be stretching the point to speak of groups in the context of southern Louisiana.

And if boundaries are as fluid as much of the evidence suggests, then there can be no significant difference in ideas, beliefs, or expectations held by individuals in these effectively overlapping sectors. If there are groups at all, it is, I am arguing, not because of cultural differentiation. This is not to say, of course, that members of groups do not often seek ways to assert and thereby prescribe differentiation from one another. But if groups were really culturally distinct, why would they make much of an effort to seek external recognition of their cultural distinctiveness? In the case of the definition of *Creole,* we see a strong difference of opinion, but we also see a widespread agreement about the status associations of being Creole, white, or black and about the social and political consequences of including or excluding those who are legally black from the group labeled Creole. Thus, both sectors of the population share basic premises about the nature of stratification in southern Louisiana and about the connections between ancestry, social status, and access to property. In fact, both sectors use these same premises to formulate their differences of opinion about Creole identity. Ironically, their efforts to differentiate themselves from each other highlight in this sense how much "culture" they actually share.

But individual manipulation of labels of identity, albeit frequent and important, tells only part of the story. Here the analysis necessarily departs from the Barthian formulation of ethnicity. Louisianians manipulate their own and other peoples' identities by playing with the available labels *subject to their current meanings.* For the manipulation of labels to be successful, the meanings of those labels must be public—shared or at least verbalized by at least a sector of the population. Whence that public meaning?

Social identities, like material objects, become public "knowledge" when they are named. Without a label to capture our conception of them, they have little social relevance because there is no "knowledge" of their existence in the first place. The emergence of a new social label, therefore, carries with it the elevation of a new social identity to the domain of public "knowledge." As it emerges as a new "thing" in the public domain, it is shaped and reshaped by other ideas and attitudes that are also part of public "knowledge." It cannot stand apart from these other ideas and attitudes because the label that officially announces its birth makes it part of that same public "knowledge." To speak of social identities, then, is to invoke all those ideas and attitudes that form part of a particular understanding of the world, an understanding that in the public sphere of a given society is that society's knowledge of the world in which its members live.

But social identities are also unlike material objects. Whereas material objects have a concrete existence whether or not people recognize their existence, social identities do not. An identity is a conception of the self, a selection of physical, psychological, emotional, or social attributes of particular individuals; it is not an individual as a concrete thing. It is only in the act of naming an identity, defining an identity, or stereotyping an identity that that identity emerges as a concrete reality. Not only does that identity have no social relevance when it is not named; it simply does not exist when it has not been conceived and elevated to public consciousness. The phrases *terms of identity, definitions of terms of identity,* and *stereotypes of identities* are therefore highly redundant. Taken together, these terms, definitions, and stereotypes are the identities themselves. They are, or represent, the conceptions of self that we commonly know as social identities.

Inherently a part of a system of conceptualizing the world that many of us have come to call culture, social identities must be described as bounded by the context of culture. But as William James implied when he argued that words have "practical cash values" (1949 [1907]: 53), specific identities emerge as concrete realities not only within some broadly defined context of culture but more particularly also within a given stream of experience. That experience is personal, situational, familial, and more generally social. It includes situations and actions whose character is primarily political and those delineated by one's access or lack of access to the means of production. Thus, the concretization of a social identity may occur, broadly speaking, within the context of culture, but usually occurs more specifically within a certain sector of a population that generally shares a common culture but also shares a more specific stream of experience. Outside that context of experience, where the identity is neither named nor defined, that identity remains never more than immanent.

Labels, then, reflect both a larger body of "knowledge," which is in itself an understanding of the world, and the context of experience of those for whom the labels are meaningful. This dual reflexivity means that the conceptualization and therefore concretization of a social identity occurs in two contexts simultaneously—one epistemological and the other social, economic, and political. Taken together, they constitute the conditions under which only *certain* choices are deemed possible—conceivable and realizable.

This is seen quite clearly when the contexts change. Social identities, thus dependent on the epistemological, social, economic, and political contexts in which they are meaningful, not only change in connotation, evaluation, and status, but also often in their very definition. We have seen racial boundaries change significantly in Louisiana. As boundaries shifted over the years, the categories of identity that they delimited shifted both in definition and composition. New criteria were applied, sometimes legally, sometimes socially, to circumscribe "racial" identities. The results were changes of identity for large sectors of the population.

Legal history epitomizes the overall process. In it we find a tradition of instituting legal constraints to racial self-determination. In it we find ample evidence of the changeability and arbitrariness of the boundaries of legally instituted racial categories. In it we document the persistent struggles between individual choices of racial identity and externally imposed limits to individual choice. And in it we see the dialectical interplay between public opinion and power politics as determinants of the principles of social classification.

But with it we have a problem. Media reactions to the Phipps case picked on Louisiana for having a statute that set the boundaries of racial identity. The implication was that such a law was by definition capricious and arbitrary and that identities so circumscribed were unreal or unnatural. Explicitly, the argument was that legal determination of identities was a blatant form of the exercise of power politics in manipulating reality. Implicitly, the argument seemed to be that such a law went against nationwide public opinion. It is as if reactions were deliberate attempts to counter the apparent confirmation in the Phipps case of conscious manipulation as the modus operandi of the law.

Law and ethnicity seem to hold a similar place in popular beliefs about American society. The tendency is to view both as above reproach: the first guided by principles of fairness and the second by the laws of nature. Manipulation counters the spirit of both. Add to it an emphasis on freedoms granted to individual citizens by the United States Constitution, and the stage is set for an a priori rejection of an easily documented fact: that identities are neither created by nature nor subject to the free exercise of individual choice. The conclusion seems radically un-American.

And yet, of course, the tradition of instituting legal constraints to racial self-determination is far from unique to Louisiana. In the twentieth century at least a third of the states of the United States have defined the boundaries of racial categories by law, and not all of these have been southern states. A number of states in the South and West have defined the boundaries of American Indian identity. A clause in the Hawaiian Homes Commission Act of July 9, 1921, which is still on the books in Hawaii, defines "native Hawaiian" to mean "any descendant of not less than one-half part of the blood of the races inhabiting the Hawaiian Islands previous to 1778" (HHCA2-201). But it is, not surprisingly, in antimiscegenation statutes that we find clauses specifying the boundaries of racial categories.

These specifications were still on the books when the United States Supreme Court finally declared antimiscegenation statutes unconstitutional in 1967 (*Loving* v. *Brace*). North Carolina, Maryland, Tennessee, and Texas prohibited marriages between whites and "persons of Negro blood to the third generation." The North Carolina statute was explicit: "All marriages between a white person and a negro, or between a white person and a person of negro descent to the third generation inclusive, are forever prohibited, and shall be void" (N.C. Gen. Stat. 14-181—passed in 1953). This North Carolina statute was not officially repealed until 1973; the Maryland analogue not until 1967; the Tennessee statute (46-402 passed in 1955) remains on the books today, although article 11, section 14 of the state constitution, which had prohibited "the intermarriage of white persons with negroes, mulattoes, or persons of mixed blood, descended from a negro to the third generation inclusive" was repealed by popular vote in 1978. Texas article 4607 (adopted in 1951) was repealed in 1969.

Florida, Mississippi, Missouri, and South Carolina prohibited marriages between white persons and persons of more than one-eighth Negro blood. Consider the inclusive wording of two of these statutes. Florida statute 741.11 adopted in 1957 read: "The words 'negro,' 'colored,' 'colored persons,' 'mulatto' or 'persons of color,' when applied to persons, include every person having one-eighth or more of African or negro blood." Missouri statute 563.240 adopted in 1953 phrased it differently: "No person having one-eighth part or more of negro blood shall be permitted to marry any white person, nor shall any white person be permitted to marry any negro or person having one-eighth part or more of negro blood; and . . . the jury trying any such case may determine the proportion of negro blood in any party to such marriage from the appearance of such a person." Like the first group of states discussed above, these four states kept their antimiscegenation statutes on the books until very recently. The 1957 Florida statute and the 1953 Missouri statutes were repealed in 1969. Article 14 of the Mississippi constitution forbidding miscegenation remains on the books, however, as does article 3 of the constitution of South Carolina.

Alabama, Arkansas, Georgia, and Virginia prohibited marriages between white persons and Negroes, mulattoes, or persons with any ascertainable trace of Negro blood. The yet unrepealed Alabama statutes (Const., art. 4 §102; Code tit. 14, §360 of 1940) prohibit marriages between whites and Negroes, or descendants of any Negroes. The wording is such as to subsume under *Negro* mulattoes and persons of color, this last type defined "as person[s] of mixed blood descended on the part of the father or mother from Negro ancestors, without reference to or limit of time or number of generations removed." Two Arkansas statutes—only recently repealed—forbade miscegenation. Statute 55-104 (from 1947) kept whites and Negroes or mulattoes from marrying legally. Statute 41-807, which prohibited "cohabitation of persons of the Caucasian race and of the negro race," specified the applicability of the anticoncubinage statute to "any person who has in his or her veins any Negro blood whatever" (Arkansas 41-808). A Georgia statute (79-103)—clearly in the books in 1958 (cf. Calhoun 1958: 237) but without a trace in the 1983 codebooks—actually defined persons of color: "All Negroes, mulattoes, mestizos, and their descendants, having any ascertainable trace of either Negro or African, West Indian, or Asiatic Indian blood in their veins, and all descendants of any person having either Negro or African, West Indian, or Asiatic Indian blood in his or her veins, shall be known in this State as persons of color" (Georgia 79-103).

A definition of *persons of African descent* appeared in the Oklahoma constitution throughout most of the 1960s. "Wherever in this Constitution and laws of this State, the word or words, 'colored' or 'colored race,' 'Negro' or 'Negro race,' are used, the same shall be construed to mean or apply to all persons of African descent. The term 'white race' shall include all other persons" (Oklahoma Constitution article 23, §11). The state's antimiscegenation statute (43, §12 dating from 1954 and repealed in 1969) used this definition to prohibit the marriage of any person of African descent to any person not of African descent. An extended definition of both colored persons and Indians remained in the Virginia statutes until 1975:

> Every person in whom there is ascertainable any Negro blood shall be deemed and taken to be a colored person, and every person not a colored person having one-fourth or more of American Indian blood shall be deemed an American Indian; except that members of Indian tribes, existing in this Commonwealth having one-fourth or more of Indian blood and less than one-sixteenth of Negro blood shall be deemed tribal Indians (Virginia 1-14, repealed in 1975).

In addition, the state of Virginia kept in its codebooks until 1968 a statute prohibiting the marriage of a white person to anyone other than whites or those descended from whites and American Indians.

Two border states—Kentucky and West Virginia—prohibited marriages between whites and Negroes, mulattoes, or persons of the Negro race through the 1960s, but unlike most of the others mentioned above, they failed to specify exactly to whom this prohibition applied.

Perhaps the most surprising of the findings is that similar statutes existed in California and that there, too, it took decades to repeal them. A proviso was added to the statutes in 1880 against issuing a license authorizing the marriage of a white person with a Negro, mulatto, or Mongolian. A 1933 amendment added the term *Malayan* to the forbidden categories. It was not until 1959 that these statutory racial restrictions on marriage were deleted, and not until 1961 that the legislature formally allowed applicants for marriage licenses *not* to state their race or color.

The list is not exhaustive. If we move away from the law strictly defined and into administrative policies and guidelines, we find ample evidence of continued severe institutional restrictions to self-determination. Affirmative action may, ironically, be the best example.

We noted earlier that the United States Supreme Court allows institutions to establish criteria of racial classification to be used to classify anyone concerned, whenever the Court deems it *necessary* for the purposes of affirmative action. Increasingly over the last twenty years, forms that have asked for racial identification include a "racial category" labeled Puerto Rican, another labeled Mexican American/Chicano, and frequently also one designated as Cuban. When the options given are any of these in addition to white and black, and the respondent is asked to check off only one box, that respondent is effectively being forced to identify himself or herself as *neither* white nor black.

Some forms, such as the admissions form used by Duke University, explicitly deny Hispanics the possibility of identifying themselves as either white or black. That form asks individuals to identify themselves as belonging to one of five categories:

White (not Hispanic)
Black (not Hispanic)
Hispanic
Asian or Pacific Islander
American Indian or Alaskan Native

It does not even offer the possibility of checking oneself off as "other."

This form is particularly deceptive. It appears to be broad-minded in indicating that there may be Hispanics who are white and Hispanics who are black. That is clearly more than is indicated on forms that simply give white, black, and Hispanic as possible alternatives. And yet the explicit separation of "Hispanics" from the rest of the population has the effect of conveying the message that it is not interested in how Hispanics identify themselves.

In addition, it is well known that many agencies and institutions ignore what the respondent checks off on a form, if the respondent has an obvious Spanish surname or indicates that he or she was born in a Spanish-speaking country and yet did not mark the box labeled Hispanic or Spanish-surnamed. Private institutions frequently do this in counting the number of "minorities" on their staffs. Clearly government affirmative action pressures are given more weight than individual choice of racial identification.

But there is, I am arguing, more in these practices than the simple manifestation of political pressure. In the case of the Spanish-surnamed, as in the case of colored Creoles, there is a rejection of the possibility of relying on them to identify themselves racially—or, to be more precise, to identify themselves as black rather than white when they have African ancestry.

In fact, the reference to the Hispanic Caribbean is telling. Indeed, when given the choice of identifying themselves as either white or black, most Spanish-speaking people from the Caribbean identify themselves as white (as was patently the case when most Puerto Ricans identified themselves as white on the 1960 United States Census before a "Puerto Rican" racial category appeared on these forms). The pattern is reminiscent of Louisiana.

Like Louisiana, the islands of the Caribbean have a history of extensive plantations and African slave labor. And like Louisiana, they have a history of extensive miscegenation, especially in the Spanish-speaking countries. Over the years, color terms other than *white* and *black* proliferated. The pattern holds throughout the Caribbean and those parts of South America with a history of African slavery. In a national sample of 100 Brazilians, Harris (1970) collected 492 terms he called racial or color terms. Sanjek (1971) discovered 116 terms in a similar study of a Brazilian village; Taylor (1959) elicited 40 terms in Runaway Bay, Jamaica, to denote 24 adult members of the community; Alexander (1977) elicited 12 terms from 9 informants in a study of middle-class Jamaicans; and Domínguez (1973) elicited 58 terms from a sample of 50 Cubans, 56 terms from a sample of 43 Puerto Ricans, and 25 terms from a sample of 11 Dominicans in a study of ethnic, racial, and social class identity among Spanish-speaking Caribbean migrants in New York City. Clearly large numbers of those with African ancestry do not label themselves black nor are they labeled by others as black in everyday discourse.

Moreover, if we look at the pattern of usage of these numerous terms, we find a flexibility and creativity that is very wide-spread. Every study of racial or color terms in the Caribbean documents widespread overlap in the use of these terms. Harris (1970), finding no obvious logic to account for the overlap, concluded that patterns of usage could only be interpreted as expressions of social class, and that racial identity was exclusively the equivalent of social class identity. Sanjek (1971) found that not all 116 terms used by his informants were socially significant but that there was still great "ambiguity" in the way the most frequently used terms were used. Alexander (1977) found middle-class Jamaicans using themselves as referential points of departure. Finding a place for themselves on the color spectrum, they tended to use a limited number of terms to refer to "grades" of lightness or darkness. The term they chose for themselves largely determined which way they skewed their own system of racial classification. Labelle (1978) found variations in the use of color terms in Haiti to be largely the product of the different positions her informants occupied vis-à-vis the means of production.

In my own sample of Spanish-speaking Caribbean people (1973), individuals tended to apply terms according to their social connotations or associations. Certain terms were considered more respectful than others; some terms were considered familiar; others had pejorative connotations. In the act of actually applying a given term to an individual, the speaker's respect, affection, or dislike for the object of his or her reference influenced the final choice of color term. The term *trigueño* was chosen over *negro, prieto* over *moreno, blanquita* (using the diminutive to connote familiarity and affection) over *india,* or *cocolo* (with negative connotations) over *trigueño.*

But the overlap is not just the product of deliberate manipulation on the part of the speaker for the sake of achieving particular social ends. It is also the product of epistemological, social, economic, and political conditions that led to the disappearance of firm boundaries between color categories in the Caribbean, except perhaps in the most elite circles of each society. For example, in Dominican and Puerto Rican Spanish, the terms *trigueño* and *indio* signify an intermediate range of the color spectrum, but the boundaries between them are often vague. There is some consensus that *trigueños* have kinky hair and *indios* have straight or slightly wavy hair, but there is no specific complex of features signified by these two terms. When the terms are used, the messages they convey depend, then, on the conceptual opposition the speaker has in mind. An individual may be identified as *indio, trigueño, blanco, prieto,* or whatever in different contexts by different people or even by the same person.

The same fluidity of boundaries is evident in censuses of the Puerto Rican population since the middle of the nineteenth century. The percentage of the population identified as *blanco* (as opposed to *mulato* and *negro*) has risen steadily and significantly, despite the fact that there has been no massive immigration of "whites" during the period. In 1846, *blancos* constituted 48.76 percent of the population. By 1910, they were 65.5 percent and, by 1950, 77 percent of the population (Rodríguez Cruz, cited in Seda Bonilla 1968). Such shifts in the "racial" composition of the population could not have occurred if whiteness had been based on the principle of purity of white ancestry. There is simply no evidence of radical differences in fertility rates. And unlike most states in the United States South, Puerto Rico did not institute legal definitions of racial categories once it repealed in 1870 the purity of white ancestry provisions it had inherited from the Spanish codes, which restricted certain elite professions and positions to those of "pure blood." Clearly a large sector of the population "became" white over three to four generations in an atmosphere that valued whiteness, stressed phenotype over ancestry, and left the government out of the process of determining its citizens' racial identities.

To force Spanish-speaking Caribbean people to choose between white and black is, then, to force them to collapse a non-dichotomous classification of color into one that is clearly dichotomous (reminiscent of the pressures that led to the transformation in mid- to late-nineteenth-century Louisiana of a ternary system of racial classification into a binary one). It is also to lead all those who usually identify themselves as anything but negro to identify themselves as white (reminiscent of the machinations of individual Creoles vis-à-vis the contemporary Creole controversy).

The refusal of these immigrants of limited African ancestry to call themselves black in the United States parallels many native-born Americans' struggle to be declared white. But the parallel is also there in the consequences of that refusal: the administrative creation of a Hispanic or Puerto Rican racial category continues the tradition of limiting the self-determination of racial and ethnic identification.

That the Louisiana story should repeat itself with Spanish-speaking Caribbean migrants now in the United States makes sense at two levels. Louisiana is both historically and geographically closely tied to Caribbean societies, and the phenotypic spread of the population in both regions testifies to a history of Afro-European coexistence and not infrequent miscegenation. But it would be a mistake, I think, to construe the Creole problem as a simple clash of *cultural* traditions—a Franco-Hispanic world view confronting an Anglo-Saxon perceptual grid—and see little implication for people or processes outside that geohistorical framework. The question I have addressed using the Louisiana Creoles as a case study concerns the extent to which institutional frameworks and epistemological discourses restrict the degree of freedom that individuals have to choose not only who but also *what* they are. In the elucidation of the limits and the manipulation that goes on within those limits, we discover, of course, at least as much about the structures and hierarchies of the larger society as we do about the characteristics and sensitivities of the group or context we have subjected to detailed scrutiny.

APPENDIX

Glendy Burke	1865
Hugh Kennedy	1865 – 1866
J. Ad. Rozier	1866
George Clark	1866
John T. Monroe	1866 – 1867
Edward Heath	1867 – 1868
John R. Conway	1868 – 1870
Benjamin Franklin Flanders	1870 – 1872
Louis A. Wiltz	1872 – 1874
Charles J. Leeds	1874 – 1876
Edward Pillsbury	1876 – 1878
Isaac W. Patton	1878 – 1880
Joseph A. Shakspeare	1880 – 1882
W. J. Behan	1882 – 1884
J. Valsin Guillotte	1884 – 1888
Joseph A. Shakspeare	1888 – 1892
John Fitzpatrick	1892 – 1896
Walter C. Flower	1896 – 1900
Paul Capdevielle	1900 – 1904
Martin Behrman	1904 – 1920
Andrew J. McShane	1920 – 1925
Martin Behrman	1925 – 1926
Arthur J. O'Keefe	1926 – 1930
T. Semmes Walmsley	1929 – 1930 (acting)
T. Semmes Walmsley	1930 – 1936
A. Miles Pratt	1936
Jesse S. Cave	1936
Fred A. Earhart	1936
Robert S. Maestri	1936 – 1946
De Lesseps S. Morrison	1946 – 1961
Victor H. Schiro	1961 – 1970
Moon Landrieu	1970 – 1978
Ernest Morial	1978 –

GOVERNORS OF LOUISIANA:

D'Iberville (leader of expedition)	1697
Sauville (first Royal governor)	1699 – 1701
Bienville	1701
Antoine de Crozat (head of monopoly)	1701 – 1717

Lamothe Cadillac (Black Prince)	1713–1716
De L'Epinay	1717 (a few months)
Bienville	1718–1724
Boisbriant (interim)	1724–1725
Perier	1725–1733
Bienville	1733–1743
Marquis de Vaudreuil	1743–1753
Kerlerec	1753–1763
Abbadie	1763–1767
Antonio de Ulloa	1767–1769
O'Reilly	1769–1770
Unzaga	1770–1777
Bernardo Galvez	1777–1784
Esteban Miró	1784–1792
Barón de Carondelet	1792–1797
De Lemos	1797–1799
Casacalvo (interim)	1799–1801
Salcedo	1801–1804
W. C. C. Claiborne (governor of the Territory of Orleans)	1804–1812
W. C. C. Claiborne (governor of the State of Louisiana)	1812–1816
Jacques Villeré	1816–1820
Thomas B. Robertson	1820–1824
Henry S. Thibodaux	1824
Henry Johnson	1824–1828
Pierre Derbigny	1828–1829
Armand Beauvais	1829
Jacques Dupré	1829–1831
Andrew B. Roman	1831–1835
Edward D. White	1835–1839
Andrew B. Roman	1839–1843
Alexander Mouton	1843–1846
Isaac Johnson	1846–1850
Joseph M. Walker	1850–1853
Paul Octave Hébert	1853–1856
Robert C. Wickliffe	1856–1860
Thomas O. Moore	1860–1864
Henry W. Allen	1864–1865
Michael Hahn	1864–1865
J. Madison Wells	1865–1867
Joshua Baker	1867

Benjamin F. Flanders	1867
Henry C. Warmoth	1868–1873
John McEnery (de jure)	1873
W. P. Kellogg (de facto)	1873–1877
Francis T. Nicholls	1877–1879
Louis A. Wiltz	1879–1881
Samuel D. McEnery	1881–1888
Francis T. Nicholls	1888–1892
Murphy J. Foster	1892–1900
William Wright Heard	1900–1904
Newton Crain Blanchard	1904–1908
Jared Young Sanders	1908–1912
Luther Egbert Hall	1912–1916
Ruffin Gavin Pleasant	1916–1920
John M. Parker	1920–1924
Henry L. Fuqua	1924–1926
Oramel Hinkley Simpson	1926–1928
Huey P. Long	1928–1931
Alvin Olin King	1931–1932
Oscar K. Allen	1932–1936
James A. Noe	1936 (four months)
Richard W. Leche	1936–1939
Sam Houston Jones	1940–1944
James H. Davis	1944–1948
Earl Kemp Long	1948–1952
Robert Floyd Kennon	1952–1956
Earl Kemp Long	1956–1960
James H. Davis	1960–1964
John McKeithen	1964–1972
Edwin W. Edwards	1972–1980
David Treen	1980–1984
Edwin W. Edwards	1984–

Sources: Soniat du Fossat 1893; Reeves 1962; various family papers, newspapers, and other political and genealogical sources in the Tulane University archives; the Historic New Orleans Collection; the Cabildo; the Louisiana State University archives.

NOTES

CHAPTER 1

1. Since the use of specific terms and phrases is an integral part of patterns of social classification throughout Louisiana history, an effort is made here to describe people as they were referred to during their lifetimes, even if the term or phrase used then is offensive to certain sectors of the population today. Thus, the terms *colored* and *persons of color* appear throughout the volume in references to patterns of self-identification. The terms *black* and *Afro-American* are used to refer to that larger sector of the North American population that has some African ancestry and identifies itself as black or Afro-American today. I make every effort to use the least offensive term available whenever such usage does not unduly bias the description and analysis of patterns of social identification.

2. Legal records are cited throughout this volume in standard legal notation. Cases that are appealed above the level of the district courts appear in volumes known as:

Martin's Reports (abbreviated as Ma.)

Robinson's Reports (abbreviated as Rob.)

Louisiana Annual Reports (abbreviated as La. Ann.)

Southern Reporter (abbreviated as So.)

Southern Reporter, Second Series (abbreviated as So. 2d)

U.S. Supreme Court Reports (abbreviated as U.S.)

Louisiana Appellate Court Reports (abbreviated as La. App.)

Volume numbers precede abbreviations; page numbers follow them.

3. The Creoles have been the focus of some scholarly research in the twentieth century—much of which I incorporate, where appropriate, in the text. But it has tended to be heavily historical and literary in orientation, to describe either white or colored Creoles, and where more social or political in orientation, to be microlevel community studies. A relatively recent example of the historical focus is Hodding Carter's *The Past As Prelude* (1968). Many of the essays in that book are solid pieces of historical research, but none deals with the very vivid problems of social classification that dominated much of the social life of New Orleans throughout its history. Published on the occasion of the 250th anniversary of the founding of New Orleans, the book stresses historical description of customs, traditions, and institutions of the city. The essays are competent but avoid topics that might be considered sensitive and controversial.

Several master's theses describe aspects of colored Creole life but restrict themselves to accounts of specific social problems within particular communities and do not ask general questions of social life or of social classification in Louisiana (Fuchs n.d.; Mott n.d.; Palazzolo 1955; Rousseau 1955; Strom n.d.; Williams and French n.d.; Wingfield 1961). Numerous bachelor's and master's theses describe images of the Creole in literature but are oriented almost uniformly towards literary criticism and to the use of the image of Creoles to enhance local color (e.g., Daspit 1936; Frotscher 1907; Guillot 1939; Pallez 1939; Smith 1926). Several other master's theses focus on limited historical periods of antagonism between Creoles and Americans. This historical research is useful, but it is concerned only with white Creoles (Adams 1939; Klein 1940; Newton 1933; Soulé 1955).

Two recent publications (Mills 1977; Woods 1972) describe a community of about ten thousand colored Creoles in northwestern Louisiana. The former is a descriptive history rather than an analytic piece; the latter is the only published work on Creoles that asks general questions about social identity and about reasons for particular forms of social classification. Woods's study is limited, however, by its exclusion of whites as subjects of study, and flawed by the underlying emphasis throughout the book on personal choice as the dominant, if not exclusive, source of all forms of self-identification. She pays little more than lip service to the broader social and historical context of classification in which the various groups and communities of Louisiana learned to define and redefine themselves.

CHAPTER 3

1. Louisiana law, following the civil law system, prescribes that a certain amount of the estate of a man or woman must go to his or her legitimate children. Such children are, therefore, considered to be forced heirs. In certain cases, parents are also the forced heirs of their deceased children. The precise percentage of an estate that must be passed on to one's legitimate children depends on the number of legitimate, surviving children of the deceased.

CHAPTER 4

1. Arpents were the standard unit of measurement of land in French Canada and Louisiana. Technically they equal just under an acre, but popularly they were assumed to be equal. People frequently used the two terms *arpent* and *acre* interchangeably.

2. My translation: That the main settlers, their children, and their legitimate descendants are noblemen in the Indies.

3. My translation: Many Creoles of St. Domingue [now Haiti] and their agricultural workers, as well as Creoles of Louisiana and others, have also died—but of an ordinary kind of illness.

4. My translation: So familiar to the Americans!

5. My translation: between two young Creoles on account of blows exchanged in public.

6. My translation: My previous Bulletin told you that the American schoolteacher, Mr. Marvin, had hit candidate A. B. Roman with his cane the sixth day of this month at the Exchange. Roman was not ashamed to take the matter to court instead of demanding satisfaction. On the eighteenth of the month, the jury that found the accused guilty and the criminal court condemned him to 100= in reparation and to two months in prison, if it is necessary to believe what they say.

This unfortunate man has been lame since childhood. Only his cane allows him to maintain his equilibrium. *And this arrogant and proud Creole* was not ashamed to hit him on the avenue as he left his help, even though he had with him several friends who were helping him along. Out of total dislike for Roman, these friends refused to let Marvin pay attention to such a humiliating insult. The victim still decided not to take his complaint to the tribunal upon his return to the city. He was reserving the moment to avenge himself when they next met. This took place in public, as I have already indicated. News of this has made Roman lose so many votes that we expect he will not get the majority of votes in the election for governor; at least we hope so with the cane test!

7. The precise geographical boundaries were the following:

First Municipality: the river, Canal Street, Esplanade Avenue, Bayou St. John, and Lake Pontchartrain from Canal to the Bayou.

Second Municipality: the river, Canal Street, Felicity Street, and the New Orleans–Jefferson parish line.

Third Municipality: the river, Esplanade Avenue, Bayou St. John, Lake Pontchartrain, and Chef Menteur.

8. My translation: Mr. Caldwell, old comedian of the American Theater, and today entrepreneur trying to light the Ejoz, submits his candidacy (but in vain) for the Mayoralty. He wants to profit from the division *between the Creoles* [in large letters], *the foreign French,* and *the American population,* since it

can only give the advantage to legitimate nationals to spend the time in all sorts of lucrative ventures. They advance a bit beyond the Creoles each day, although our new governor has already indicated his impartiality on this matter. This gives credit to his wise posture.

We continue to expect that Mr. Denis Prieur *Créole* will remain mayor. He has always done his job honorably, and we will support his reelection in order to avoid electing a less qualified citizen.

9. My translation: If art only exists under certain conditions, poetry is the opposite: it exists everywhere. . . . The word woman is the secret of art. This magic word, this cabalistic power, the Abracadabra, and Abracalan of the poet, is found deep in all intellectual endeavors. In the age of enchanted dreams, it is synonymous with the glory of hope. It is senseless to represent poetry in the form of an angel. . . . The Creole is a houri without the Koran, a Sultaness of beauty but without the seraglio; a daughter of Smyrne or of Georgie who does not say, "Allah is great, Mohammed is his prophet!" when you bid her good morning; she is an angel on the wings of fire . . . but one who speaks French. One would say upon reading the works of these poets that they were all born on the banks of the Mississippi. They paint the original, even when they believe they make portraits only of fantasy: chimeras found yonder are realities here. Here they have family names and certificates of baptism.

10. My translation: of about seventy years old, a *Louisiana Creole,* made mattresses for a living on Conde Street near the corner of St. Philip and of the public baths, capitalist owner of many houses in this neighborhood. She also had some cash, but they say that her two sons did not respect her when she was alive but will take advantage of this inheritance to live leisurely.

11. My translation: Also dead is the widow Madame Pierre Canué, old Louisiana and colored Creole, who was the rich owner of many beautiful houses of this city and of one in the Metairie. She was a woman who was thought to be very respect-

able, so much so that her death deserves to be noted regretfully.

12. My translation: a handsome young Creole from St. Domingue, son of a respectable and still young family.

13. My translation: The lovely Creoles through intrigue as much as through personal connections have almost all come to occupy honorable positions in government today, as well as the most lucrative posts, whose administrative condition is sterner now than under their predecessors. One must regret that they handle their jobs with more ease, as can be seen from the taxes imposed on the industrial enterprises of the unfortunate.

14. *Daily Crescent,* February 25, 1861, p. 4; March 8, 1861, p. 4; March 9, 1861, p. 1; March 11, 1861, p. 1; March 23, 1861, p. 1. *Daily Times Delta*—March 9, 1861, p. 5.

15. See, for example, Victor Grima's letter to his sister Marie in New Orleans on October 6, 1865, from Paris (Grima Family Papers 1788–1921, at the Historic New Orleans Collection):

Nous avons appris qu'il régnait en ce moment à la Nouvelle-Orléans une véritable épidémie, qui menace notre jeune population, dont elle semble ne devoir épargner personne; déjà j'ai appris que grand nombre de mes anciens condisciples avaient peri victimes des atteintes du fléau; plus de vingt autres, m'assure-t-on, sont aujourd'hui condamnés . . . au mariage!!! Est-il possible, grands Dieux, que au moment òu il règne un pareil état de choses vois songiez à me rappeler dans notre malheureuse ville, moi l'ennemi-né des unions anticipées. Tu connaissais bien peu, ma chère soeur, ton pauvre vieux frère, quand tu as écrit quelques unes des petites lignes qu'accompagnent ta naive réclamation d'autorité de jeune fille, cette espèce de déclaration d'indépendance faite avec ingénuité qui m'a franchement amusé. Si j'avais le temps aujourd'hui, nous pourrions dire bien des choses, mais je voudrais entendre tes objections si nous parlions, ce qui serait inévitable, des différences que les moeurs de la vieille Europe ont apportées à la *négociation* des mariages; on pourrait faire à ce sujet une comparaison avec ce qui se pratique dans notre bon pays, et c'est là un sujet plein d'enseignements utiles; tout n'est pas mauvais, il faut bien le savoir, dans la vieille expérience du vieux monde: on ne fait pas souvent en Europe, en France du moins, l'étrange folie dont on se rend, hélas! Trop souvent coupable chez nous, je veux dire; de laisser arriver dans les familles des étrangers dont personne ne connaît l'origine, et auxquels on donne en mariage les premières filles du pays. Je ne comprends pas que, dans un pays ouvert à tous les chevaliers d'industrie que rejette l'Europe, on soit assez simple pour recevoir chez soi un étranger dont on ne connaît pas l'histoire de la manière la moins equivoqué combien d'individus font aujourd'hui partie des familles les plus respectable de notre pays, sans que jamais personne ait cherché à savoir d'où vien-nent ces individus, ce qu'ils ont été dans leur pays, ce que sont leurs familles, et pour quelle raison ils sont émigré à l'étranger; il faut bien savoir qu'en Europe les gens qui appartiennent à une sphere sociale élevée ne s'en vont pas vivre a l'étranger; il y a assurément des exceptions, mais elles sont très rares aujourd'hui; on allait en Amérique autre-fois, dans des temps qui ne ressemblent plus à ceux où nous vivons, mais les choses ont changé au point qu'il nous est légitimement permis de nous défier de tout étranger qui aborde sur notre sol; notre pays offre des ressources que chacun a le droit d'exploiter, et je suis le premier à vouloir que chacun en profite; mais, en dehors de ce qui appartient à tout le monde, j'ai dans mon pays que j'aime à voir ouvert à l'étranger, un sanctuaire où je ne veux pas qu'il pénètre, avant d'avoir fait connaître ses faits et gestes, avant que je sache ce qu'il vaut et ce que volent les siens.

My translation:

We have learned that there is a real epidemic in New Orleans at the moment threatening our youth, and that it seems not to be sparing anyone. Already I've learned that a large number of my old peers have fallen victim to "blows"; more than twenty others, they assure me, are condemned today to marriage!!! Is it possible, my God, that just when this kind of thing is taking place in our unfortunate city, you mean to tell me this—I who am the born enemy of anticipated unions. You knew your poor old brother very little, my dear sister, when you wrote those few lines that accompany your naive reclamation of authority (that of a young woman), like a declaration of independence that is so ingenuous that it frankly amused me. If I had the time today, we would be able to discuss many things, but I would want to hear your objections (and it would be inevitable that you would have objections if we could talk about this) to the difference that the mores of old Europe have made in the process of *negotiating or arranging marriages*. One could draw a comparison between these and the practices of our good country, and this would be very instructive. You have to realize that the old (and tried) experiences of the old world are not all bad. Europeans don't surrender themselves frequently to strange follies, at least not in France. Alas! We are too frequently the ones to blame, I would say, for letting ourselves get connected to families of strangers whose origin we do not know, and to whom we give in marriage the most eligible young women of the country. I do not understand how in a country that welcomes all the gentlemen of industry who reject Europe, one can be so simple-minded that one would welcome into one's home strangers whose backgrounds one didn't know at all. How many people come and go through the most respectable families of our country without anyone trying to find out where these people came from, what they were in their own countries, what their families were, and why they emigrated abroad? One should realize that the Europeans who belong to the highest social status do not emigrate abroad. Of course, there are exceptions, but exceptions are rare today. They used to go to America in the old days, when things were different. But things have changed so much that we can now justifiably look down on any and all foreigners who come to our part of the world. Our country has resources that everyone has a right to exploit, and I am the first to say that all should profit from it. But beyond that which belongs to all, there is in this country (which I would like to see open to all) a sanctuary that I consider mine and that I do not want them to penetrate (or invade) unless I first learn more about their backgrounds and their manners, unless I first know what they are (socially) worth and what their families are worth [perhaps also a play on words—"and whether they steal"].

CHAPTER 5

1. Nightmares and stories about whites being sold into slavery were common but in most cases fictional. Whites did serve as indentured servants in Virginia and North Carolina, in the eighteenth century in particular, but never quite as slaves since theirs was by law a limited period of servitude.

2. At lower levels of political influence we do find a few other ex-slaves, namely David Young, James B. Lewis, and Theophile T. Allain (son of a white planter and a mulatto slave mother). But none of these ever came close to dominating black politics in nineteenth-century Louisiana.

3. Reconstruction and colored disenfranchisement have been popular topics for graduate theses as well as professional

publications. For more details and some argumentation, see Blassingame 1973; Campbell 1971; Duboca 1924; Ford 1933; Leavens 1966; Lestage 1935; Luke 1939; Perkins 1929; Reddick 1939; Rest 1962; Robert 1932; Singletary 1949; Smith 1940; Tunnell 1966; Uzee 1950; Vincent 1968, 1976; Warren 1965; Webb 1962; Williams 1946; Windham 1948.

4. My translation: "From One Side or From the Other"

The time has come to indicate what the sons of Louisiana want—that one must be either WHITE or BLACK, that each person must decide for himself. There are two races here: one superior, the other inferior. . . . Their separation is *absolutely* necessary. So let us separate ourselves as of today into two distinct parties—the White Party and the Black Party. Positions will be made clear—between white Louisiana and black Louisiana. *Le Carillon* displays the white's flag, with the profound conviction that only within its folds can Louisiana be saved.

5. My translation: "The Mixture of Races"

The racial hybrid is fickle and fugitive for physiological reasons. Different from his ancestors, he gives life to descendants who just don't look like him. From one generation to another, the flow of blood moves towards one of two sources, so as to regain its identity. If the three or four million individuals of African origin that there are in the South were distributed throughout the whole territory of the U.S., it wouldn't be long before they'd be absorbed by the great expanse of the white race. But concentrated in a small area, as they are at present, where they nearly equal the number of whites, if miscegenation continued between them and the whites, our South would soon provide the same kind of spectacle of human chaos that created the irremediable misery of Spanish America.

So, what will come of these mixed, weakened populations—unhappy descendants of brave Confederate soldiers? It is not hard to foresee it. The ever-increasing flow of white Northern immigrants, whose identity they are careful to maintain, will drive out the "troubled waters" resulting from Afro-Caucasian mixtures. The unrecognizable remainder of the Louisiana population will disappear in exile under West Indian skies, in Mexico, or in the anarchic "republics" of South America.

6. My translation: "Francoése and the Races"

Antouène, I am *smarter* than you;
Listen to me carefully and you'll see;
You say that prejudice is dead,
That equality has replaced it!
You must be very dumb to believe that!

Those who are white will never be black!
Those who are black will never be white!
Those who are yellow and think of themselves as white
Will never consider themselves black.
You must be dumb not to know that!

The day that a single mulatto believes
That we, the Negroes, are his equal,
That day you'll turn into a horse,
And I, I'll become white, I think.
You must be dumb not to understand that!

Against us the prejudice of the mulattoes
Will never end.
They despise us; so rest assured,
Mulattoes will be our Pontius Pilate:
You're not too dumb to understand that!

Equality, unification
Will create a peculiar [or funny] sort of race, I think,
Since the child of such a union
Will be neither white, nor yellow, nor black.
You're not too dumb to understand that!

Antouène, if we don't watch out
The mulattoes are going to trick [deceive] us;
They say they are talking for us
But . . . I prefer to deal with whites.
Pure milk is more valuable than that which is mixed!

Whites—they're a real race;
Blacks—they're a real race;
Horses—they're a real race;
Cattle—they're a real race;
Havana cigars—they're a real race;
But mulattoes—they're no more a race

Than mules are a race,
Or mixed cigars are really a race.

The poem was published anonymously, but all indications are that it was written by a white French-speaking Creole trying to copy the "voice" of Creole-speaking blacks. Not sure that I could fully trust my own knowledge of French Creole, I sent a copy of the poem and my tentative translation of it to French Creole expert Alexander Hull. His detailed reply seems to corroborate my suspicions. He wrote:

> The Creole in this text is exactly the same sort that was being used at about this time for the publication of folktales by such "scholars" as Alfred Mercier and Alcée Fortier, both for the spelling (*ein* for *un*, *tournin* and *gagnin* for *tourner* and *gagner*, for example), and the grammar, normed on the basilect (*yé méprisé nu*, obviously habitual present, where mesolectal creole very likely used, as today, a short form of the verb for this meaning: *méprise*, not *méprisé*). The author obviously knew French, and fell into it inadvertently (?) from time to time (*puisque l'enfant de cette union. . .*). At a pretty good guess, the poem was written by a white man. Would that fit?

7. My translation: "A daring mulatto"

> Last Thursday, after taking care of its routine matters, the Fifth Ward Club of the White League closed its doors and began its executive session. Just before the reading of a very important message from the Supreme Council of the League—a message that can only be heard by the pure—we noticed a small gentleman, who did not belong to the club, sitting comfortably amidst the members of the League. He had the audacity to try to disrupt the quiet proceedings of the assembly, and evidently report these proceedings to our enemies—because he was a *pure-blooded* mulatto, if it is possible for mulattoes to be pure-blooded, of course.
>
> The trespasser was expelled. He did well to leave without starting any commotion, since the tiniest insolence on his part would have meant work for the funeral director the following day.

8. My translation: The Arabs beautiful and true mulattoes, some Negroes.

9. My translation: What should our fellow Spanish citizens, who are descended to a large extent from Arabs, think of that assertion? The Arabs are white, essentially white, just tanned by exposure to light and to the sun, as are all whites who live out in the open in hot countries. They are a pure people, without mixtures. They're a well-marked type that has preserved itself without change throughout the centuries. They are like the Jews and the Phoenicians, of Semitic race, and claim to be direct descendants of Shem, one of Noah's sons.

CHAPTER 6

1. The labels included in the questionnaire are frequently used by the New Orleans public today. I have already discussed the relationship of *Creole* to *Cajun*. *Creole* is juxtaposed to *Cajun* in certain social circles but not in others; hence, the term *Cajun*, too, has more than one set of referential meanings and, by implication, conflicting connotations of social status. The fact that these words have meanings that are in dispute may make them less attractive as labels of self-identification than words like *French* or *American* whose meanings are not regarded as ambiguous.

CHAPTER 7

1. These figures come from the same census sources cited for Table 4.2 in Chapter 4. I have computed the percentages myself.

2. These computations are included in the text to show the extent to which contemporary definitions of *Creole* differ from contemporary patterns of identification of Creoles. I call this disagreement "underrepresentation," even though it is quite clear that the number of people who identify themselves as Cre-

oles today or are identified by others as Creoles does not under-represent contemporary "Creole" social categories. The point is that Creole definitions (or metasemantic statements) of the Creole identity do not themselves conform to the semantic categories of "Creole" and "non-Creole." Many people who meet the requirements set forth in the definitions Creoles give of Creole identity do not identify themselves and are not identified by others as Creoles.

CHAPTER 8

1. Indeed, one could also find antireligious Creole women and some very pious Creole men, but the image that remains is not that. As in other Mediterranean societies, there is a sense in Louisiana that religion is a crutch of the weak. It is proper for a Creole lady to be religious, since she is a member of "the weaker sex"; it may be a sign of mental or physical weakness for a Creole man to be observant.

2. The Sisters of the Holy Family seem to guard their history perhaps more than others. The Xavier University library once had copies of a master's thesis and a bachelor's thesis on the history of the order and its role in the education of nonwhites in Louisiana. But both theses disappeared from the university's archives long ago. A journalist preceded me in the search for information and was equally unsuccessful. The order does stand by the biography of Sister Henriette Delille, published as a pamphlet by a member of the order who wishes to remain anonymous.

3. Debuts in New Orleans are coordinated with Mardi Gras activities. For most debutantes, the year of the debut culminates when the girls appear as queens or maids in Mardi Gras balls. Although many of the girls who appear in the courts of Mardi Gras krewes are not official debutantes, most of the debutantes become queens or maids in the most prestigious balls.

4. Creole and non-Creole blacks usually say that the Zulus are black but not Creole. However, the founding father of the club was a Metoyer of the well-known Creole Cane River family. Some Creoles do belong to the organization now, and some Creoles attend the ball. The claim that Zulu is not Creole has probably more to do with the difference of style between the so-called Creole and non-Creole balls than with the characteristics of actual members or invited guests. The Zulus stage a parade as well as a ball. About thirty minutes before Rex hits the streets on Mardi Gras each year, Zulu floats, cars, and decorated trucks begin to roll. Originally begun as a spoof on Mardi Gras, the parade retains much of the irreverence of its earlier years. Its entertainment value is great. Those who ride on the floats throw small plastic coconuts to the crowds as well as the usual beads. They wear colorful, often extravagant, costumes and attract large crowds. To the propriety-minded Creole, public behavior of this sort is downright vulgar. Though the Zulu Club selects a king and a queen each year, like the other krewes, and stages dressy if not totally formal balls, its association with "the masses" of blacks in Louisiana is strong enough to keep most Creoles from identifying with it.

BIBLIOGRAPHY

I. Demographic information
   United States, Bureau of the Census.
   Social and economic characteristics of the population. Censuses of 1810,
      1820, 1830, 1840, 1850, 1860, 1870, 1880, 1890, 1900, 1910,
      1920, 1930, 1940, 1950, 1960, and 1970. Washington, D.C.:
      United States Government Printing Office.

II. Legal records
   Cases argued and determined in the courts of appeal and the Supreme
   Court of the State of Louisiana (1830–1978).
      Published in chronological order in:
         Martin's Reports
         Robinson's Reports
         Louisiana Annual Reports
         Southern Reporter
         Southern Reporter, Second Series
         Louisiana Appellate Court Reports
   Civil District Court Archives (suits, wills, trials)
   Codes of law and constitutions of Alabama, Arkansas,
         California, Florida, Georgia, Hawaii, Kentucky, Maryland, Missis-
         sippi, Missouri, North Carolina, Tennessee, Texas, Virginia, and
         West Virginia.
   Dainow, Joseph, ed.
      1961   *Civil Code of Louisiana.* Revision of 1870 with Amendments to
               1960. Second Edition. St. Paul, Minn.: West Publishing Co.
      1972   *Compiled Edition of the Civil Codes of Louisiana.* Baton Rouge:
               Louisiana State University.
      1973   *West's Louisiana Statutes Annotated Civil Code,* vol. 17. St. Paul,
               Minn.: West Publishing Co.
   Notarial Archives of the City of New Orleans
      (Records of Property Transfers and Successions)
   Recopilación de las Indias (Spanish Colonial Code)
   United States Supreme Court Reports

III. Manuscript and Tape Collections
  Amistad Research Center, Dillard University:
    Rosa (Freeman) Keller Collection
    Natalie Midlow Collection
    Alexander Pierce Tureaud Papers
  Corpus Christi Parish Records, New Orleans
  Friends of the Cabildo, Oral History Project, Dorothy
    Schlesinger, director, New Orleans
  The Historic New Orleans Collection:
    Beauregard Letters
    Dauberville-Bouligny Family Papers
    Free Persons of Color Collection
    Louis Moreau Gottschalk Collection
    Grima (Mrs. Alfred) Collection
    Laussat Papers
    Nott (George William) Family Papers
    St. Gème Collection
    Slavery in Louisiana Collection
    Spanish Colonial Land Grant Papers
    Stouse Collection
    Vieux Carré Survey
    Villeré (Ernest Caliste) Family Papers
    Villeré (Jacques Philippe) Family Papers
  Library of Congress, Washington, D.C.:
    Jefferson Papers
    Microfilm of Records of the Catholic Church in Louisiana
        to 1803; originals are at the archives of Notre Dame University.
    Melrose Collection
    Miscellaneous Collection
    RSVP Collection
    Safford Collection
    Williamson Collection
  Louisiana State University Archives, Baton Rouge:
    Carondelet Papers
    Nathaniel Evans Papers
  New Orleans Archdiocesan Archives:
    St. Louis Cathedral Records
  St. Peter Claver Parish Records, New Orleans:
    Records of the Activities of Josephite Brothers
      in New Orleans
  Special Collections Division, The Howard-Tilton Memorial

Library, Tulane University:
  Augustin-Wogan-Labranche Family Papers
  Craig-Eshleman Family Papers
  Cruzat Family Papers
  De la Vergne Family Papers
  Favrot Family Papers
  Connell Family Papers
  New Orleans Cabildo Records (includes Morales Papers)
  New Orleans Jazz Collection
  New Orleans Municipal Papers
  Nott (George William) Papers
  Poydras Home Collection
  Rainold Collection of Mardi Gras Organizations
    (1955–1972)
  Schmidt Family Papers
  Superior Council Records
  Urquhart Collection (Trist Wood Papers)
  Albert Walker Papers
  WPA Records
Special Collections Division, Eugene P. Watson Memorial
  Library, Northwestern State University, Natchitoches,
  Louisiana:
  Cloutierville Church Records
  Colonial Documents Collection
  Dormon Collection
  Fontenot Collection
University of New Orleans Archives:
  Autocrat Club Records
  James Bezou Papers
  Louis Charbonnet Papers
  Jeunes Amis Collection
  Knights of Peter Claver Records
  Monnot-Lanier Family Papers
  Plasterers' Union Records
  Société des Francs Amis Records

IV. Newspapers
  L'Abeille
  The Anglo American
  Le Carillon
  Clarion Herald

Durham Morning Herald
Figaro
International Herald Tribune
The Josephite Harvest
Louisiana Creole
Louisiana Weekly
Le Moniteur de la Luisiane
New Orleans Commercial Bulletin
New Orleans Courier
New Orleans Daily City Item
New Orleans Daily Creole
New Orleans Daily Crescent
New Orleans Daily Delta
New Orleans Daily Orleanian
New Orleans Daily Picayune
New Orleans Daily Times Delta
New Orleans Louisiana Advertiser
New Orleans Mercantile Advertiser
New Orleans States Item
New Orleans Times Democrat
New Orleans Times Picayune
New Orleans Tribune
New York Times
People
San Francisco Chronicle
L'Union

V. References Cited

Adams, Ben Avis
> 1939 "A Study of Indexes of Assimilation of the Creole People in New Orleans." Master's thesis, Tulane University.

Alexander, Jack
> 1977 "The Culture of Race in Middle-Class Kingston, Jamaica." *American Ethnologist* (August).

Anonymous
> 1892 *Biographical and Historical Memoirs of Louisiana,* 3 vols. Chicago: Godspeed Co.

Arena, Carmelo R.
> 1954 "A Social Study of the Spanish Land Tenure System in Spanish Louisiana, 1762–1803." Master's thesis, Tulane University.

Argüedas, Jeanne Wogan
  1936 "A List of all the French Societies in New Orleans." From *The New Orleans Courier*, April 17. Unpublished records, Special Collections Division, Howard-Tilton Memorial Library, Tulane University.
  n.d. "A Visit to Popo and Mémé d'Abadie." Unpublished ms.

Arthur, Stanley Clisby, ed., and de Kernion, George
Campbell Huchet, collab.
  1931 *Old Families of Louisiana*. New Orleans: Joseph S. W. Harmanson.

Asad, Talal
  1972 "Market Model, Class Structure and Consent: A Reconsideration of Swat Political Organisation." *Man*, n.s. 7(1):74–94.

Augustin, James M. and Thomas H. Ryan
  1893 *Sketch of the Catholic Church in Louisiana on the Occasion of the Centenary of the Erection of the See of New Orleans in 1793*. New Orleans.

Backer, Leola
  1930 "A Study of the Adoption Law and Its Administration in Louisiana." Master's thesis, Tulane University.

Barth, Fredrik
  1966 *Models of Social Organization*. Royal Anthropological Institute Occasional Paper No. 23. London.

Barth, Fredrik, ed.
  1969 *Ethnic Groups and Boundaries*. Boston: Little, Brown & Co.

Baudier, Roger
  1939 *The Catholic Church in Louisiana*. New Orleans.
  1943–1951 "Historic Old New Orleans" weekly column in New Orleans' *Catholic Action of the South*.

Beckwith, Paul
  1893 *Creoles of St. Louis; A Genealogy of the Descendants of René Auguste Chouteau of Bearn, France, who came to New Orleans in the eighteenth century.* St. Louis: Nixon-Jones Printing Co.

Beer, William, ed.
  1911 *Early Census of Louisiana*. Publications of the Louisiana Historical Society V.

Bennett, Joan W.
  1976 "Diane Weysham Ward v. Director of the Bureau of Vital Statistics, Louisiana State Health Department." *Perspectives in Biology and Medicine* (Summer):582–592.

Bernard, Amelie C.
  1944 "Adoption Laws and Practices in the State of Louisiana, 1943–1944." M.S.W. thesis, Tulane University.

Berquin-Duvallon

1803 *Vue de la Colonie Espagnole du Mississippi ou des Provinces de la Loui-siane . . . en l'Année 1802*. Paris. Translated by John Davis as *Travels in Louisiana and the Floridas*. New York, 1806.

Bezou, James

1967 "Remembrance of Creole Days." Address to Le Petit Salon, December 7. Unpublished ms.

1969 "L'Athénée Louisianais." Unpublished ms.

1972a "L'empreinte de la France en Louisiana." April 3. Unpublished ms.

1972b "French—A Limpid Language." Address to the Round Table Club on November 9, 1972, and to the Executives Club on May 31, 1974. Unpublished ms.

n.d. "Le Reveil Francais." Unpublished ms.

n.d. "New Orleans Half a Century Ago." Unpublished ms.

Birmingham, Stephen

1977 *Certain People: America's Black Elite*. Boston: Little, Brown & Co.

Blanchet, Osceola

1941 "Investigation of Negro Business in New Orleans, 1930–40." Master's thesis, Xavier University.

Blassingame, John

1973 *Black New Orleans, 1860–1880*. Chicago: University of Chicago Press.

Boehm, Christopher

1980 "Exposing the Moral Self in Montenegro: The Use of Natural Definitions to Keep Ethnography Descriptive." *American Ethnologist* 7(1):1–26.

Borgia, Sr. M. F. (S.S.F.)

1931 "History of the Sisters of the Holy Family of New Orleans." Bachelor's thesis, Xavier University.

Bossu, Jean-Bernard

1962 *Travels in the Interior of North America, 1751–1762*. Translated and edited by Seymour Feiler. Norman: University of Oklahoma Press.

Braithwaite, Edward

1971 *The Development of Creole Society in Jamaica, 1770–1820*. Oxford: Clarendon Press.

Briede, Kathryn C.

1937 "A History of the City of Lafayette." Master's thesis, Tulane University.

Brinton, Crane

1936 *French Revolutionary Legislation on Illegitimacy, 1789–1804*. Cambridge: Harvard University Press.

Brito Figueroa, Federico
  1966 *Historia Social y Económica de Venezuela.* Caracas: Universidad Central de Venezuela.
Buck, Paul H.
  1925 "The Poor Whites of the Ante-Bellum South." *American Historical Quarterly* 31.
Cable, George Washington
  1879 *Old Creole Days.* New York: Charles Scribner.
  1880 *The Grandissimes.* New York: Charles Scribner.
  1881 *Madame Delphine.* New York: Charles Scribner.
      1884a *The Creoles of Louisiana.* New York: Charles Scribner.
  1884 *Dr. Sevier.* Boston: J. R. Osgood and Co.
  1959 *Creoles and Cajuns: Stories of Old Louisiana.* Arlin Turner, ed. Garden City, N.Y.: Doubleday.
Caire, R. J.
  1976 "Letter to the Editor." *New Orleans Magazine* (July): 10.
Cajun, André [pseud.]
  1943 *Why Louisiana Has Parishes, Policejurymen, Redbones, Cajuns, Creoles, Mulattoes, Quadroons, Octoroons, Griffes.* New Orleans: Harmanson. The New Orleans Public Library Archives lists Andrew J. Navard as author.
Calhoun, John C.
  1958 "Who Is a Negro?" *University of Florida Law Review* 11:235–240.
Campbell, Clara López
  1971 "The Political Life of Louisiana Negroes, 1865–1890." Ph.D. dissertation, Tulane University.
Carter, Clarence C., ed.
  1940 *The Territorial Papers of the United States,* vol. 9: *The Territory of Orleans 1803–1812.* Washington, D.C.
Carter, Hodding, ed.
  1968 *The Past as Prelude. New Orleans 1718–1968.* New Orleans: Pelican.
Catharine, Sr. M. (S.S.F.)
  1933 "The Origin and Development of the Welfare Activities of the Sisters of the Holy Family." Bachelor's thesis, Xavier University.
  1917 *A History of the United States,* vol. 4. New York: Macmillan Co.
Clark, John G.
  1970 *New Orleans, 1718–1812: An Economic History.* Baton Rouge: Louisiana State University Press.
Cochran, Estelle Mina Fortier
  1963 *The Fortier Family and Allied Families.* San Antonio: Estelle Cochran.

Comaroff, John L., and Roberts, Simon
    1981 *Rules and Processes: The Cultural Logic of Dispute in an African Context.* Chicago: University of Chicago Press.

A Creole of St. Domingue
    1959 *My Odyssey; Experiences of a Young Refugee from Two Revolutions.* Translated and edited by Althea de Puech Parham. Baton Rouge: Louisiana State University Press.

Dargo, George
    1975 *Jefferson's Louisiana: Politics and the Clash of Legal Traditions.* Cambridge: Harvard University Press.

Daspit, Florence Driscoll
    1936 "Cable and the Creoles of New Orleans." Bachelor's thesis, Loyola University of the South.

Davis, Kenneth
    1976 "Racial Designation in Louisiana: One Drop of Black Blood Makes a Negro!" *Hastings Constitutional Law Quarterly* 3:199–228.

De Bow
    1857 "The Free Black Population, North and South." *De Bow's Review* 23 (August).

Degler, Carl N.
    1971 *Neither Black Nor White: Slavery and Race Relations in Brazil and the United States.* New York: Macmillan Co.

Deiler, John
    1909 *The Settlement of the German Coast of Louisiana and the Creoles of German Descent.* Philadelphia: American Germanica Press.

Desdunes, Rodolphe
    1911 *Nos Hommes et Notre Histoire.* Montreal.

Detiege, Sister Audrey Marie
    1976 *Henriette Delille, Free Woman of Color.* New Orleans: Sisters of the Holy Family.

De Ville, Winston
    1968 *The Gulf Coast.* New Orleans.

Domínguez, Virginia R.
    1973 "The Middle Race." Scholar of the House thesis, Yale University.
    1975 *From Neighbor to Stranger: The Dilemma of Caribbean Peoples in the United States.* Occasional Papers no. 5. New Haven: Antilles Research Program, Yale University.
    1984 "The Language of Left and Right in Israeli Politics." *Political Anthropology* 4:89–109.

Domínguez Ortiz, Antonio
    1955 *La sociedad española en el siglo XVIII.* Madrid.

Drouet, Adele
1927 "Creole Lullabies." *New Orleans Times-Picayune,* June 15, magazine sect.:5.

Dubroca, Isabelle C.
1924 "A Study of Negro Emancipation in Louisiana, 1803–1865." Master's thesis, Tulane University.

Duchein, Annette
1932 "Creole Duelists of 1832 Would Be Amazed to See Women Descendants Fence." *New Orleans Times-Picayune,* February 28:28.

Dufour, Charles
1967 *Ten Flags in the Wind: The Story of Louisiana.* New York: Harper and Row.
1968 "The People of New Orleans." In *The Past as Prelude,* edited by Hodding Carter. New Orleans: Pelican.

Eagleson, Dorothy Rose
1961 "Some Aspects of the Social Life of the New Orleans Negro in the 1880's." Master's thesis, Tulane University.

Enciclopedia Universal, Europea-Americana
1925 "Barcelona: Hijos de J. Espase."

Evans, Sally Kittredge
1974 "Free Persons of Color." In *New Orleans Architecture,* vol. 4: *The Creole Faubourgs,* edited by R. Toledano, S. K. Evans, and M. L. Christovich. Gretna, La.: Pelican.

Everett, Donald
1950 "Legislation concerning free Persons of Color in in New Orleans Parish, 1840–1860." Master's thesis, Tulane University.
1952 "Free Persons of Color in New Orleans, 1803–1865." Ph.D. dissertation, Tulane University.

Field, Flo
1927 "A la Creole!" Play reviewed by Hermann B. Deutsch, March 15, 1927, "Hail 'A la Creole!' a Perfect Whimsical Play of Quarter; And Flo Field Doing It All." *New Orleans Item.*

Fischer, Roger
1967 "The Segregation Struggle in Louisiana, 1850–1890." Ph.D. dissertation, Tulane University.

Ford, Alma Louise
1933 "The Negro in Louisiana Politics, 1878–1898." Master's thesis, University of Texas.

Fortes, Meyer
1955 "Names among the Tallensi of the Gold Coast." *Afrikanistische Studien* 26:337–349.

Fortier, Alcée
  1892 "A Few Words about the Creoles of Louisiana." Address delivered
       at the 9th annual convention of the Louisiana Educational Associa-
       tion. Baton Rouge: Truth Books.

Frazier, Franklin
  1957 *Black Bourgeoisie: The Rise of a New Middle Class in the United States.*
       New York: Collier Books.

Frotscher, Lydia Elizabeth
  1907 "George Cable and His Louisiana Studies." Master's thesis, Tulane
       University.

Fuchs, Sister Helen Rose
  n.d. "Contact and Prejudice Reaction from the Viewpoint of Colored
       Creoles." Master's thesis. Cited by Sister Frances Jerome Woods in
       Marginality and Identity. Baton Rouge: Louisiana State University
       Press, 1972.

Gayarré, Charles
  1886 "Creoles of History and Creoles of Romance." Typescript of
       limited circulation, Tulane University, Special Collections Divi-
       sions of the Howard-Tilton Memorial Library.

Geertz, Clifford
  1975 *The Interpretation of Cultures.* London: Hutchinson.

Gill, Richard, and Sherman, Ernest
  1973 *The Fabric of Existentialism.* Englewood Cliffs, N.J.: Prentice-Hall.

Glazer, Nathan, and Moynihan, Daniel P., eds.
  1963 *Beyond the Melting Pot.* Cambridge: Harvard University Press and
       MIT Press.

  1975 *Ethnicity: Theory and Experience.* Cambridge: Harvard University
       Press.

de Gournay, P. F.
  1886 "Creole Pecularities." *Magazine of American History:* 542–549.

Gray, Lewis C.
  1941 *History of Agriculture in the Southern United States to 1860.* New
       York: P. Smith.

Guillot, Raymond A.
  1939 "The Picture of the Creole and Acadian in Modern Literature."
       Bachelor's thesis, Loyola University of the South.

Hagelberg, G. B.
  1974 *The Caribbean Sugar Industries: Constraints and Opportunities.* Occa-
       sional Papers no. 3. New Haven: Antilles Research Program, Yale
       University.

Hall, A. Oakey
  1851 *The Manhattaner in New Orleans; or Phases of "Crescent City" Life.*

New York: J. S. Redfield, Clinton Hall; New Orleans: J. C. Morgan.

Haring, C. H.
1963 *The Spanish Empire in America*. New York: Harbinger Books.

Harris, Abram L.
1936 *The Negro as Capitalist: A Study of Banking and Business among American Negroes*. Philadelphia.

Harris, Lancelot
1897 "The Creoles of New Orleans." *Southern Collegian* 30(3):192–212.

Harris, Marvin
1970 "Referential Ambiguity in the Calculus of Brazilian Racial Identity." *Southwestern Journal of Anthropology* 26(1).

Harris, Marvin, and Kottak, Conrad
1963 "The Structural Significance of Brazilian Racial Categories." *Sociologica* 25.

Haskins, James
1975 *The Creoles of Color of New Orleans*. Drawings by Don Miller. New York: Thomas Y. Crowell.

Herrin, M. H.
1952 *The Creole Aristocracy: A Study of the Creole of Southern Louisiana*. New York: Exposition Press.

Herzfeld, Michael
1982 "When Exceptions Define the Rules: Greek Baptismal Names and the Negotiation of Identity." *American Ethnologist* 38(3):288–301.

Huber, Leonard V.
1974 "New Orleans Cemeteries: A Brief History." In *New Orleans Architecture*, vol. 3: *The Cemeteries*, edited by Mary Louise Christovich. Gretna, La.: Pelican.

Ingraham, J. H.
1841 *The Quadroone; or, St. Michael's Day*, vol. 1. New York: Harper and Brothers.

Irvine, Judith T.
1978 "When Is Genealogy History? Wolof Genealogies in Comparative Perspective." *American Ethnologist* 5(4):651–674.

Isaacs, Harold
1975 "Basic Group Identity: The Idols of the Tribe." In *Ethnicity: Theory and Experience*, edited by Nathan Glazer and Daniel P. Moynihan. Cambridge: Harvard University Press.

Jackson, John Robert
1935 "The Poor Whites of Ante-Bellum Louisiana." Master's thesis, Tulane University.

Jackson, Luther Porter
   1942   *Free Negro Labor and Property Holding in Virginia 1830–1860.* New
           York.
James, William
   1949   *Pragmatism: A New Way for some Old Ways of Thinking.* New York:
           Longmans. Reprint of 1907 ed.
Jenkins, Samuel Willis
   1965   "The People of Hybrid Island." Master's thesis, Louisiana State
           University.
Jones, Joseph H.
   1950   "The People of Frilot Cove." Ph.D. dissertation, Louisiana State
           University.
Kane, Harnett T.
   1944   *Deep Delta Country.* New York: Duell, Sloan, and Pearce.
   1958   *The Southern Christmas Book; The Full Story from Earliest Times to
           Present: People, Customs, Conviviality, Carols, Cooking.* New York:
           McKay.
Kapferer, Bruce, ed.
   1976   *Transaction and Meaning: Directions in the Anthropology of Exchange
           and Symbolic Behavior.* Philadelphia: Institute for the Study of Hu-
           man Issues.
King, Grace
   1921   *Creole Families of New Orleans.* New York: Macmillan Co.
King, James F.
   1951   "The Case of José Ponciano de Ayarza: A Document on *Gracias al
           Sacar. Hispanic American Historical Review* 31(4):642–644.
Klein, Selma Louise
   1940   "Social Interaction of the Creoles and Anglo-Americans in New
           Orleans, 1803–1860." Master's thesis, Tulane University.
Kmen, Henry A.
   1961   "Singing and Dancing in New Orleans: A Social History and
           Growth of Balls and Opera, 1791–1841." Ph.D. dissertation,
           Tulane University.
Kniffen, Fred B.
   1968   *Louisiana: Its Land and People.* Baton Rouge: Louisiana State Uni-
           versity Press.
Knight, Franklin
   1970   *Slave Society in Cuba during the Nineteenth Century.* Madison: Uni-
           versity of Wisconsin Press.
Labbé, Dolores Egger
   1971   *Jim Crow Comes to Church: The Establishment of Segregated Catholic*

Parishes in South Louisiana. History Series no. 4. Lafayette, La:
    University of Southwestern Louisiana.

Labelle, Micheline
  1978 *Idéologie de couleur et classes sociales en Haiti.* Montreal: University of
    Montreal Press.

Lacour, Arthur Burton
  1952 *New Orleans Masquerade.* Stuart O. Landry, collab. New Orleans:
    Pelican.

Lanusse, Armand
  1945 *Creole Voices: Poems in French by Free Men of Color,* edited by E. M.
    Coleman. Washington, D.C.: Associated Publishers. Reprint of
    1845 ed.

Latrobe, Benjamin H. B.
  1951 *Impressions respecting New Orleans: Daily Sketches 1818–1820.*
    Edited by Samuel Wilson, Jr. New York: Columbia University
    Press.

Leavens, Finnian Patrick
  1966 "L'Union and the New Orleans Tribune and Louisiana Reconstruc-
    tion." Master's thesis, Louisiana State University.

LeBreton, Dagmar Renshaw
  1947 *Chahta-Ima: The Life of Adrien-Emmanuel Rouquette.* Baton Rouge:
    Louisiana State University Press.

Le Gardeur, Jr., Rene
  1954 "Les Prémières Années du Théâtre." *Comptes Rendus de l'Athénée
    Louisianais.*

Lestage, N. Oscar, Jr.
  1935 "The White League in Louisiana and Its Participation in Recon-
    struction Riots." *Louisiana Historical Quarterly* 18:616–695.

Luke, Josephine
  1939 "From Slavery to Freedom in Louisiana, 1862–1865." Master's
    thesis, Tulane University.

Lussan, Auguste
  1837 "La famille creole, drame en cinq acts et en prose. Représenté pour
    la prémière fois, sur le théâtre Français de la Nlle. Orléans, le 28
    Fevrier 1837. . . ." New Orleans: chez Fremaux et Alfred Moret.

McCants, Sister Dorothea Olga, ed. and trans.
  1973 "Translator's Introduction." In *Our People and Our History.* Baton
    Rouge: Louisiana State University Press.

Martineau, Harriet
  1838 *Retrospect of Western Travel,* vol. 2. London.

Martínez Alcubilla, M.
  1891 *Diccionario de la administración española.* 5th ed. vol. 7. Madrid.

Martínez-Alier, Verena

1974 *Marriage, Class and Colour in Nineteenth-Century Cuba: A Study of Racial Attitudes and Sexual Values in a Slave Society.* Cambridge: Cambridge University Press.

Menn, Joseph Karl

1964 "The Large Slaveholders of Louisiana in 1860." Master's thesis, Louisiana State University.

Miceli, Augusto

1964 *History of the Pickwick Club.* New Orleans: Pickwick Press.

Mills, Gary B.

1977 *The Forgotten People: Cane River's Creoles of Color.* Baton Rouge: Louisiana State University Press.

Moore, Sally Falk

1978 *Law as Process.* London: Routledge and Kegan Paul.

Mott, Vincent V.

n.d. "The Creole de Couleur: A Sociological Study of a Racial Sub-Group." Master's thesis, Fordham University.

Narroll, Raoul

1964 "Ethnic Unit Classification." *Current Anthropology* 5(4).

New Orleans City Council

1936 *New Orleans in 1805: A Directory and a Census.* New Orleans: Pelican Gallery.

Newton, L. W.

n.d. "Creoles and Anglo-Americans in Old Louisiana." *S W Social Service Quarterly* 14:31–48.

Nolte, V.

1934 *Fifty Years in Both Hemispheres: or, Reminiscences of a Merchant's Life.* New York: G. Howard Watt. Reprint of 1854 ed.

Norman, Benjamin M.

1845 *Norman's New Orleans and Environs.* New Orleans.

Nott, G. William

1926 "The Haunting Melodies of Creole Songs." New Orleans Times-Picayune. July 18, magazine sect.:3.

Overdyke, W. Darrel

1933 "The History of the American Party in Louisiana." *Louisiana Historical Quarterly* 16:409–410.

1950 *The Know-Nothing Party in the South.* Baton Rouge.

Palazzolo, Charles Santo

1955 "Corpus Christi: A Sociological Analysis of a Catholic Negro Parish in New Orleans." Master's thesis, Louisiana State University.

Pallez, Mildred A.
   1939 "Cable's Treatment of the Creoles." Master's thesis, Fordham
        University.
Parks, Jessica
   1974 "Social Classification of Race: The Case of the Houma of Louisiana."
        Bachelor's honors thesis, Newcomb College, Tulane University.
Pascal, Robert
   1962 *Readings in Louisiana Family Law.* Baton Rouge: Louisiana State
        University Press.
Peacocke, James S.
   1856 *The Creole Orphans: or Lights and Shadows of Southern Life. A Tale of
        Louisiana.* New York: Derby and Jackson; Cincinnati: H. W.
        Derby.
Perkins, A. E.
   1929 "Some Negro Officers and Legislators in Louisiana." *Journal of
        Negro History* 14:523–528.
   1943 "Oscar J. Dunn." *Phylon* 4:105–107.
Poché, Judge F. P.
   1886 "Speech of the Honorable J. P. Poché on Creole Day at the 1886
        American Exposition in New Orleans." *New Orleans Daily Pica-
        yune,* February 8.
Price, Richard, and Price, Sally
   1972 "Saramaka Onomastics: An Afro-American Naming System."
        Ethnology 11(4):341–367.
Priestley
   1929 *The Coming of the White Man.* New York: Macmillan Co.
Puckett, Erastus P.
   1907 "The Free Negro in New Orleans to 1860." Master's thesis, Tulane
        University.
Pulzskys, Francis, and Pulzskys, Theresa
   1853 *White, Red, Black.* New York: Redfield.
Radcliffe-Brown, A. R.
   1952 *Structure and Function in Primitive Society.* London: Cohen and West.
Rama, Carlos M.
   1970 "The Passing of Afro-Uruguayans from Caste Society into Class
        Society." In *Race and Class in Latin America,* edited by Magnus
        Morner. New York: Columbia University Press.
Reddick, Dunbar
   1939 "The Negro in the New Orleans Press, 1850–1860: A Study in
        Attitudes and Propaganda." Ph.D. dissertation, University of
        Chicago.

Reed, Germaine A.
1965 "Race Legislation in Louisiana, 1864–1920." *Louisiana History* 6(4):379–392.

Reeves. Miriam G.
1962 *The Governors of Louisiana.* New Orleans: Pelican.

Reinders, Robert
1965 "The Free Negro in the New Orleans Economy, 1850UN–1860." *Louisiana History* 6.

Rest, James
1962 "The Louisiana Constitutional Convention of 1867–1868." Bachelor's honors thesis, Tulane University.

Riley, M. L.
1936 "The Development of Education in Louisiana Prior Statehood." *Louisiana Historical Quarterly* 19.

Robert, Mary Elizabeth
1932 "The Background of Negro Disenfranchisement in Louisiana." Master's thesis, Tulane University.

Robertson, W.
1812 *The History of America.* Philadelphia: J. Broien and T. L. Plowman. Reprint of 1777 ed.

Rodríguez Casado, Vicente
1942 *Primeros años de investigaciones científicas.* Madrid: Instituto Gonzalo Fernández de Oviedo.

Rohrer, John H., and Edmonson, Munro S., eds.
1960 *The Eighth Generation: Cultures and Personalities of New Orleans Negroes.* New York: Harper and Brothers.

Rouquette, Adrien
1880 "Critical Dialogue between Aboo and Caboo on a New Book; or, a Grandissime Ascension." Pamphlet published anonymously in New Orleans by a fictitious publisher. Turner (1966: 102) and LeBreton (1947: 319ff) attribute it to Rouquette.

Rousseau, Kara Enid M.
1955 "Cultural Patterns of Colored Creoles: A Study of a Selected Segment of New Orleans Negroes with French Cultural Orientations." Master's thesis, Louisiana State University.

Roussève, Charles B.
1937 *The Negro in Louisiana. Aspects of His History and His Literature.* New Orleans.

Rowland, Dunbar
1917 *Official Letter Books of W. C. C. Claiborne.* Madison: Democrat Printing Co.

Runyan, Glenn M.
1967 "Economic Trends in New Orleans, 1928–1940." Master's thesis,
Tulane University.

Sahlins, Marshall
1976 *Culture and Practical Reason*. Chicago: University of Chicago Press.

Samuels, Ruth
1974 "Relationships between the Sexes in an Afro-American Community in New Orleans." Ph.D. dissertation, Tuane University.

Sanjek, Roger
1971 "Brazilian Racial Terms: Some Aspects of Meaning and Learning."
American Anthropologist 73:1126–1143.

Saunders, Eugene
1925 *Lectures on the Civil Code of Louisiana*. New Orleans: E. S. Upton
Printing Co.

Saxe-Weimar-Eisenach, Bernhard
1828 *Travels through America during the Years 1825–1826*. Philadelphia:
Carey, Lea and Carey.

Saxon, Lyle
1929 *Old Louisiana*. New York: Century Co.
1939 *Fabulous New Orleans*. New York: D. Appleton-Century Co.

Seda Bonilla, Eduardo
1968 "Dos modelos de relaciones raciales: Estados Unidos y América
Latina." *Revista de Ciencias Sociales* 12(4):569–598.

Shugg, Roger
1968 *Origins of Class Struggle in Louisiana*. Baton Rouge: Louisiana State
University Press. Reprint of 1939 ed.

Silverstein, Michael
1976 "Shifters, Linguistic Categories, and Cultural Description." In
Meaning in Anthropology, edited by Keith Basso and Henry Selby.
Albuquerque: University of New Mexico Press.

Singletary, Otis A.
1949 "The Reassertion of White Supremacy in Louisiana." Master's thesis, Louisiana State University.

Smith, Irene Dixon
1926 "The Louisiana Creole in Fiction." Master's thesis, Tulane
University.

Smith, Samuel D.
1940 *The Negro in Congress, 1870–1901*. Chapel Hill: University of
North Carolina Press.

Soniat du Fossat, Mrs. Eugene
1893 *Biographical Sketches of Louisiana's Governors from D'Iberville to Foster*.
Baton Rouge: Advocate Book and Job Office.

Soulé, Leon Cyprian, Jr.
  1955 "The Creole-American Struggle in New Orleans Politics,
      1850–1862." Master's thesis, Tulane University.
Stahl, Annie
  1942 "The Free Negro in Ante-bellum Louisiana." *Louisiana Historical
      Quarterly* 25.
Strom, Florence Alwilda
  n.d. "The Outmigration Pattern of a Colored Community in the
      South." Master's thesis. Cited by Sister Frances Jerome Woods in
      Marginality and Identity. Baton Rouge: Louisiana State University
      Press 1972.
Taylor, Council
  1959 "Class and Colour: A Comparative Study of Jamaican Status
      Groups." Ph.D. dissertation, Yale University.
Thompson, Edgar T.
  1972 "The Little Races." *American Anthropologist* 74(5):1295–1306.
Tinker, Edward L.
  1953 *Creole City: Its Past and Its People.* New York: Longmans, Green.
Toledano, Roulhac
  1974 *New Orleans Architecture*, vol. 4: *The Creole Faubourgs.* Gretna, La.:
      Pelican.
Tregle, Joseph G.
  1952 "Early New Orleans Society: A Reappraisal." *Journal of Southern
      History* 18:20–36.
Tunnell, Teddy B.
  1966 "The Negro, the Republican Party, and the Election of 1876 in
      Louisiana." *Louisiana History* 7:101–116.
Turner, Arlin
  1966 *George W. Cable: A Biography.* Baton Rouge: Louisiana State Uni-
      versity Press.
Turner, Victor W.
  1967 *The Forest of Symbols.* Ithaca, N.Y.: Cornell University Press.
Uzee, Philip D.
  1950 "Republican Politics in Louisiana." Ph.D. dissertation, Louisiana
      State University.
Villeré, Paul
  1921 "Le Créole—Réflexions l'Après-Guerre." *Comptes Rendus de l'Athé-
      née Louisianais:* 65–85.
Vincent, Charles
  1968 "Negro Leadership in Louisiana, 1862–1870." Master's thesis,
      Louisiana State University.

1976 *Black Legislators in Louisiana during Reconstruction.* Baton Rouge: Louisiana State University Press.

Voorhies, Jacqueline
1973 *Some Late Eighteenth Century Louisianians.* Lafayette: University of Southwestern Louisiana History Series.

Warren, Millard W.
1965 "A Study of Racial Views, Attitudes, and Relations in Louisiana, 1877–1902." Master's thesis, Louisiana State University.

Webb, Allie B.
1962 "A History of Negro-Voting in Louisiana, 1877–1906." Ph.D. dissertation, Louisiana State University.

Wilkie, Mary E.
1977 "Colonials, Marginals and Immigrants: Contributions to a Theory of Ethnic Stratification." *Comparative Studies in Society and History* 19(1):67–95.

Williams, Louretta, and French, William H.
n.d. "Attitudes toward Public Assistance in a Nonwhite Rural Community." Master's thesis. Cited by Sister Frances Jerome Woods in *Marginality and Identity.* Baton Rouge: Louisiana State University Press, 1972.

Williams, T. Harry
1969 *Huey Long.* New York: Alfred A. Knopf.

Windham, Allie B.
1948 "Methods and Mechanisms Used to Restore White Supremacy in Louisiana, 1872–1876." Master's thesis, Louisiana State University.

Wingfield, Roland
1961 "The Creoles of Color: A Study of a New Orleans Subculture." Master's thesis, Louisiana State University.

Wonk, Dalt
1976 "The Creoles of Color." *New Orleans Magazine* (May):47–57.

Wood
1912 *Wood's Directory of Colored Businesses in New Orleans.* 3rd ed. New Orleans.

Wood, Minter
1938 "Life in New Orleans in the Spanish Period." Master's thesis, Tulane University.

Woods, Sister Frances Jerome
1972 *Marginality and Identity: A Colored Creole Family through Ten Generations.* Baton Rouge: Louisiana State University Press.

Woodson, Carter G.

1924 *Free Negro Owners of Slaves in the United States in 1830 together with Absentee Ownership of Slaves in the United States in 1830.* Washington, D.C.

1925 *Free Negro Heads of Families in the United States in 1830.* Washington, D.C.

Wright, James M.

1921 *The Free Negro in Maryland.* New York: Columbia University Studies in History, Economics and Public Law no. 222.

INDEX